Internet Marketing Research: Theory and Practice

Ook Lee
University of Queensland, Australia

IDEA GROUP PUBLISHING
Hershey • London • Melbourne • Singapore

Acquisitions Editor:	Mehdi Khosrowpour
Managing Editor:	Jan Travers
Development Editor:	Michele Rossi
Copy Editor:	Beth Arneson
Typesetter:	Tamara Gillis
Cover Design:	Deb Andree
Printed at:	Sheridan Books

Published in the United States of America by
    Idea Group Publishing
    1331 E. Chocolate Avenue
    Hershey PA 17033-1117
    Tel: 717-533-8845
    Fax: 717-533-8661
    E-mail: cust@idea-group.com
    Web site: http://www.idea-group.com

and in the United Kingdom by
    Idea Group Publishing
    3 Henrietta Street
    Covent Garden
    London WC2E 8LU
    Tel: 44 20 7240 0856
    Fax: 44 20 7379 3313
    Web site: http://www.eurospan.co.uk

Library of Congress Cataloging-in-Publication Data

Lee, Ook, 1965-
  Internet marketing research : theory and practice / Ook Lee.
    p. cm.
  Includes bibliographical references and index.
  ISBN 1-878289-97-7 (pbk.)
   1. Internet marketing. I. Title.

  HF5415.1265 .L43 2001
  658.8'4--dc21   00-066969

British Cataloguing in Publication Data
A Cataloguing in Publication record for this book is available from the British Library.

Internet Marketing Research: Theory and Practice

Table of Contents

Preface i
Ook Lee, University of Queensland, Australia

1   Online Marketing Strategies in the Information Economy:
    A Comparative Analysis 1
    Bharat Rao, Institute for Technology and Enterprise,
    Polytechnic University, USA
    Louis Minakakis, Chase Manhattan Bank, USA

2   Leveraging Online Information to Build Customer
    Relationships 15
    Christian Bauer, Working Systems Solutions,
    *   Western Australia*
    Arno Scharl, Vienna University of Economics and
    *   Business Administration, Austria*

3   The Evolution of Web Marketing Practice 31
    Malu Roldan, San Jose State University, USA

4   Pricing Strategies for Digital Books: Issues and
    Directions for Research 47
    P. K. Kannan, University of Maryland, USA
    Barbara Kline Pope, National Academy of Press, USA
    Eva Guterres, University of Maryland, USA

5   Factors Influencing Marketing Performance
    On the Web 61
    Ashok Ranchhod, Julie Tinson, and Fan Zhou
    Southampton Business School, UK

6   Positioning in Cyberspace: Evaluating Telecom
     Web Sites Using Correspondence Analysis 77
     Pierre Berthon, University of Bath, UK,
     Leyland Pitt, Michael Ewing, Nimal Jayaratna,
     and B. Ramaseshan, Curtin University of Technology, Western
     Australia

7   Investigating Social Motivations for Internet Use 93
     Thomas F. Stafford, Texas Woman's University, USA
     Marla Royne Stafford, University of North Texas, USA

8   Turning Browsers into Buyers: User Interface
     Design Issues for Electronic Commerce 108
     Rex Eugene Pereira, Drake University, USA

9   4I: A New Premise for Marketing Online 150
     Amit Pazgal and Sandeep Sikka
     Washington University, USA

10   Exploring Consumers' Willingness to Contribute
     to Internet Web Sites 176
     Benedict G.C. Dellaert
     Tilburg University, The Netherlands

11   The Theory Behind the Role of Leverage and the
     Strategic Alignment of Organisations While Creating
     New Markets (Internet Marketing and E-Commerce) ... 187
     S.I. Lubbe, Vista University, South Africa

12   Beyond CPMs and Clickthroughs: Understanding
     Consumer Interaction with Web Advertising 209
     Patrali Chatterjee, Rutgers University

13   Comparing Consumer Purchase Behavior on the
      Internet and in Brick-and-Mortar Stores:
      An Overview of Recent Research 218
      Jie Zhang, University of Michigan, USA

14   Satisfaction, Frustration, and Delight: A Framework
      for Understanding How Consumers Interact
      with Web Sites 231
      Jennifer Edson Escalas, University of Arizona, USA
      Kapil Jain, University of Arizona, USA
      Judi E. Strebel, San Francisco State University, USA

About the Authors 252

Index   259

Preface

Internet marketing has become an important issue for many businesses around the world which have any form of commercial presence on the net. It is often perceived that doing business on the Internet mostly requires competency in the technology area. However as many dot com companies are failing due to lack of revenue generation, which could be induced by the inadequate marketing and marketing research, practitioners and scholars of e-commerce are keen to obtain a better understanding of the whole phenomenon of Internet marketing. To understand what's working as an Internet marketing strategy or tactic, one needs to conduct marketing research using rigorous statistical methodology.

In this book, early chapters introduce concepts of Internet marketing and its tools. For example, Rao and Minakakis' chapter does comparative analysis of Internet marketing companies with real-life company profiles. Bauer and Scharl's chapter gives an explanation on the technology used in collection of online consumers' information and on how online information can be utilized by Internet marketing context. Roldan's chapter gives an excellent survey of technical capabilities of Internet marketing practicing companies. Kannan, Pope, and Guterres' chapter concentrates on the marketing of e-books. They suggest that there could be various pricing tactics in order to prevent cannibalization with the printed books.

Subsequent chapters deal with rigorous statistical analysis in order to find what's working as a marketing tactic. For example, Ranchhod and Zhou conducted analysis of 122 UK companies to find out factors influencing marketing performance on the Web. Berthon, Pitt, Ewing, Ramaseshan, and Jayaratna conducted correspondence analysis of 15 telecom companies with Web presence in order to obtain objective evaluation technique of Web sites. Stafford and Stafford utilized regression analysis of questionnaires of 98 subjects to identify motivations for the use of commercial Web sites. A very extensive statistical analysis was completed by Pereira in order to investigate the interaction effects between the search strategy of software agents and the consumer's product class knowledge.

Later chapters contain mostly conceptual papers which envision the new paradigm for Internet marketing area. Pazgal and Sikka suggest that instead of Porter's 4P, we should adopt 4I (Intensity, Integration, Interaction, and Identification) for the fundamental marketing mix for Internet marketing. Dellaert applies household production theory to explain the causes of consumers' willingness to contribute to Internet Web sites including buying/selling/etc. Lubbe investigates the theory behind the role of leverage and the strategic alignment of organizations while creating new markets in Internet marketing and e-commerce.

The last chapters deal with more practical issues regarding Internet marketing such as measurement/consumer behavior/consumer interaction. Chatterjee gives a detailed tour of currently available Web advertisement measurement techniques and provides a framework for better metrics of Web advertisement effectiveness. Zhang overviews current research on comparing consumer purchase behavior on the Internet and in brick-and-mortar stores. Escalas, Jain, and Strebel's research provides a fascinating look into what goes on in the mind of a consumer while surfing the net; they include emotions such as satisfaction, frustration, and delight.

Internet marketing research can provide lots of useful information and insight to not only academics but also practitioners since knowledge obtained through this kind of research usually represents the statistically significant sample of real population. Thus research on this area should continue by collaboration between industry and academics for the purpose of acquiring and sharing valuable consumer data.

Chapter 1

Online Marketing Strategies in the Information Economy: A Comparative Analysis

Bharat Rao
Polytechnic University, USA

Louis Minakakis
Chase Manhattan Bank, USA

On-line marketers are fast pushing the boundaries of the field through a combination of creative content, the use of in-depth market knowledge, and the deployment of interactive and analytical technological tools. Targeted on-line marketing has emerged as a viable form of reaching customers on the Internet. In addition to providing a cheap and effective way of reaching qualified and interested end customers, it offers several other advantages in the way marketers can establish long-term customer relationships, leading ultimately to retention and loyalty. In this paper, we offer an introduction to the phenomenon and describe typical business models for targeted marketing online. We do this through a comparative case analysis of Netcentives, Inc., a leading integrator of interactive media technology; Agency.com, a leading interactive media agency and NetPerceptions, Inc., a provider of collaborative filtering software. We then outline some of the challenges and opportunities in this new medium going forward, including issues related to consumer privacy and the changing nature of intellectual property.

BACKGROUND

Direct marketers spent approximately $163 billion in the U.S. in 1998. Recent figures show the U.S. retail sales are growing at about three percent annually, while catalog and direct-mail sales are growing at about seven percent. This confirms the trend that more households purchasing in response to these catalogs and direct mailings, mostly based on mailing lists obtained by the marketers. Although catalog marketing remain one of the most popular forms of off-line direct marketing, direct marketers do not mail catalogs to every household in the country, due to resource constraints. Instead, they purchase mailing lists that break down customer groups by income segments, household size, purchase history, or hobbies and interests. By using these lists, direct marketers can target their prospective consumer and limit the amount of extra catalogs being mailed.

In the early days of direct marketing, efforts at reaching prospective customers could be best described as using a "shotgun approach." By packing an envelope full of advertisements and coupons and mailing them out to a large amount of households, it was discovered that customers would actually respond by buying some of the promoted products. Gradually, such efforts gave way to more targeted campaigns. 1-800 numbers grew in popularity as marketers fled to the television seeking immediate response. Today, with the creation of large-scale databases that systematically collect information on households and individuals, direct marketing is fast approaching the Promised Land of one-to-one promotions and incentives, and incorporating new types of interactivity[1]. By using mail, telephones, computers and television, knowledge on prospective customers is being converted to revenue dollars. Knowledge of this sort is tremendously useful and is used in turn to create powerful online brands[2]. Thus, online marketing radically changes the way in which information about customers is collected, analyzed and put to use.

The competitive dynamics of the direct marketing industry are changing fast with the advent of the Internet. At the present time, nearly 30% of the 97 million U.S. households are online. Electronic commerce generated $32 billion in online purchases in 1998. Correspondingly, expenditures on online ad spending (including media and direct marketing) have been growing steadily and are expected to rise to $9 billion in 2002 from $3.3 billion in 1999. This represents a small chunk of spending if one considers the total amount spent by direct marketers in 1998 ($163bn). It comes as no surprise that online advertising has emerged as one of the hottest growth areas for direct marketers. As a recent Forrester Research study put it,

> Direct marketers are flocking to the Internet, drawn by the promise of cheaper marketing, deeper customer relationships, and access to a worldwide audience. With the ability to connect instantly to the customer, the Internet promises to become the ultimate one-to-one marketing vehicle…[3]

Several interesting business models have emerged in order to tap into some of the advantages offered by the Internet. In the following sections, we profile three business models that tap into some of these possibilities.

COMPANY PROFILES AND ANALYSES

Netincentives: Taking Incentives Online

What Is Incentive Marketing?

Incentive-based marketing is a technique where the consumer is rewarded or compensated for completed purchase transactions. Similar to the concept of "rebates" in the physical marketplace, online marketing "incentives" are driving the explosive growth in advertising and marketing revenues. The key difference, however, is that marketers can extract information from online consumers by providing them additional incentives. This information can then be used in conjunction with other direct marketing plans to design and deliver targeted messages.

One of the key objectives of online marketers is to increase their look-to-buy ratio[4]. In addition, they want to build relationships with customers so that they return and be retained for repeat purchases. In addition to a major new marketing channel, the online world offers a cheap and cost-effective way of reaching a large number of qualified customers. Of the $163 billion spent on online advertising, about $34 billion was spent on online direct marketing in 1998. However, it is estimated that online direct marketing will account for between 30% and 50% of the total online advertising expenditures in 2001, up from 21% in 1998. Online direct marketing can take the form of e-mail or Web-based promotional offers. The online channel is particularly attractive because advertisers can use tools that are not available in traditional media, such as measurement of "click-through" rates and one-click response to e-mail offers. Further, online sites can record and track user behavior, and these data can be used in conjunction with responses to online advertising messages. These tools give advertisers rapid feedback on their marketing campaigns. This feedback can be used to tailor new messages and targeted offers, when integrated with existing data about customers, and purchase and post-purchase behavior.

Netcentives, Inc.: Company Background

Netcentives, Inc. is one of the leading integrators of interactive media technology. Combining its expertise in interactive media, and traditional promotion incentives, Netcentives is one of the leaders in the use of online incentive plans for advertisers and marketers. In order to understand how this program works, one must look closer at the business model in question. In the following section, we describe a typical set of transactions that may be conducted and the role of a media integrator.

Netcentives holds the sole rights to an important set of systems, procedures, and a method for providing online rewards programs. On June 30, 1998, Netcentives was granted U.S. Patent 5,774,870, "Online Interactive Frequency and Award Redemption Program," which gives the company ownership of intellectual property pertaining to the online incentive business process. Customers who shop online can earn points or other units of value for their purchases, and then redeem those points online for items from an award catalog. A user may access the program online and may browse a product catalog for shopping. The user may electronically place an order, upon which the program automatically checks the user's credit and electronically issues a purchase order to the supplying company. The program also calculates award points, updates the award account of enrolled users, and communicates that number of awarded points to the user. Enrolled users may browse through an award catalog and electronically redeem an amount of awarded points towards an award. The program then electronically places an award-redeeming order with the fulfillment house and updates the user's award account.

Netcentives, Inc.: Products And Services

ClickRewards™ is the flagship product for Netcentives[5]. It is a promotional program that allows consumers to earn valuable rewards for completing activities on participating Web sites. Consumers earn ClickMiles™ for doing things like purchasing products, downloading software or filing out surveys. ClickMiles are Netcentives' version of a digital currency that Internet marketers can provide to consumers as an incentive for completing online activities. Consumers can redeem ClickMiles for a number of valuable rewards, including frequent flyer miles, car rental and hotel discounts, as well as goods and services on the Web. The basic premise of ClickRewards.com is to shop at various partner sites outlined on the ClickRewards.com home page. While shopping at these sites, the customer collects ClickMiles, which may be redeemed for diverse types of services and products.

The partner sites and methods for obtaining ClickMiles are quite diverse. Each partner site has its own link on the ClickRewards.com Web site that delineates how ClickMiles are obtained. The total amount of the ClickMiles received is dependent upon which site is visited and how much is spent. ClickMiles can also be received for trying out a product or service offered by the one of the partner sites. In addition, ClickRewards.com also publicizes certain specials throughout the year. This serves as a direct incentive to join ClickRewards.com and further to utilize their membership to benefit from shopping with ClickRewards.com affiliated retailers. ClickRewards.com has taken the basic concept of frequent flyer miles and has expanded the ways a person may accumulate more mileage through their partner sites. This concept is not new but rather a reinvention. This reinvention serves as a great avenue for consumers to a) shop online and b) gather ClickMiles to put toward rewards. This interactive campaign can be easily imitated, but one of the things that differentiates ClickRewards.com from other incentive Web sites is its diverse relationship with popular physical and online retailers.

Netcentives is also involved in the consulting business. With their ClickRewards Enterprise Incentive Solutions program, Netcentives offers the ClickRewards incentive program to corporate intranets and extranets. Netcentives is providing the tool for customers to archive any motivational objectives; it could be a program to inspire performance growth from both direct and channel sales forces. Netcentives also offers two types of loyalty programs: Site Specific and Network. Netcentives offers in-depth analysis of the business and determines what drives shareholder value then and in the future, as well as what the brand stands for. Next, they collaborate with the customer to create a complete profile of their customer base, enabling them to determine what motivates each segment. Armed with this extensive knowledge, Netcentives designs, unique and powerful Custom Loyalty Program. They determine the right currency, the most motivating rewards, the proper number and type of earning opportunities, even the look and feel of the entire campaign. Finally, they customize the technology necessary to build the custom program to the design specifications.

The Netcentives Professional Services (NPS) team is an additional area formed to better service customers. This group specializes in creating architectures, providing thoughtful analysis, constructing quality software, and planning careful deployment of enterprise applications. They use object-oriented tools, techniques and methods. Their comprehensive approach provides clients with the tools necessary to move both developers and organizations toward Distributed Systems and Object Architectures. NPS team members are comfortable with technologies that include all major relational databases, Java, PowerBuilder, application servers and other middleware, and transaction technologies for processing electronic transactions.

Netcentives Business Model

ClickRewards provides ClickMiles as the currency unit that users accumulate from sites in the Netcentives network. ClickMiles accrue across a network of sites with participating sites rewarding online customers with Netcentives' ClickMiles for activities like registering or subscribing to the site, buying goods, or using online customer service. Their business model is mainly premised on the fact that participating sites will buy ClickMiles from Netcentives at a cost of three cents for each ClickMile. Netcentives, in fact, pays the airlines less than two cents for each frequent flyer mile, keeping the difference in return for managing the tracking, reporting, online adjustments, and fulfillment. By consolidating the technology infrastructure and gaining access to a wide audience, Netcentives stands to make a small profit out of every transaction.

Since consumers already understand and collect rewards like frequent flyer miles from car rentals, credit card use, etc., Netcentives is not dependent on changes in consumer behavior. In fact, the promotional offers have immediate appeal because most customers are adding to existing mileage accounts. The success to their model is dependent on the amount of partners that they can generate as well as a total number of actual members. Most frequent flyer miles programs, unless they are having a special two for one offer, give customers miles one for one on their dollars spent. ClickRewards can offer more miles for the customer dollar.

ClickRewards feels they set themselves apart from programs like CyberGold and MyPoints.com by first focusing on electronic commerce. ClickMiles are awarded for shopping online, which means partners with physical stores as well as Web sites, such as OfficeMax, can only grant ClickMiles for purchases from their Web site. Secondly, ClickRewards is the only program to give consumers frequent flyer miles from six major airlines with the well-understood value of one ClickPoint equals one mile. Thirdly, they feel they that some of the best and most popular merchants as partners.

While a number of firms are catching up with Netcentives in this domain, the business model is inherently robust and will increase in effectiveness with wide-spread adoption and an expanded set of business relationships.

Agency.com: The Rise of Interactive Relationship Management

Corresponding to the rise of interactive online services like the one described above, there are a host of service providers that seek to deliver solutions in areas ranging from interactive advertising and marketing programs, to in-depth market research and media campaigns. In the following section we will describe the role of interactive ad agencies and point out the key similarities and differences from their physical counterparts. Agency.com, a leading interactive ad agency based in New York, has spearheaded the initial forays into new media branding and marketing.

Background: New Media in New York

In order to understand the success of Agency.com, it is important to understand the context of new media in New York's "Silicon Alley." New York has been the hub of the advertising and media industries. Today, these traditional strengths have been bolstered by bold forays into the new media space by many pioneering firms like Agency.com. The new media industry in New York is a collection of more than 5000 companies, mainly small entrepreneurial firms that developed and marketed Internet sites, multimedia software, on-line entertainment and other digital offerings. Together, these firms now employ more workers in the city than traditional media industries like television, book publishing or newspapers[6].

The new media industry has also flourished in New York because of the city's ample pool of young designers, artists, writers and programmers, fluent in digital technology and thus able to take advantage of the rapid spread of personal computers and the Internet. The hub of the region's industry has been in so-called Silicon Alley, which is broadly defined as all new media firms south of 41st Street in Manhattan[7]. Further, New York City has a number of educational institutions including New York University and Columbia University that prepare students for success in the high-tech arena. In addition, there are focused programs offered by the likes of the Parsons School of Design and Manhattan's School of Visual Arts, which offers a concentration in digital design and computer art.

What Does Agency.com Do?

Agency.com develops and builds "end-to-end interactive solutions" that allows client companies to manage marketing relationships, by offering superior communications, customer service and commerce capabilities online. Agency's objective is to go beyond providing an online presence. The idea is to provide the technological solution that makes the interactive strategy work in an integrated interactive relationship-management framework. Various accounts in the trade press suggest that Agency.com is an interactive advertising agency, a full service, e-commerce enabler, a management consulting firm, and an interactive marketing and digital communication provider, among others. However, from the inside looking out, Agency.com does not see themselves as an interactive advertising agency. By deploying solutions in interactive business and marketing consulting, graphic user interface design, e-commerce, e-dentity and brand management, E-media planning, buying and ad production, and systems integration, Agency.com has positioned itself as an interactive relationship-management company.

Chan Suh, Agency's founder, believes that they have become an "agency", since they are a group of agents acting on behalf of their clients. But he does not consider them to be an advertising agency. Agency.com agents are in interactive relationship management. "We are not a traditional consultancy, advertising agency or technology company."[8]

Agency.com Business Services

As opposed to traditional advertising firms, Agency.com provided a range of services. These included helping companies set up sites on the World Wide Web and placing 'banner' advertisements on other Web sites to bring more traffic. While the work by Agency.com included the kind of writing and design skills used in traditional advertising agencies, a lot of the work done in the 'interactive' agencies closely resembled the detailed computer programming typically provided by technology companies. Due to their programming excellence, one of Agency.com's main strengths is in developing solutions and applications for all types of interactive platforms, including the Internet, Intranets, Extranets, CD-ROMs, Web-ROMs, Kiosks and iTV. Agency.com is thus in a unique position to provide e-business consulting to browser developers, such as Microsoft, by developing powerful, low-cost personalization applications.

Partnerships and Growth

Omnicom, Agency.com's parent company, is the second largest advertising agency holding company in the world, with stakes in four of the top fifteen interactive agencies. Financial backing from Omnicom has helped Agency.com to acquire and merge with several companies, such as Online Magic (the company's European division), Interactive Solutions and Spiral Media. In August of 1998, Agency.com acquired Eagle River Interactive—making it the largest interactive agency in the world. According to CEO Chan Suh, the merger added additional and qualified resources to meet customer demand and geographic reach in places where they didn't have it. Agency.com has also partnered with NetGravity, market leader in online advertising and direct marketing management solutions. The purpose of these mergers was to gain a "center for excellence" with the newly acquired specialized skills and client base network. Recently, in January of 1999, they added an Asian influence with the acquisition of Edge Consultants. Agency.com saw the importance of becoming affiliated with agencies overseas, since clients around the world had sought out their shops. Agency.com international offices included sites in England, France and Singapore.

The market for Web strategy and services is expected to grow from $4 billion today to $15 billion by 2002.[9] A Web site price tag of $50,000 easily turns into more than $1M when including the interactive development strategies. The growth in Agency's revenue is representative of the growth in the industry. In 1998 revenues increased to $80 million well above competitors such as iXL, Modem Media, Think New Ideas, Reinvent Communications, and organic Online.[10]

ADVERTISING NETWORKS

In addition to reaching aggregate groups of consumers through individual online ads, marketers are also using the power of ad networks to reach a more targeted audience. Ad networks enable advertisers (like Intel, E-Trade, Nissan, etc.) to work with online publishers (like Yahoo, The New York Times, etc.) and deliver custom advertising based on the knowledge of the target audience. By serving as a link between traditional advertising agencies (like Ogilvy and Mather, Leo Burnett, etc.) and Web publishers, ad networks like DoubleClick, 24/7 Media, Flycast, Xoom Network, etc. are able to make targeted affinity buys at multiple publisher sites for their customers. In this way, they reach a wider yet measurable audience. Publishers also stand to gain as they can outsource many key functions like the ad sales force and ad management technology, and gain access to large, branded advertisers who might have been otherwise reluctant to move online.

NETPERCEPTIONS: PERSONALIZING THE ONLINE EXPERIENCE

One of the major opportunities facing online marketers is the ability to personalize users online experiences through technology. One of the prime examples of personalization has been the use of product recommendations, made popular by the likes of Amazon.com. In fact, it is NetPerceptions' collaborative filtering technology that drives Amazon.com's product recommendation capabilities. NetPerceptions is a first mover in knowledge management for online retailers and others interested in real-time business-to-customer potential sales prediction and recommendation technologies. NetPerceptions provides powerful solutions for capturing both explicit and tacit knowledge gained from online consumers' interaction and browsing activities, which can then be put to good use in marketing efforts. NetPerceptions provides its services based on the premise that conventional knowledge management is not enough.

Company Background

NetPerceptions began as a research project at the University of Minnesota in 1992 with the objective of helping people to cope with the enormous amount of information available on Usenet Internet discussion groups. The core idea was to sort the information according to each individual's interests. The underlying technology was known as collaborative filtering, which identifies communities of like-minded people then taps each community's collective experience to recommend information that would be relevant to the individuals within those communities.[11]

NetPerceptions was founded in 1996 to bring this collaborative filtering technology to market. Its founders included the original members of the research project, as well as software engineers from Cray Research. In 1998, NetPerceptions developed the first Real-time Recommendation Platform, which today is incorporated in all NetPerceptions solutions. This platform seamlessly integrates the latest enhancements of collaborative filtering technology, with associative filtering, fuzzy logic, and genetic algorithm technologies, so the optimum technology can be applied to whatever real-time recommendation task is at hand.[12] This technology produces a high level of predictive accuracy and solutions. Thus, real-time recommendation technology predicts an individual's preferences and makes specific recommendations accordingly. These recommendations include cross-selling and up-selling, and they even go as far as recommending Web site content and how a company should advertise. The company handles these tasks by observing the behavior of consumers. It looks at the amount of click-throughs and recalls past behavior, purchasing histories, as well as a rating system that customers fill out. The technology used draws upon this knowledge to make recommendations with high predictive accuracy. Because this acts in real-time, the technology learns more and gets smarter with every transaction.

Products and Services

NetPerceptions offers a competitive array of products and services. The company claims that during the first year following installation, a suggestive selling strategy based on the collaborative filtering technology can conservatively contribute 34% of total Web site sales revenue by:
1. increasing the conversion of browsers to buyers by 2% each month,
2. increasing order size by 4% beginning at $35 per average order, and
3. growing the percentage of orders from repeat customers from 30% to 35%.

NetPerceptions E-Commerce 5.0

NetPerceptions' real-time personalization technology called *E-commerce 5.0* is the software product that interacts with online customers capturing their preferences in real time. The e-business can then get recommendations from this software based on the knowledge it acquires after pooling this information together with relevant information about different products and services offered, past customer preferences and other customer trends. The company also offers other e-commerce products with similar objectives. NetPerceptions' Personal Shopper and NetPerceptions Smart Merchant are two examples. These products consolidate multiple data sets to develop cross-sell strategies, move overstocked items, promote new products, and strategically classify customers and track items that take off unexpectedly as well as items that lag in sales (i.e., "hot sellers" and "dogs").

NetPerceptions for Call Centers 2.0

NetPerceptions for Call Centers 2.0 helps companies to cross-sell and up-sell during a call and also provide incentives to get the customer to come back. By using the same real-time recommendation engine used by Internet marketers and bringing it into call centers, the technology becomes powerful because it takes previously untapped information customer bases and turns them a powerful knowledge base. The Call Center suggests cross-sell recommendations based on the customer's preferences and past history in real time. This is one step better than traditional data-mining and statistical analysis, given the real-time recommendation and learning capabilities of the product.

NetPerceptions for Ad Targeting

NetPerceptions for Ad Targeting is software that targets advertisements to individual tastes and interests of the customer at hand. The end result is higher click-through rates, which enhances the ability for a site to increase advertising revenue. The company claims that NetPerceptions for Ad Targeting can show measurable improvements in targeting in less than 24 hours and that no other real-time ad targeting solution can be deployed so quickly and enjoy measurable results.

NetPerceptions for Marketing Campaigns 2.0

NetPerceptions for Marketing Campaigns 2.0 is the latest release of software designed to personalize email. This enables marketers to use customer-based knowledge obtained in real time and customize email messages and solicitations. By allowing individual marketers to design, deploy and continuously evaluate any number of concurrent campaigns, including ongoing campaigns that are automatically triggered by marketer-defined events such as a customer placing an order, this package focuses on streamlining marketing campaign management. All campaigns deliver content that is personally relevant to each customer and is driven by the marketer's acquisition, interaction, and retention goals. None have to wait for help from chronically backlogged system administrators of external service bureaus.

Finally, NetPerceptions is working on developing software for knowledge management. This will enable an organization to view its knowledge base. The technology recommends documents and data sources as well as frequently asked questions from other employees that can be used to help an individual to learn more about the task at hand. This concept could increase productivity by decreasing search time. It can also be used in training to help someone with a vast amount of knowledge share that knowledge with those who need it. NetPerceptions gives eBusinesses the ability to find the documents, data sources, frequently asked questions, and fellow employees that can help them make the most of any given task in real time. This is one of the first knowledge management solutions that leverages both explicit and tacit knowledge based on each individual's immediate informational needs. While conventional search engines have been a step in the right direction, the real-time recommendation and learning capabilities of NetPerceptions technology, combined with its unique ability to share tacit knowledge, take everything to the next level. By giving an eTailer the tools needed to be more informed and proactive than ever before, NetPerceptions for Knowledge Management helps optimize return on investment of knowledge capital.[13] The company also offers a variety of advertising solutions designed to maximize customer traffic.

Partnerships

One of the driving factors behind the company's success is the numerous partnerships in the industry. These partnerships were formed to create effective e-commerce environments for clients. All of these partnerships have helped to forge, leverage, and enhance relationships with their clients online. Some of these partner firms include BroadVision (which provides one-to-one relationship management applications to business customers), DoubleClick, (a global Internet advertising solutions company), as well as technology vanguards like Microsoft and IBM. The company has aggressively built a customer base that includes many of the world's best known brands including: Art.com, Bertelsmann, CDNOW, Egghead.com, eToys.com, , Fingerhut, Hudson's Bay Company, J.C. Penney, Procter & Gamble, Tower Records, Walgreen's and SBC Communications.

Increasing numbers of businesses are recognizing the potential of the personalization movement through call centers, e-mail, the Internet or within their corporate Intranets. The earnings potential for NetPerceptions is attractive if they can continue to retain customers and attract new ones with their software, consulting and conference fees. "Upside Magazine's "E-Business Winners" list[14], compiled by the leading technology business magazine after surveying 200 analysts, recognizes the 20 technology, telecommunications and biotechnology companies most likely to continue their success in the future. NetPerceptions, which ranks No. 12 on the list, was cited for its innovative software, large customer base, strong financial performance and predicted revenue growth. "The number of households shopping online could grow to 49.9 million by 2004," the magazine said, "and technology like NetPerceptions' could increase the cross-sell rate to those buyers by 20 to 25 percent." These trends bode well for NetPerceptions and others firms like it, who are striving to deliver a new stream of value-added software products to facilitate electronic commerce.

CHALLENGES AND FUTURE DIRECTIONS

All the business models outlined above tap into the opportunities offered by the Internet. However, all these models are based on solid marketing foundations. These include the collection and use of marketing information, the ability to reach and target the right audience for a product or service, and finally, the ability to respond to market demands based on customer feedback.

There are several challenges to these models going forward. There are increasing demands by customer advocacy groups to protect online privacy. Some of these demands are justified, as eager marketers have jumped on the online bandwagon without heed for the fundamental ethic of protecting consumer interest. Growth in credit-card fraud and junk-mail solicitations is a direct result of such exuberance. Over time, marketers will have to strike a balance between online privacy and the ability to provide more targeted campaigns and one-to-one marketing efforts. Another serious concern to such models is external: It is not clear if the current system of patents is well suited to business models based on information and software. For example, several of the patents granted in the recent past to online marketing-related innovations are too broad-based, and undermine the importance of serious new innovation in this sector. It remains to be seen if a new regulatory framework is put into place to take into account the nature and scope of content based and software based innovation[15].

Further, it should be realized that the Internet fundamentally alters traditional marketing models. First, the networked model of competition dramatically increases the speed of change in every part and function of the organization, be it in building and delivering a marketing campaign or altering product or service characteristics based on feedback. By its very nature, it leads to discontinuous innovation that can supersede existing modes or channels of doing business. For example, several innovative marketers have abandoned traditional mass media and used alternative and new-media based channels to create completely new brands[16]. Second, the Internet gives small marketing outfits the ability to extend market reach and impact using technological excellence and know-how, and an aggressive partnering strategy. Thus, a successful business model can be scaled dramatically, and threaten existing players. Finally, the rate of innovation diffusion through the online medium is faster than through conventional channels, and thus requires firms to be acutely aware of their "time to market", and the "time to market response". In addition, many Web-based businesses have discovered that wired customers make their views and opinions known, and are extremely involved with their consumption experience[17]. The feedback loop between buyers and sellers is shrinking fast. Firms who seek to compete in this domain need to understand the dynamics of viral digital marketing, and the formation of extremely loyal customer communities. By constantly listening to what customers have to say, observing their purchase and consumption behavior, and interacting with them in a dynamic environment, marketers will be able to fine-tune the products or services offered. Customers are demanding convenience, participation, and anticipation[18]—the firms that deliver these effectively will be tomorrow's winners.

REFERENCES

Agency.com Web Site, URL: http://www.agency.com.

Bass, Bill, Mary Modahl and Kerry Moyer (1997), 'Internet Direct Marketing,' *The Forrester Report*, 1(6).

Deighton, John (1996), 'The Future of Interactive Marketing,' *Harvard Business Review*, p. 151, November-December.

Farrell, G. (1998), 'Agency.com', *Business 2.0*, December.

Glazer, Rashi (1999), 'Winning In Smart Markets,' *Sloan Management Review*, 59.

Joachimsthaler, Erich and David A. Aaker (1997), 'Building Brands Without Mass Media,' *Harvard Business Review*, January-February, 39.

Kadison, Maria LaTour, David E. Weisman, Mary Modahl, Ketty C. Lieu, Kip Levin (1998), The Look-To-Buy Imperative, 'The Look-To-Buy Imperative,' *The Forrester Report*, 1(1).

Netcentives Web Site, URL: http://www.netcentives.com.

Netperceptions Web Site, URL: http://www.netperceptions.com.

Neuborne, Ellen and Robert D. Hof (1998), 'Branding on the Net,' *Business Week* No. 3603, November 9, 76.

Rao, Bharat (1999), 'The Internet and the Revolution in Distribution: A Cross-Industry Examination and Synthesis,' *Technology in Society*, 21(3), Pergammon Press.

Red Herring Magazine, URL: http://www.redherring.com.

The Industry Standard (1998), 'I-Builders You Should Know: Agency.com,' www.thestandard.com, November 16.

The Industry Standard, URL: http://www.thestandard.com.

Thurow, Lester (1997), 'Needed: A New System of Intellectual Property Rights,' *Harvard Business Review*, September-October, 95.

Tsuruoka, Doug (1998), 'If Net Can Make It There, It Can Make It Anywhere,' *Investor's Business Daily*, October 7, A10.

Upside Magazine, URL: http://www.upside.com.

Wang, Nelson (1997), ' New York's Silicon Alley: A Hub for Creative Talent,' *Internet World*, Mecklermedia Corp., December 8.

ENDNOTES

1 Deighton, John (1996), 'The Future of Interactive Marketing,' *Harvard Business Review*, p. 151, November-December.

2 Neuborne, Ellen and Robert D. Hof (1998), 'Branding on the Net,' *Business Week,* No. 3603, p. 76, November 9.

3 Bass, Bill, Mary Modahl and Kerry Moyer (1997), 'Internet Direct Marketing,' *The Forrester Report*, Vol. 1, No. 6, February.

4 Kadison, Maria LaTour, David E. Weisman, Mary Modahl, Ketty C. Lieu, Kip Levin (1998), The Look-To-Buy Imperative, 'The Look-To-Buy Imperative,' *The Forrester Report*, Vol. 1, No. 1, April.

5 www.clickrewards.com.

6 Tsuruoka, Doug (1998), 'If Net Can Make It There, It Can Make It Anywhere,' *Investor's Business Daily*, p. A10, October 7.

7 Wang, Nelson (1997), 'New York's Silicon Alley: A Hub for Creative Talent,' *Internet World*, Mecklermedia Corp., December 8.

8   www.agency.com.
9   The Industry Standard (1998), 'I-Builders You Should Know: Agency.com,' www.thestandard.com, November 16.
10 Farrell, G. (1998) Agency.com', *Business 2.0*, December.
11 www.redherring.com/companyprofile/netperceptions.htm.
12 www.netperceptions.com/company/history.
13 http://www.netpercetions.com.
14 http://www.upside.com/texis/mvm/ebiz/story?id =38a1fd20.
15 Thurow, Lester (1997), 'Needed: A New System of Intellectual Property Rights,' *Harvard Business Review*, p. 95, September-October.
16 Joachimsthaler, Erich and David A. Aaker (1997), 'Building Brands Without Mass Media,' *Harvard Business Review*, p. 39, January-February.
17 Rao, Bharat (1999), 'The Internet and the Revolution in Distribution: A Cross Industry Examination and Synthesis,' *Technology in Society*, Vol. 21, No. 3, Pergammon Press.
18 Glazer, Rashi (1999), 'Winning In Smart Markets,' *Sloan Management Review*, p. 59.

Chapter 2

Leveraging Online Information to Build Customer Relationships

Christian Bauer
Working Systems Solutions, Western Australia

Arno Scharl
Vienna University of Economics, Austria

Collecting and analyzing the available information about customers is at the core of building customer relationships. This chapter categorizes potential sources of online customer information and presents examples for their utilization in an Internet business context. Methods to gather and analyze customer preferences and expectations as well as to visualize the actual behavior of Web Information Systems users are identified and categorized according to information source. In analogy to customer tracking in traditional retailing outlets, the chapter demonstrates the need to capture and visualize how users approach and navigate through Web Information Systems in order to maximize the customer delivered value in global electronic commerce.

INTRODUCTION

Since the commercialization of the Internet, marketing in general and advertising in particular were at the forefront of utilizing the new media for establishing a relationship with potential customers. The starting point for any relationship building, automated or manual, is the identification, collection and analysis of information about virtual business partners as the basis for individualized communication. The Internet offers numerous opportunities for implicit and explicit data capturing, which enables organizations to build better relationships with consumers and maximize the value of electronic transactions. This paper presents an inclusive framework of all information sources available to commercial Web Information Systems operators and provides examples of how these information sources can be capitalized upon.

In contrast to systems supporting Electronic Data Interchange (EDI) and wholesale trading, Web Information Systems for online markets exclusively target individual customers. Web Information Systems as a sub-category of mass information systems rely on the hypertext functionality and transfer mechanisms of the World Wide Web ((Scharl & Brandtweiner, 1998); see Figure 1). Mass information systems in general are global systems that support online information retrieval and routine tasks by way of self-service for a large number (thousands or millions) of occasional users who are spread over various locations (Hansen, 1995).

Being characterized by interactivity, dynamic updating, hypertextuality, and global presence they incorporate the concept of electronic catalogs (Palmer, 1997) which represent any collection of documents "that contains information about the products and services a commercial entity offers" (Segev, Wan & Beam, 1995). While the role of Web Information Systems as disseminators of information has been generally acknowledged, the notion of Web Information Systems for personalized consumer communication is frequently considered more of academic interest than of practical commercial relevance. The traditional mass media advertising model still dominates corporate strategies but needs to be replaced by new models of marketing communication making use of the full potential of the World Wide Web (Hoffman & Novak, 1997). As formulated by Hoffmann, Novak and Chatterjee (Hoffman, Novak & Chatterjee, 1995): "The interactive nature of the medium can be used by marketers to hold the attention of the consumer by engaging the consumer in an asynchronous 'dialogue' that occurs at both parties' convenience. This capability of the medium offers unprecedented opportunities to tailor communications precisely to individual customers, allowing individual consumers to request as much information as each desires. Further, it allows the marketer to obtain relevant information from customers for the purposes of serving them more effectively in the future."

Figure 1. The Web information systems environment

Focusing on the added value created for individual companies, marketing-oriented research efforts in this field have to include the identification of necessary preconditions for adaptive technologies, being the key element for an in-depth analysis of the evolution of distributed hypertext environments. As a result from reduced barriers to market entry, Web Information Systems transactions are more dynamic and potentially less predictable than their traditional counterparts. This is one of the reasons why sociocultural characteristics of the Internet and the World Wide Web in particular have to be considered as external parameters by the participating institutions when designing their retailing applications. Emerging standardized description models like the **O**pen **P**rofiling **S**tandard (OPS; http://www.firefly.net/company/OPS.fly) or the **P**latform for **P**rivacy **P**references Initiative (P3; http://w3c.bilkent.edu.tr/P3/) will provide valuable insights for the personalization of Web Information Systems regarding geographic and demographic segmentation criteria. The role of customers is getting transformed in the virtual marketspace of Web Information Systems. "Individual customers can act, if they choose to, as the analyst, the portfolio manager and the broker" (Dutta, Kwan & Segev, 1997). Based on these insights and observable shifts within the corporate value chain (e.g., the convergence of production and communication), intuitive modeling frameworks for gathering and integrating customer-specific information into retailing applications of Web Information Systems are required and have to consider the distinct features of Web Information Systems mentioned above.

CATEGORIZATION OF ONLINE CUSTOMER INFORMATION

Collection of information about customers is a necessary prerequisite for any form of relationship marketing, from face-to-face contact to global electronic media. A cornerstone and major obstacle of relationship marketing on the Internet, therefore, is the availability (or lack) of data about potential Internet customers. Consumers use anonymous Web clients and communication is provided through stateless HTTP (Hypertext Transfer Protocol). Customers will be willing to provide information about themselves under certain circumstances. However, the quality of user input remains questionable and companies rely on the cooperation of Internet users. To lay the foundations of any customer information analysis a framework for assembling potential customer information is needed.

A categorization based on the information source is developed in the following. The Web client respectively the network parameters, the user (customer) as well as third parties constitute potential information sources. These information sources and their respective attributes are summarized in Table 1. Various methods are available to obtain customer information. These (implicit or explicit) acquisition methods obviously depend on where the data is sourced from with the information gain being closely related to the efficiency and the scope of the acquisition method being employed.

Table 1: Sources of electronic customer information

Source			Acquisition Methods	Information
I	Client/ Network [Im- plicit]	Network Information	Environment Variables, HTTP Log-Files	e.g., Remote Host (Name), Browser, etc.
		Browser Support	Cookies, Java-Applets, Hidden CGI data	Visited Pages, Clickstream Analysis
II	User [Ex- plicit]	Interactive	Online Forms, etc.	Questionnaires, etc.
		Records	Customer Database	All of the Above
III	Third Party [Explicit]		Network Infrastructure	Verified Network Information

IMPLICIT GATHERING OF CUSTOMER INFORMATION

The two distinct types of implicit information gathering are presented first. Network information is available in all Internet transaction scenarios, regardless of the customer's preferred software, but contains only limited customer-specific information. Exploiting browser support enables Internet marketers to gather far more exhaustive customer information, but relies on cooperative software technology on the customer's side.

Network Information

Information from the Web client and HTTP is obtained most easily and always available. This data is passed along in environment variables when a Web server invokes a CGI-script on (Web) client request (CGI = Common Gateway Interface). For general HTML pages, the HTTP information is stored in configurable log-files. This information is usually very reliable, although it is possible to mask or maliciously change these parameters on both client and server side.

Unfortunately, the information content of this data is very poor. In regard to Web client information the following information is included: HTTP connection status, browser type, hostname or IP number of the Web client, and operating system. The standard HTTP log-files contain the remote host(name), date and time of request, the client request string, the HTTP status code (error code) and the number of bytes sent. If configured accordingly, the time taken to serve the request, any environment variable, or the port number used can be recorded as well.

To explain the poor value of this type of information for relationship marketing, the hostname is picked as an example and investigated in greater detail. A "host" can roughly be defined as a computer connected to the Internet with a unique IP number assigned. A single host may "mask" several hundreds or thousands of users (i.e., all use the same hostname respectively IP number). Security measures like firewalls or IP masquerading and caching facilities like proxy servers add more confusion to the relation of hostname and single users. The usage of the same browser by several users is another potential "danger" and might add noise to the data, decreasing the results' validity. The significance of direct HTTP information for keeping track of Web Information Systems customers, therefore, remains relatively limited. Valuable analysis based on network information is only feasible in very distinct environments.

An example would be a campus bookshop, where the vast majority of customers are students of that university. Moreover, it is very likely that computer laboratories and remote access facilities are all linked together in a campus network with the same Internet domain. The campus network infrastructure might even allow them to distinguish between faculties with IP numbers assigned to certain computer laboratories. If a Web Information Systems document of the bookshop is requested from a computer laboratory of the business school, it is quite obvious that a business student was interested in that particular page. If a user from computer science searches for a particular textbook, this search indicates demand for this book from computer science students. As a consequence, the Web Information Systems can be designed to suit specific customer target groups. Of course, such an analysis is only feasible in distinct settings, but the simple example stated above also illustrates the potential power of customer data analysis.

Browser Support

More sophisticated methods for the acquisition of customer information can be implemented using some of the features offered by modern Web clients. The most well-known and efficient method are "cookies", originally developed by Netscape (*http://developer.netscape.com/docs/manuals/communicator/jsguide4/ cookies.htm*). With this technology, a piece of information (which can be a unique identification token) is sent from the Web server to the client and stored on the client computer. Usually, the Web client will send this information back to the Web server when it requests another document (regardless of whether this request happens five minutes or five months later). Web servers can set attributes for "cookies", limiting them to certain (Internet) domains, expiration dates, or secure communication channels. Although users can change information contained in "cookies", this is not likely to happen considering the considerable efforts necessary to do this. A more serious threat to the validity of this information source is the option in most Web browsers to turn "cookies" off.

"Hiding" information in CGI *variables (http://hoohoo.ncsa.uiuc.edu/cgi/)* is a much less powerful method. It usually only works for continuous browser „sessions" and – in contrast to cookie implementations relying on modern Web browsers like Netscape Communicator 4.x supporting different user profiles – does not distinguish between users working on the same Web browser. Possible options include "hidden" fields in online forms or characters appended to URLs.

Much more cooperation from the client-side is involved when Java-Applets are employed to track customer behavior, although some users may not be aware of these actions. The interactivity and client-server communication capabilities of Java-

Applets allow for more detailed information gathering than cookies or hidden CGI information, but are slowing down response time and are increasing complexity and difficulty of Web Information Systems development. As for cookies, most Web browsers allow users to disable Java functionality which will prevent the remote execution of applets.

What information can be gained through these methods? The effective identification of a certain user or customer has the huge advantage over simple network information that connections between singular resource requests can be derived from the available data. Eventually, this leads to complete "clickstream" analysis which may be regarded as a detailed Web Information Systems discourse transcript (compare Jasper, Ellis & Wajahath, 1998). We define clickstream analysis as looking at the "path" (i.e., the entry and exit points to Web Information Systems documents) through the Web Information Systems rather than looking at statistics of singular Web pages alone. Variables of interest include entry and exit point, access time or sequence of requested HTML documents. The analysis will usually focus on both single sessions *(sequential accountability)* and on analogies between subsequent sessions initiated by the same user *(distributional accountability; compare* Jasper, Ellis & Wajahath, 1998*)*. Opportunities and requirements of this acquisition method and of visualizing aggregated clickstreams in particular are investigated in greater detail a bit later.

The data collected with these methods provides more accurate and detailed information about online customer behavior. An Internet shopping center, for example, with a whole variety of products can track down the interests of individual customers by logging their "request history" based on cookies.

If a customer takes a closer look at the available home entertainment products, an accurate list of items she was interested in before making the final decision to purchase one particular product represents valuable feedback for optimizing the placement of goods in virtual Web Information Systems environments. Frequently visited products which show low access (review) times and lead to many exits will either be presented in a different way or eliminated from the range of products offered online. Such features also add value to customers as their search process and associated transaction costs (in terms of time spent browsing and comparing offers) are cut down drastically.

VISUALIZATION OF AGGREGATED CLICKSTREAMS

The customer-oriented regular gathering of stimulus-response-data and its integration with stored information for creating dynamic user models in conformity with observable real-world patterns help the information provider to map and classify the customer's behavior, to describe its geographic and temporal distribution, and to accurately predict future behavior (Link & Hildebrand, 1995; Jaspersen, 1997). The granularity and quality of the resulting database entries determine the degrees of freedom for the information provider, the ability to maximize the customer delivered value, as well as the overall economic potential of every single project relying on this important source of information.

In the early stages "clickstream" applications exclusively focus on the processing of HTTP log-file data, enhancing the representations of commercially available analysis software for Web Information Systems. Some examples for this category of applications based on HTTP log-file data are listed in Table 2 (compare Busch, 1997; Malchow & Thomsen, 1997):

These tools, however, only provide statistically oriented representations embedded in various reports (including tables, bar charts, etc.) usually being generated directly in HTML or in a file format compatible with popular word processing software. In contrast to that, an integrated approach to Web Information Systems development and customer interaction requires the provision of easily comprehensible, visual information to decision-makers from all corporate areas. Such tools are envisaged to be analogous to traditional customer tracking diagrams which are quite common for real-world retailing outlets (see Figure 2; also Becker, 1973).

The integration and visualization of customer information will help companies running commercial Web Information Systems in their efforts to map and classify the customer's behavior, to predict future trends, to advertise more effectively, and to maximize the customer delivered value of electronic transactions. As envisaged by evolutionary Web Information Systems development efforts the optimal organizational response to customer preferences can only be achieved by the constant observation of Web Information systems usage and appropriate (re-)design. The resulting feedback cycle of (Web Information Systems) (re-)design, implementation, usage and analysis is depicted in F_Ref481227844 Figure 3. Only the implementation of business processes to enable such a cyclical approach allows

Table 2: Commercial Web-tracking software packages

Product	Company	URL
ARIA	Andromedia	http://www.andromedia.com
Bazaar Analyzer Pro	Aquas	http://www.aquas.com
GuestTrack	GuestTrack	http://www.guesttrack.com
HitList Professional	Marketwave	http://www.marketwave.com
I/PRO	Nielsen Interactive Media	http://www.nielsenmedia.com
Net.Analysis Pro	Net.Genesis	http://www.netgen.com
NetIntellect	WebManage Technologies	http://www.webmanage.com
NetTracker	Sane Solutions	http://www.nettracker.com
WebTrends	WebTrends	http://www.webtrends.com

Figure 2. Customer tracking in traditional retailing outlets (Becker 1993)

organizations to successfully employ Internet marketing and build lasting relation-ships with online customers (Bauer, Glasson & Scharl, 1999).

As illustrated in Figure 3, the examples for the design and analysis modeling are taken from a particular Web Information Systems methodology, eW3DT. For visualizing behavior and access patterns of Web Information Systems customers, the meta model of the *Extended World Wide Web Design Technique (eW3DT)* will be used in a modified version, taking into account the specific requirements of Web Information Systems analysis. Originally, eW3DT was intended to provide design-ers with a graphical notation for the construction of conceptual Web Information Systems models. Due to space limitations and our focus on Web Information Systems customer analysis the syntax of eW3DT will not be described in this paper (please refer to Scharl, 1997; Scharl, 2000; Bichler & Nusser, 1996). Independent of iconic similarity and real equivalence to a given object (hypermedia compound document), every information object type of eW3DT defines a general profile for

Figure 3. The iterative Web development process in a cybernetic feedback loop

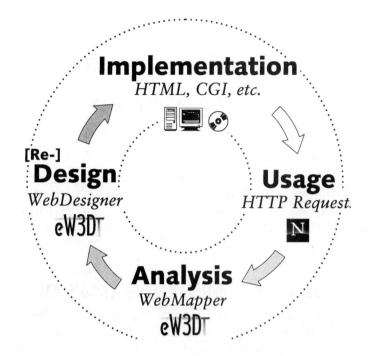

describing the characteristic attributes of this document. Each of these profiles corresponds to a set of abstractions commonly found in Web Information Systems.

With regard to the application domain of Web Information Systems analysis, however, the rectangular symbols representing different types of hypertext compound documents will incorporate a completely different set of attributes. While the color respectively the shading of objects represents their number of HTTP requests [N_Hits], the thickness of connecting links between the documents represents the frequency with which these links where followed by customers. In addition to that, the average viewing time of Web Information Systems documents in seconds is displayed in the field [Avg_VTime]. With the [Info] button, detailed information about the object in question is accessible (e.g., a list of host names / IP addresses of the most important visitors, aggregated number of entries and exits, etc.). Being part of the user interface, the two arrow symbols in the bottom right corner do not represent an attribute of the object but provide the analyst with the option to move between lower-level and upper-level diagrams.

Figure 5 contrasts the traditional customer tracking diagram with the new and integrated approach to online customer tracking. The right side of the figure contains both the design and analysis view from eW3DT for a particular Web Information System. With the proposed methodology we try to enhance the representations used by commercially available analysis software for Web Information Systems (in most cases only statistically oriented) with a graphical overview analogous to physical customer tracking which is quite common for traditional retailing outlets. This will help commercial information providers in their efforts to map and classify the customer's behavior, to predict future trends, and to advertise more

Figure 4. WebMapper standard symbolic element

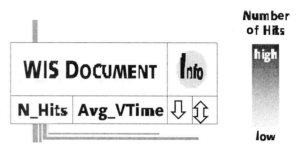

effectively. In the long run maximizing the customer delivered value of electronic transactions will lead to lasting and loyal relationships with customers – one of the basic concerns of companies investing into the infrastructure for Web Information Systems-based forms of business.

EXPLICIT GATHERING
OF CUSTOMER INFORMATION

Explicit gathering of customer information always relies on the conscious cooperation of customers at some point of the data life cycle. The data collection can be manual or automated, and in the latter case online or offline. For the purposes of Web-based Information Systems the distinction between (online collected) interactive customer response data and information gathered from existing (electronic)

Figure 5. Customer tracking for traditional retailing outlets versus eW3DT and WebMapper

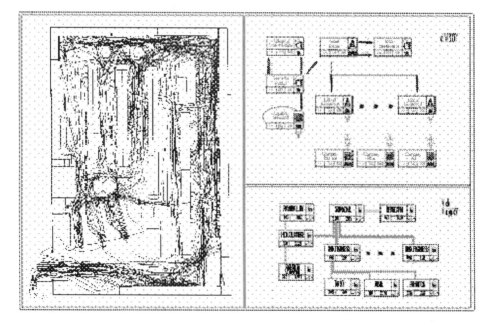

user records, which might have been created for other applications, appears most important.

Interactive Customer Response

Being explicit forms of data gathering, the remaining categories of Web Information Systems customer information indicated in Table 1 rely on the cooperation of the customer. HTML forms, the online equivalent of paper-based questionnaires, are a very simple method of direct customer interaction. Potentially, these input documents represent a very valuable source, but major shortcomings include the self-selection of customers or the fact that they may not be willing to provide information at all. In addition to that, it is most often impossible to check the quality of the provided information. However, for some information the customer is the only available source.

Simple implementations employ online forms and CGI-scripts to gather user data and response accordingly. But besides the universally employed feedback form, more sophisticated systems have been developed. Successful companies provide customized goods, services, or Web documents that are only available via Web Information Systems and from this source. Among the most popular examples are customized news services like MyYahoo! *(http://my.yahoo.com/)*, MSNBC *(http://www.msnbc.com/news/default.asp)*, CNN Custom News *(http://customnews.cnn.com/cnews/pna.myhome)*, or the push-oriented *PointCast (http://www.pointcast.com/)*, to name just a few. In addition to specifying their individual news preferences (e.g., regarding detailed weather reports for certain cities, portfolios for personalized stock market information, world news updates according to the user's main topics of interest, and so forth), users are usually asked to provide basic demographic information as well (see Figure 6).

User Records

Customer databases build the core of so-called "database marketing" systems, where multidimensional attributes of customers are recorded. The most often employed method of exploiting these databases has become part of our daily life in the form of personalized mass mailings. In the virtual age, Web Information Systems can take these technologies to the next step by synchronously keeping track of all the information sources mentioned above.

Additional information can be included from "conventional" customer databases with data sourced from past customer records, where "traditional", face-to-face business has been conducted rather than electronic transactions. Through the combination of all the data stored about an individual customer, new aspects might occur which would have been neglected otherwise.

The potential of relationship marketing solutions based on this data seems to be high compared with the relatively easy implementation at rather low costs. Companies that cannot include all products into their online catalogues may combine demographic information with user requests to select an online product mix tailored to specific target groups. More powerful marketing tools can be supported from this analysis. Consider the following example from the financial services industry: Retail banks offer their customer all sorts of discounts based on criteria such as account balance, customer loyalty, age, profession, or income. Confronting a customer with advertising or special offers primarily intended for other target groups, however, is not a wise decision. In Internet-banking authentication is a necessity for security reasons. Once a customer is authenticated online, her requests for Web Information Systems pages are logged and her records are looked up in a customer database. Information about her interests (from the observable online customer behavior) and her demographics (from the customer database) are linked and the according marketing communication material will be mailed to her. Young customers will receive advertisements about student discounts while older customers with large credit balances will receive information about investment opportunities.

THIRD PARTY NETWORKS

So far, only the customer-specific data resulting from interactions between companies and their customers has been discussed. With the commercialization of the Internet utilization of network resources is the obvious next step. Associations or service providers specializing in offering digital customer data can extend the analysis tools mentioned above and generate information otherwise unobtainable by individual enterprises. Until now, only few ventures offer such services with limited functionality to companies. The simplest advertising idea using third party information are context-specific banner ads in search engines (Yahoo!, AltaVista, HotBot, etc.) based upon user input. More sophisticated information could be provided by online shopping networks. These "Internet Malls" already provide their member companies with services such as Web Information Systems implementation or maintenance, payment transaction processing or logistics support. This close relationship can be expanded to relationship marketing, if information is shared amongst all involved companies under central management. Much more accurate customer profiles will result from such databases. These advantages need not be restricted to companies operating closely together. Loose associations of companies and other available information sources can be managed through providers of distributed (database) networks. The main goal of these ventures is to share customer-specific information and to add value to their respective relationship marketing efforts.

Early examples for the potential of such networks are Engage Technologies *(http://www.engagetech.com/)* or Firefly with the Passport Network Hub *(http:// www.firefly.net/studio/products/Passport_Network_Hub/).* It goes without saying that high attention has to be paid to issues of consumer privacy when implementing such applications.

Figure 6. MyYahoo! ID card

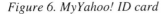

STRATEGIC CONSEQUENCES
The Convergence of Productive and Dispositive Data Processing

The strong specialization of academic research and practice in formulating, analyzing and implementing global marketing strategies for Web Information Systems was a direct result from the insight that abstract marketing instruments cannot generally be applied to different sectors and industries without taking into account the specific features of these heterogeneous segments. The necessary consideration of core competencies is reflected in a number of highly specialized approaches of analyzing market-oriented decision behavior (Haller, 1997).

In the early seventies the first textbooks were published which explicitly dealt with trade marketing and emphasized the institutional function of trade. Prior to this rather focused approach trade was primarily regarded as a mere distribution channel of productive industries. With the gaining popularity of direct marketing the increasing importance of IT support was recognized as well. Direct marketing represents a targeted, carefully planned communication process with known customers (active or potential) which relies on historic and context-specific information usually being stored in corporate database systems, uses different media synchronously, and provides instant customer feedback. The increasing convergence of product design, presentation, and communication goes hand in hand with the parallel use of customer-related information for specifying a company's product and communication policy. This implies an integrated architecture for both productive and dispositive data processing (compare, for example, the marketspace model of Dutta, Kwan & Segev, 1997).

Tailored solutions at a cost level comparable to that of mass marketing increase the degree of freedom for price policy, attract new customers, reduce price elasticity of demand, and create barriers to market entry for potential competitors (Reiss & Beck, 1995). The convergence of information retrieval and usage as far as adaptive marketing systems are concerned obsoletes the usual distinction between market research and market management. Nevertheless, isolated and sequential approaches are still quite common in business practice. Seen as a closed loop consisting of conceptual design, pre-test, stimulus, customer response, and performance analysis, adaptive systems contribute to a more realistic, dynamic user model and a more efficient allocation of limited marketing resources.

Maximizing the Customer Delivered Value

There is an ongoing discussion about anonymity and privacy on the Internet in general and on the World Wide Web in particular. These issues are of rather societal interest and, though important, were not discussed in this chapter. Obviously related are legal issues, such as privacy laws and regulations, which vary from country to country. These legal barriers have to be addressed at an international level for global media like Web Information Systems, and the leading industrial nations still have to agree on a global solution. However, for reasons of clarity and in order to ensure a comprehensive research framework, absence of legal restrictions was assumed for this discussion.

Gathering high-quality data about Web Information Systems users is a prerequisite for combining marketing instruments in order to effectively analyze and influence the information retrieval, decision and usage patterns of active and potential customers (Belz, 1997). Some authors vehemently criticize these manipulative intentions although many customers – no matter which specific target group they belong to – demand both communication and product design to be tailored specifically to their personal needs and preferences. Customizing Web Information Systems content to user profiles, therefore, aims at identifying potential customers and offering them the required products at the right time and conditions, using appropriate representations and terminology (Link & Hildebrand, 1995). Using the definition of Kotler et al. (Kotler et al., 1996), this target may be expressed by maximizing the customer delivered value, which is calculated as the difference between the *total customer value* (product, services, personnel, image values) and *the total customer cost* (monetary, time, energy, and psychic costs).

Analogous to traditional markets, users of Web Information Systems buy the required products and services from the (information) provider that they believe offers the highest customer delivered value. Due to the immaterial, non-tangible, and transitory nature of services and due to the fact that production and consumption take place synchronously, the value of product-oriented market research in the traditional sense is drastically reduced. The focus on products has to be replaced by an in-depth analysis of customers and target groups including personal needs, preferences, and expectations, which provides essential feedback for product design as well as for strategic and operative decisions of the sales department (Huettner, 1997).

CONCLUSION

When analyzing Internet business operations instead of their traditional counterparts, important choices such as how to optimally place physical goods are replaced by decisions concerning the appropriate depth and width of electronic product catalogs and the recommended hierarchical layer for presenting certain products or services. Electronic business models that integrate Web Information Systems with sophisticated analysis tools and adaptive system components provide far more opportunities for capturing and leveraging behavioral data than currently utilized by most companies. The classification of sources for this category of information represents the basis for more detailed analyses. Customer-specific information can be derived from client/network sources, users or third-party networks. All of these channels have to be considered synchronously when customer behavior in Web Information Systems is to be analyzed.

The design of interactive Web Information Systems that maximize the delivered value and build lasting relationships with customers has to incorporate available data into structured communication channels. This paper presented a categorization for available sources of information about online customers, which provides Internet marketers with a starting point for designing Web Information Systems and successfully transforming the corporate value chain.

REFERENCES

Becker, W. (1973). *Beobachtungsverfahren in der demoskopischen Marktforschung.* Eds. O. Strecker and R. Wolffram (= Bonner Hefte für Marktforschung, Bd. 9), Ulmer, Stuttgart.

Belz, C. (1997). *Strategisches Direct Marketing: Vom sporadischen Direct Mail zum professionellen Database Management*, Ueberreuter, Vienna.

Bichler, M.; Nusser, S. (1996). W3DT – The Structured Way of Developing WWW-Sites, *Proceedings of the 4th European Conference on Information Systems*, Lisbon, 1093-1101.

Busch, (1997). Count your blessings. *Internet World*, June, 75-83.

Dutta, S.; Kwan, S.; Segev, A. (1997). Transforming business in the marketspace – strategic marketing and customer relationships. *CMIT Working Paper*. University of California, Berkeley.

Haller, S. (1997). *Handels-Marketing*. Ed. H.C. Weis (Modernes Marketing für Studium und Praxis). Kiehl, Ludwigshafen.

Hansen, H.R. (1995). Conceptual framework and guidelines for the implementation of mass information systems. *Information & Management*, February, 125-142.

Hoffman, D.; Novak, T. (1997). A new marketing paradigm for electronic commerce. *The Information Society*, 13 (1), 45-54.

Hoffman, D.; Novak, T.; Chatterjee, P. (1995). Commercial Scenarios for the Web: Opportunities and Challenges. *Journal of Computer-Mediated Communication*, 1 (3), 1995, http://jcmc.huji.ac.il/vol1/issue3/hoffman.html.

Huettner, M. (1997). *Grundzuege der Marktforschung*. Oldenbourg, Munich/Vienna.

Jasper, J.; Ellis, R.; Wajahath, S. (1998). *Towards a Discourse Analysis of User Clickstreams on the Web*, Institute of Gerontology, Wayne State University, 1998, http://giw.iog.wayne.edu/manuscripts/webdiscourse/.

Jaspersen, T. (1997). *Computergestütztes Marketing: Controllingorientierte DV-Verfahren für Absatz und Vertrieb*. Oldenbourg, Munich/Vienna.

Kotler et al. (1996). *Principles of Marketing – The European Edition*. Prentice Hall, London.

Link, J. and Hildebrand, V.G. (1995). Wettbewerbsvorteile durch kundenorientierte Informationssysteme – Konzeptionelle Grundlagen und empirische Ergebnisse. *Journal fuer Betriebswirtschaft*, 45 (1), 46-62.

Malchow, R. and Thomsen, K. (1997). Web-Tracking. *Screen Multimedia*, September, 57-61.

Palmer, J. (1997). Retailing on the WWW: The use of electronic product catalogs. *EM – Electronic Markets*, 7 (3), 6-9.

Reiss, M.; T.C. Beck, T. (1995). Performance-Marketing durch Mass Customization. *Marktforschung & Management*, February, 62-67.

Scharl, A. (1997). *Referenzmodellierung kommerzieller Masseninformationssysteme – Idealtypische Gestaltung von Informationsangeboten im World Wide Web am Beispiel der Branche Informationstechnik*. Peter Lang, Frankfurt, .

Scharl, A. (2000): Evolutionary Web Development. London: Springer, http://webdev.wu-wien.ac.at/.

Scharl, A.; Brandtweiner, R. (1998). A Conceptual Research Framework for Analyzing the Evolution of Electronic Markets. *International Journal of Electronic Markets*, 8 (2), 39-42.

Segev, A.; Wan, D. and Beam, C. (1995). Designing electronic catalogs for business value: results of the CommerceNet pilot. *CMIT Working Paper*. University of California, Berkeley.

Chapter 3

The Evolution of Web Marketing Practice

Malu Roldan
San Jose State University, USA

This chapter reviews the current state of Web marketing practice and presents a framework on the relationships among Web technology capabilities, marketing approach and customer orientation. We present a discussion of how Web technology capabilities — such as data, network reach, traceable traffic, portability, interactivity, and high-bandwidth transmission — enable different marketing approaches – specifically, matching, branding, customer experience, and viral marketing. The viability of these approaches is determined by how well they match the orientations of target customers – be it recreational, experiential, convenience, or economic. Propositions regarding the interaction between current practices and shopper orientations are presented as a basis for determining effective Web marketing practices.

This chapter discusses the second generation of Web marketing practice. As the Web platform enters its adolescence (in Internet years), we are in a promising juncture in the evolution of these practices. Browser-accessible applications, networks, and Web marketing are growing in sophistication. The Web-reachable user population has mushroomed as well, thanks to the proliferation of cheap to free Web access and personal computers. In the U.S. alone, the growth of the online population has reached 64% saturation (ACNielsen Homescan, 2000) and there is a strong push for growing wired populations globally (Lynch, 2000; Baker, Gross, Kunii and Crockett, 2000). Nevertheless, companies are still struggling to come up with means of harnessing this technology to effectively reach and maintain their target markets. It is, thus, an interesting time in which to capture the state of marketing practice – in effect to take a reading of a range of forms vying for survival in the current ecosystem of marketing practice. Among these forms are clues to the form of future Web marketing practice – as future practices will likely be formed of combinations or elaboration of the forms we see today. In addition to describing these approaches, we will discuss how they exploit the capabilities of Web technologies and how well suited they are for targeting customers of different orientations.

This chapter will assume two typical goals of marketing efforts – customer acquisition and monetizing markets (Rayport, 1999). Customer acquisition is a major buzzword of the current internet era. In lieu of profits, many dot-coms are seeking high growth in market size or revenues as a way of signaling the market that the company is worth the investment – by venture capital, stock market, or corporate acquirer. Thus, much of Web marketing, particularly for dot-coms, is geared towards attracting customers and getting them to initiate a recognized relationship with the company – usually by registering as a member (e.g., one-click shopping at amazon.com), signing up for services (e.g., e-mail service from hotmail.com), or setting up a custom default page (e.g., MyYahoo at yahoo.com). Once a customer is acquired, the second goal — monetizing markets — kicks in. At this point, marketing efforts are focused on developing and maintaining an economic relationship with an "acquired" customer, making sure that they continue to remain a part of the company's customer base while contributing to the company's revenue stream. Companies expect such a relationship to become monetized in the form of profit. Presumably, a company can charge loyal customers a premium for their products and services, increasing the likelihood of generating healthy profits.

We propose a three-dimensional framework for discussing the marketing approaches used to achieve these goals of customer acquisition and monetizing markets. The three dimensions are customer orientation, technology capability, and marketing approach. *Technology capabilities* cover the significant characteristics of Web technologies that enable them to provide an excellent platform for marketing. *Marketing approaches* are the strategies that companies have used to exploit the capabilities provided to them by this Web platform. Lastly, *Customer orientation* refers to a customer's general predisposition towards acts of shopping (Li, Kuo, and Russell, 1999). The next section will discuss these dimensions in detail.

THREE DIMENSIONS
OF WEB MARKETING PRACTICE

The three dimensions of Web marketing practice of concern here are technology capabilities, marketing approaches, and customer orientation. This section discusses each dimension separately and in detail, providing examples to illustrate the categories comprising each dimension. Technology capabilities enable different marketing approaches. These marketing approaches, in turn, have different applications and impacts on customers, depending on their orientations. The following

Figure 1. Conceptual framework relating technology, marketing approach and customer orientation

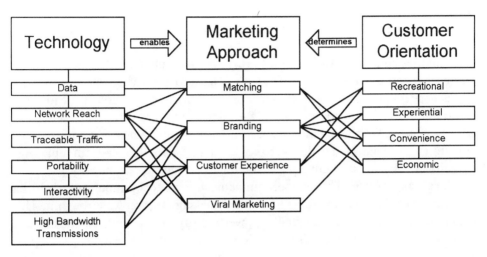

discussion will mirror this sequence of relationships among the three dimensions, as summarized in Figure 1.

TECHNOLOGY CAPABILITIES

Web technologies provide a powerful infrastructure for marketing approaches. This power stems from six characteristics to be described here – data, network reach, traceable traffic, portability, interactivity, and high-bandwidth transmission.

Data. The Web consists of banks of Web servers accessible to client machines over a collection of networks. A key aspect of Web server software is the ability to track activity at a given server. Additionally, more sophisticated software packages and services for collecting and analyzing data on customers are emerging, among them: comprehensive trend and usage monitoring organizations like Media Metrix (http://www.mediametrix.com/usa/index.jsp), online market research services like QuickTake (http://www.quicktake.com/qt/default.asp), collaborative filtering technology such as MacroMedia's Like Minds (http://www.macromedia.com/ebusiness/likeminds/), and trend intelligence services like the Worth Global Style Network (Agins, 2000 – http://www.wgsn.com). The struggle to understand the nature and potential of the Web has resulted in a proliferation of services that track Web trends at various levels of analysis. This, coupled with the fact that the TCP-IP protocol renders most Web activity traceable, has resulted in huge amounts of data being collected on customer activity. Granted, much of these data remain poorly analyzed (Ryan, 1999). But the fact that the data have been collected offers up the prospect of mining this data for key information on customers. Such information can serve as a basis for designing and evaluating marketing programs.

Network Reach. The growing popularity of the Web platform and the associated hype has stimulated the growth of data networks to run on various conduits – from cable to phone lines to wireless. Phone companies, cable companies, media content providers, and various entrepreneurial investors (e.g. Paul Allen's Vulcan Ventures) are allocating huge resources to building data networks, controlling content, and signing up customers. Deregulation and highly energetic mergers and acquisitions activity among these companies (Cresswell, 2000) provide rapid network growth and a presence in multiple conduits for their data network services. Offers like free Web services (e.g., NetZero.com) and equipment rebates in exchange for internet service provider contracts (e.g., Compuserve) have lowered the cost of PCs and network access, and fueled recent growth in the number of users tapping into the Web. Now more than ever before, with almost 135 million (and growing) users connected to the Web (CyberAtlas, 2000), this platform represents a significant channel for delivering marketing messages to customers.

Traceable traffic. The Internet communication protocols require an identifier for every node in the network and for every message that flows through it. This requirement results in a potentially powerful way of tracking customers and targeting marketing messages. By knowing the source of a given message, marketers are able to track which Web sites direct traffic towards the sites they are promoting. It is also a way of targeting the messages to nodes in the network that may be most receptive to them. The growing popularity of email marketing exploits this capability perfectly. With the ability to associate consumers with their Web activities, marketers can use relatively cheap email channels to send targeted email advertising directly to the customers who would be most receptive to it (O'Brien, 2000).

Portability. A new trend in Web technologies is the growing miniaturization and specialization of Web access points, in the form of information appliances or IP-addressable embedded computing. At this juncture, there is a battle for control of the standard information appliance at both the hardware and software platforms. A variety of devices are vying for the consumer choice for portable Internet access (English, 2000), among them handheld personal data assistants (PDAs) like Palm Pilots and Compaq's iPaq, clamshell profile PCs like the Hewlett-Packard Jornada 820, e-mail readers like Sharp's Pocketmail, Web-enabled cell phones like the Motorola Timeport, and just about any handheld device in general use that could be outfitted with Web access capability — from Walkmans to Gameboys (Baker, Gross, Kunii, and Crockett, 2000). On the software side, Microsoft is angling to mount a strong challenge to the PalmOS dominance in the handheld PDA space with the release of its PocketPC software (Carvajal, 2000). This competition promises to stimulate the rapid enhancement of the capabilities of these devices as the companies try to one-up each other with new introductions. More importantly, and pertinent to the purpose of this paper, these devices enable customers to access marketing messages without being tethered to their home computer or bulky laptops. This enables the consumer to obtain "just-in-time" marketing messages that could enhance and inform their customer experience in any location – including a store where they can purchase products they are interested in Weber (2000).

IP-addressable embedded computing is built on the premise that any device –

from washing machines to clothing – that can embed a computer chip, can possess the capability to patch into networks like the Internet (Wildstrom, 1999). Once connected, these devices not only can display marketing messages, but they can also send out information on their status – e.g., to repair and maintenance centers. They may even alter the characteristics of the product itself to fit the situation at hand. For example, software upgrades that provide greater capabilities can be sent directly to these embedded chips via the Internet.

Interactivity. Web communications are in their essence two-way conversations between client devices and servers. As such, a client device (and a customer working through it) can send messages to a server that uniquely identifies a customer and his/her preferences and characteristics. This information can be obtained directly by asking the customer or by tracking a customer's activities while he/she is on the Web – within the fuzzy limits of still evolving Internet privacy laws. This information can be used to customize marketing messages that are sent back to the customer in reaction to the information provided by him/her. A growing trend is to place human experts in the space between the server and the client (Kirsner, 1999). These experts can provide advice and information to customers via a chat, discussion group, or email interface. Particularly for products or services that have ambiguous features, the give-and-take provided by these interactive tools – particularly text and voice chats – can help experts hone in on the needs of a customer and, hopefully, better match him/her with the products and services provided by the company.

Another capability enabled by interactivity is an engaging customer interface. Interactivity makes it possible to involve the consumer in game and game-like situations that hook a customer via activities that involve play and competition. Core to the engaging nature of these activities is the fact that an intriguing, entertaining, and/or informative reply is provided in response to entries by a customer. The customer is then more likely to continue the interaction because his/her interest has been piqued. A compelling example of the power of interactivity for engaging customers is the profitable frenzy created in auction sites like ebay.com around bidding wars for the most ordinary products.

High-bandwidth transmissions. Note that this refers to the messages being sent through Internet wires, not the wires themselves. The ability to send out large files that require high-bandwidth pipes, while currently stymied by low-bandwidth networks, nevertheless holds the promise for providing rich, omnimedia, Web marketing settings. Already there are efforts to experiment with the transmission of virtual smell and touch sensations aside from the readily available visual sensations (Platt, 1999). This holds the promise for developing Web approaches that allow customers to experience the product, and the shopping activity, through simulations — without ever leaving their desktops. Ultimately, it will be possible to introduce a virtual version of the customer him or herself. This virtual customer can try on clothes, not only to show the customer product characteristics like color and styling, but also to actually preview how an outfit will look on the customer. At the same time, the look, smell, and ambiance of a store can be simulated so that customers can feel that they are trying the clothes on and shopping around at their favorite stores and malls.

These technologies alone and in combination enable a variety of marketing approaches, as discussed in the next section.

MARKETING APPROACH

Marketing approaches enabled by Web technologies can be classified under four categories – matching, branding, customer experience, and viral marketing.

Matching. Matching is the alignment of a company's products and services with the preferences of its customers. It includes among the earliest approaches to Web marketing, commonly referred to as one-to-one marketing or mass customization (Brady, Kerwin, Welch, Lee, and Hof, 2000). Matching is enabled primarily by the pervasive data collection capabilities of Web technologies. These data, when mined effectively, can provide rich profiles of customer requirements. A company can then use this information to customize its product to match each customer's unique profile.

Currently, much of this customization occurs for the most information rich products. For example, customers can select what types of information are available to them when they fire up their browsers – via the "My—" pages provided by portals – e.g., MyYahoo. Portals also provide targeted ads aimed at the demographics of customers – e.g., matching banner adds to the customer's gender – or based on customer behavior – e.g. matching banner adds to the search engine requests of customers (an add for Toyota trucks might pop up when a user enters a search for pick-ups into the search engine).

This approach can evolve to a point where even hard goods, such as home appliances, can be customizable on the fly. The portability capabilities of this technology allow the embedding of computing and network capabilities within these hard goods. For example, a small computer monitor on an oven can display instructions for cooking a meal, specific to the abilities of the cook. This message can be sent periodically to the oven from a menu planning service according to the parameters set by the customer. The same service can coordinate the shopping required to complete the meals in its plan, say for a given week, either by providing a printable list or by directly coordinating with a grocery delivery service. These services are already partially available through companies such as Streamline.com. A customer gets set up with the service by having the company scan the UPC of the items in its pantry and allowing the company to install a lockbox with a refrigerated section in an accessible area of his/her house, such as the garage. A customer then uses a UPC reader to scan all items as he/she uses them up. This generates an order list that Streamline fills automatically by delivering the goods to the lockbox. By partnering with a menu planning service, Streamline can not only replenish a customer's pantry with commonly used goods, but also bring the ingredients, and even equipment, necessary for completing a week's worth of meals – or a day's worth, depending on the preferences of the customer.

Branding. The branding approach contrasts with the matching approach by taking the perspective that customers cannot always tell marketers what they want – whether in focus groups, individual interviews, or surveys. Also, inferences about customer preferences based on their past Web surfing activities or purchases are, at this stage, imperfect educated guesses at best. Data mining techniques, particularly for Web data, are at their infancy and cannot yet provide reliable profiles of customer preferences. So matching approaches are problematic because it is hard to determine what customer preferences need to be matched, let alone what product or service characteristics can match those preferences. An alternative approach would be for a company to aim to prescribe and shape customer preferences. This ability accrues to companies that build strong brands (Kirsner, 1999).

Web technologies, particularly because of capabilities like network reach and high-bandwidth transmissions – e.g., omnimedia – have great potential for brand building approaches. Especially when coordinated with traditional channels for brand building, the Web can significantly extend the basket of tools available to marketers aiming to build a brand. Like traditional broadcast media, the Web can deliver materials used to build a brand image to any desktop patched onto the Internet. Such materials can range from advertising to the look and feel of a Web site. Coordinating Web advertising and Web site look with traditional advertising can be a powerful way to establish a brand image (Dayal, Landesberg, and Zeisser, 2000).

Other Web technology capabilities augment the brand building potential created by a coordinated broadcast effort. In particular interactivity and portability can be exploited to provide novel ways for customers to connect and attach to a brand. Interactivity can be used in conjunction with high-bandwidth transmissions to create virtual environments where customers can experience a brand – for example, by playing a game that incorporates concepts from the company's brand image. With portability, these virtual environments can be experienced by the customer in any setting, enabling a bricks-and-clicks approach to brand building. Customers can take a portable device with them as they roam the aisles of a store, for example. The portable device can provide advertising messages that coordinate with the store environment customers are walking through. Such advertising messages can add to the ambiance of the store by reinforcing the brand image with complementary advertising material. They can also provide a medium for interacting with a virtual environment – e.g., customers can be involved in a game that requires information collected from the bricks and mortar store. This combination of the virtual and bricks-and-mortar environments can provide engaging, novel experiences that increase the likelihood that the customer will form a strong emotional connection with a brand (Weber, 2000).

Customer Experience. The customer experience is a combined approach that aims at applying Web technologies to the full experience surrounding a given product or service. This includes providing customers with the information and product characteristics they prefer as well as building and maintaining a strong product brand (Kirsner, 1999). In effect, a company taking a customer experience approach builds a brand and builds credibility to a level that it can meet, exceed, anticipate and dictate customer preferences through its products and services. In the past, Web marketers aimed at achieving this purely on the Web platform. Recent developments of Web technology's portability and network reach capabilities have stimulated the evolution of customer experience approaches that assume a bricks-and-clicks platform, that is, a coordination between the virtual platform and the bricks-and-mortar platforms available to a given company.

As with branding, combining Web technologies' network reach, high band-width capabilities, and interactivity goes a long way towards creating a virtual environment that is engaging and informative. Early Web marketers such as those with amazon.com were extremely savvy with the use of Web technologies to provide customers with efficient and clean Web storefronts. Search engines and intelligent agents have empowered customers by providing them with the tools and information necessary to research a given product or service and identify the best value among a set of choices.

Bricks-and-clicks platforms significantly extend the power of customer experience approaches. On a bricks-and-clicks platform, a customer can access just-in-time information pertinent to a product or service that they are using or purchasing. For example, biztravel.com provides their customers with up-to-the-minute flight information downloadable to their PDAs. Thus, a biztravel.com customer can make decisions about his/her schedule and flight alternatives at any point during a trip – in between meetings, on the way to the airport. This gives customers greater flexibility with scheduling and, potentially, helps them make more effective use of their time (Kirsner, 1999).

Several mall developers are experimenting with powerful ways of incorporating PDAs to extend customer experiences at their malls. PDAs are used to scan in items that a customer wishes to purchase at different stores in a mall. Marketers can use the PDAs to cross-sell merchandise to these customers – suggesting other products that complement the items that they have purchased. When ready, customers can take the PDA to a mall checkout station, pay for the goods, then either have them delivered or pick them up at one spot. PDAs can also be used to build gift registries – parents who have little time to shop can have their teens shop around and scan items that they would like to put on a wish list. Mom and Dad can then select items to give their teens as gifts from these wish lists (Groover, 2000).

Perhaps most intriguing is the way that PDAs can empower customers, particularly with their bricks-and-clicks buying activities. Customers who have identified items to purchase can refer to their PDAs to determine which stores in the local area carry comparable items. The customers can compare prices of similar items that are for sale in stores that they can conveniently get to from their current locations. If products are out of stock at a given store, customers can check to see if they are available at other stores in the general vicinity of the current store. Customers can also access information about products themselves – e.g., check out buyer guides and product comparisons – that help them make informed choices before purchasing products (Weber, 2000).

Viral Marketing. A highly effective marketing application of Web technologies is viral marketing. Similar in approach to network marketing, direct mail, and pyramid schemes, viral marketing made a significant impact on Web marketing practice when its effectiveness was clearly demonstrated in the early days of Hotmail (Bronson, 1999). With only a few thousand dollars budgeted for marketing, the company was able to grow its customer base to 100,000 in a matter of weeks. On the strength of Hotmail's success, viral marketing has become one of the most prevalent marketing approaches particularly among dot-coms (Ransdell, 1999). Start-ups are giving away for free everything from internet service to personal computers to a vast array of Web applications (e.g., group support software from egroups.com). This approach directly addresses the customer acquisition goal of marketers. A company's customer base grows rapidly when products and services are provided free of charge.

Viral marketing leverages the network reach and traceable traffic capabilities of Web technologies. Essentially, this approach grows a customer base by using existing customers as focal points. Each customer brings with him/her a network of potential customers — ideally, captured in an MS Outlook address book. Viral marketers can then, with the permission of the customer, send email invitations to people in the customer's network. Usually the growth in the network benefits the customer as well since he/she will be able to use the company's products and services with the people in his/her network, should they decide to become customers. Thus, the network reach of the Internet makes it possible to connect an even wider range of customers to the network, while traceable traffic enables marketers to determine where a customer is located on the Web and where potential customers may be reached.

Clearly, the Web platform and its extension into bricks-and-clicks can be a powerful marketing medium. The following section explores the effective appropriation of these approaches to reach a range of customer types.

CUSTOMER ORIENTATION

Customer orientation is an important dimension in assessing the viability of various Web-marketing approaches. Since not all approaches will work for all customers, this very viability is highly dependent on the type of customer that is being targeted by the marketing approach. If companies can match approaches to customers, they can more efficiently tap their marketing budgets, focusing the resource intensive campaigns only on those customers that will be receptive to them. In this discussion, customer orientation is defined in terms of the shopping behavior of customers – incorporating aspects of customer activities, interests and opinions regarding the relationship of shopping to their lifestyle. Among the numerous taxonomies of customer orientation, we will use here one that has been associated with the behavior of electronic commerce customers.

This taxonomy classifies customers into four orientations – *recreational*, *experiential*, *convenience*, and *economic*. While this is intended as a classification system, it is important to say here that customers that tend towards only one of these orientations, are rare. Generally, customers will display a combination of these orientations; though have a tendency towards one of them. The following definitions of the four orientations use the example of a clothing purchase as a way of differentiating and clarifying the definitions.

Recreational Orientation. Customers with a recreational orientation shop for pleasure. In a survey of 999 internet users, Li, Kuo, and Russell (1999) found that these customers strongly agree with statements that characterize them as enjoying window shopping, enjoying shopping around and looking at window displays, and never feeling bored when shopping. Recreational customers will likely value the ambiance surrounding a shopping purchase as much as – or even more than – the item being purchased on its own. For example, a recreational shopper looking to make a clothing purchase will drive the extra distance to purchase it at a mall or upscale store that provides entertainment or a special atmosphere. Once there, they are likely to spend extra time browsing through stores and engaging in activities unrelated to the clothing purchase – e.g., sitting down for a cup of coffee at an outdoor café.

Experiential Orientation. Customers with an experiential orientation like to inspect and try products before purchasing them. Li, Kuo, and Russell (1999) found that these customers strongly agree with statements that characterize them as wanting to see and touch products before buying them, not wanting to buy things without seeing them, and wanting to try a product before buying it. An experiential customer looking to make a clothing purchase will visit a clothing store to check on the adequacy of a piece of clothing in terms of features like fit, color, styling and workmanship.

Convenience Orientation. Customers with a convenience orientation like to minimize the time and effort associated with the purchase of a product. Li, Kuo, and Russell (1999) found that these customers strongly agree with statements that characterize them as not wanting to wait in long lines for checking out goods, placing great importance on saving time while shopping, and wanting to be able to shop at any time of day. Convenience customers will likely purchase products from stores that are easy to reach and have efficient checkout procedures. A convenience customer looking to make a clothing purchase will obtain the product from a store that is most accessible to them or from a mail-order catalog.

Economic Orientation. Customers with an economic orientation like to conduct a lot of research to make sure that they obtain the best value for their money when making a purchase. Li, Kuo, and Russell (1999) found that these customers strongly agree with statements that characterize them as wanting to shop around for the best buy, wanting to consider a wide selection before making a purchase, and feeling great when they get a good deal. They also strongly agree that a being a smart shopper is worth the extra time it takes and that having a wide selection of goods to choose from is very important. Before making a purchase, an economic shopper will conduct a number of activities to obtain information on the clothing he/she intends to purchase – e.g., consulting all available resources, checking comparisons and consumer reports – and to obtain the best price – e.g., comparison shopping, using coupons and other offers.

As suggested by the above discussion, these orientations have strong potential to impact the way customers might react or relate to on-line marketing approaches. In the next section, we present propositions on the relationship between marketing approach and customer orientation.

Customer Orientation Determines Marketing Approach

It is tempting to assume that all marketing approaches apply to all customers. It is often stated that one-to-one marketing – matching products to customer preferences – is the way to form lasting relationships with customers. However, this statement seems to miss the point that customers not only have preferences regarding product attributes, they also have preferences – conscious or not — regarding the marketing approaches used on them. Different customers respond differently to different marketing approaches. It is our argument that this mechanism will be a strong determinant of the forms of Web marketing approaches in the future. In this section we present several propositions regarding marketing approach preferences of customers with varying orientations.

The reader should note that while there is variation in the mix of approaches that each type of customer relates to, it is significant that the discussion below identifies branding as an approach that connects with every customer type. The reason for this is that every customer relates to different aspects of a given brand – using it as a signal for status or quality, for example. As such, brands not only connect products and services with social and emotional factors, they also act as shorthand for customers seeking other qualities from products and services. In the fast-paced world of the Internet era, every shopper appreciates convenience at least some of the time, regardless of his/her primary orientation. Brands provide a convenient, expedient way of determining if a product meets a customer's requirements.

Customers with recreational orientations shop for pleasure. They will thus be most responsive to the ambiance that surrounds a given product or service. This ambiance is generally built with branding and customer experience approaches. These customers respond to the social and emotional experiences associated with a given brand. For example, they would be willing to pay a premium to purchase a tin of tea that connects a story to the leaves it contains – e.g., tazo teas, republic of tea. Online, they would be willing to purchase from a site that associates social or emotional significance to a product. For example, they would pay a premium to buy wines at wine.com because of "Chief Cork Dork" Peter Granoff's expertise and humor.

Multimedia experiences that simulate off-line shopping could be powerful draws to customers with recreational orientations. However, much of the technology — and certainly current bandwidth — prevent online marketers from providing the experiences that could draw these customers away from the bricks-and-mortar experiences that they most strongly connect with. Current bricks-and-clicks approaches could provide an interim solution. Customers can still experience a mall while gaining the benefits of online shopping via a PDA. Bricks-and-clicks also provides online marketers with an opportunity to learn about the shopping habits of these customers – ultimately, incorporating elements of the mall experience into the Web platform when feasible. At the same time, this platform will likely have impact on the customers themselves – slowly incorporating online elements into their mental models of a shopping experience. Moreover, Web technologies are rapidly being augmented with multimedia capabilities that go beyond sound and visuals. Synthesizers like those being developed at Digiscents (Platt, 1999) can be used to simulate a rich spectrum of the sensory aspects of an online shopping experience. This could result in the evolution of shopping experiences with major online components that satisfy and draw even customers with recreational orientations.

Proposition 1. Customers with recreational orientations will respond most strongly to branding and customer experience approaches.

Proposition 2. Customers with recreational orientations will respond to the emotional and social significance of a brand.

Customers with an experiential orientation like to inspect and try products before purchasing them. On the surface, they will tend to be most responsive to approaches that recreational orientation customers respond to — branding and customer experience approaches. However, while customers with recreational orientations respond to the social and emotional associations of a brand or customer experience, experiential orientation customers largely use brand and customer experience as a way of learning more about a product or service. They may use a brand as a signal that a given product or service will have the product characteristics they desire – e.g., right fit. For example, the dimensions of clothes from a given brand generally stay consistent, particularly for well-established brands that institute good quality control. A customer with an experiential orientation can thus have some confidence that products with a given brand will fit him/her as expected. Because of this confidence, such a customer may forgo a trip to the store to check out sizing and instead purchase products from a trusted brand online. Additionally, online marketers may encourage online purchases from experiential orientation customers by striving to build an online brand that is associated with standardized, predictable product characteristics – good fit, colors that match the colors of online graphics, rich product descriptions and photographs, sending product samples and swatches out to the customer.

Customers with experiential orientations will respond most strongly to customer experiences that focus on product characteristics rather that on the ambiance of a shopping experience. Multimedia experiences that help the customer assess the suitability of a product are most useful. Many experimental multimedia-shopping applications address just these needs of experiential orientation customers. For example, a customer's dimensions and preferences could be scanned and digitized. This digital representation of the customer can then be used to "try on" various products that the customer would be interested in – e.g. clothes, accessories, and sports equipment. Placing the digital representation on the Web greatly expands the number and variety of products that could be fitted to the customer's digital representation. The customer could then quickly see which products would be acceptable and, perhaps with some experience, trust this mode of shopping enough to make purchases without having to go to a store and actually touch and feel a product. These experiences could be augmented with samples and swatches sent via traditional means to the customer. Moreover, developments in digital synthesizers like the odor synthesizers being developed by DigiScents (Platt, 1999) portend a future where customers can touch, see and smell a product without taking their eyes off their flat panel displays.

Proposition 3. Customers with experiential orientations will respond most strongly to branding and customer experience approaches.

Proposition 4. Customers with experiential orientations will use a company's brand as a proxy for identifying products that possess the attributes that match their requirements.

Customers with convenience orientations like to minimize the time and effort associated with the purchase of a product. They will thus respond most strongly to marketing approaches that help them make their purchase decisions and the actual purchase quickly. These approaches include matching, branding and viral marketing. Matching and viral marketing work similarly in this case. They both push or prescribe products to the customer. Matching approaches determine products to be pushed based on a profile of the customer – built from a combination of measures such as customer surveys, customer behavior logs, and intelligent agents. Viral marketing pushes products through the associations that a customer has. Usually, a viral marketing product or service invitation arrives at a customer's inbox because one of the customer's friends or associates has used the product and would like to recommend it to his/her friends. This loosely targeted spam provides a measure of filtering that generally insures that the convenience orientation shopper gets information on products that they would like but don't have the time or inclination to seek out. In both cases – the matching and viral marketing approaches – the effort by the convenience orientation customer is minimized. Wise marketers make the next steps easy – minimizing the clicks necessary to purchase a product and/or requesting only the most essential data in membership forms.

Convenience orientation customers save time by using brands as proxies for their product or service requirements. At the purest, all they might want is quick, convenient service so they are attracted to shop at online retailers that build a reputation and track record of providing accessible Web sites, easy interfaces, powerful search features, and quick shopping cart checkouts. Amazon.com's one-click shopping is a very good example of this. Often, a customer combines a convenience orientation with other orientations like recreational or experiential ones. In these latter cases, customers use brands to minimize or eliminate the time spent searching for products or services that match their combined orientations. For example, a customer with a combination of recreational and convenience orientations may prefer to shop at a site like gap.com which maintains strong associations with the company's advertising campaigns and store image by providing a clean-cut, all-American, trendy Web site – thereby meeting the customer's recreational needs. At the same time, the site meets the customer's convenience needs by facilitating online purchases.

> *Proposition 5.* Customers with convenience orientations will respond most strongly to matching, branding, and viral marketing approaches.

> *Proposition 6.* Customers with convenience orientations will use a company's brand as way of quickly identifying products and services that match their requirements.

Customers with economic orientations like to get the best value for their money and are willing to do the extra research to obtain it. The matching marketing approaches will be most useful for these customers. These customers, especially if they also possess a convenience orientation, will appreciate any timesaving services that help with their research. Also, by minimizing the time and effort spent in research, a product's value increases because its price is not augmented by the opportunity costs a customer incurs by allocating resources to research. At least some of the research activity of these customers can be relegated to online shopping bots (Somers, 2000). Aside from the bots, these customers would appreciate online resources like consumer reporting services (www.consumerreports.org), word-of-mouth shopping advisory communities (Epinions.com), and online retailer ratings (bizrate.com). Despite the best research and tools, many products will not match a customer's requirements perfectly. In these situations, products with IP-address-able components make it possible to customize products "on the fly" to meet most closely the general and situational requirements of an economic orientation customer.

As with other types of customers, an experiential orientation customer will use a company's brand as a proxy for the product characteristics he/she prefers – in this case a good value. These customers will look for brands that are associated with a long track record of quality and dependability, much like the Honda brand for cars. Online, a customer with an experiential orientation may tend towards the brands known for providing products with good value – Honda for cars, Gap for clothes, Charles Schwab for online brokerage services. Additionally, economic orientation customers may also select online sites for the value that their service provides. Established online retailers like amazon.com or buy.com enhance the value associated with the brands of the products they sell by assuring that products will ship on time, will arrive on time and in good condition, and will be easily returnable should there be problems.

> *Proposition 7.* Customers with economic orientations will respond most strongly to the matching and branding approaches.

> *Proposition 8.* Customers with economic orientations will use a company's brand as a proxy for identifying products and services with good value.

The propositions presented in this section underscore the importance of paying attention to customer orientation when planning a marketing program. Failure to address the preferences of certain types of customers could seriously undermine the customer acquisition and monetizing activities of a company. The discussion also suggests that building a strong brand helps to smooth out the rough edges of a marketing program. A strong brand attracts all customer types, particularly when associated with the aspects that each customer type desires.

CONCLUSION

The marketing approaches discussed in this chapter are clearly in flux and still steeped in traditional marketing practice. The evolution of Web marketing practice will involve the transformation of this practice through creative exploitation of Web technologies and their capabilities. Ultimately, the market will determine future forms of Web marketing practice. As captured in the conceptual framework presented in this chapter, customer orientation will play a significant role in this selection process.

REFERENCES

ACNeilsen Homescan (2000). "Two-thirds of Americans Online" http://cyberatlas.internet.com/big_picture/demographics/print/0,1323,5901_358791,00.html.

Agins, Teri (2000). "Apparel Firms Use the Web For Help Tracking Fashions." *Wall Street Journal*, May 11.

Baker, Stephen, Neil Gross, Irene M. Kunii, Roger O. Crockett (2000). "Wireless in Cyberspace." *Businessweek Special Report*, May 29.

Brady, Diane, Katie Kerwin, David Welch, Louise Lee, and Rob Hof (2000). "Customizing for the Masses." *Businessweek*, March 20.

Bronson, Po (1999). *The Nudist on the Late Shift.* New York: Random House.

Carvajal, Doreen (2000). "Push Made for Digital Books." *San Jose Mercury News,* May 23.

Cresswell, Julie (2000). "Telecom's Mixed Signals." *Fortune,* April 3.

Cyberatlas (2000). http://cyberatlas.internet.com/big_picture/traffic_patterns/article/0,1323,5931_363591,00.html.

Dayal, Sandeep, Helene Landesberg, and Michael Zeisser (2000). "Building Digital Brands." *McKinsey Quarterly*, Second Quarter.

English, David (2000). "Pocket Power." *ComputerShopper,* May.

Groover, Joel (2000). "On Cyber Pond." *SCWonline,* April 20.

Kirsner, Scott (1999a)."Brand Matters." *NetCompany,* Fall.

Kirsner, Scott (1999b). "The Customer Experience." NetCompany, Fall 1999.

Li, Hairong, Cheng Kuo and Martha G. Russell (1999). "The Impact of Perceived Channel Utilities, Shopping Orientations, and Demographics on the Consumer's Online Buying Behavior." *Journal of Computer Mediated Communication,* December.

Lynch, David (2000). "Internet's Made-In-USA Label Fading." *San Jose Mercury News,* May 23.

O'Brien, Jim (2000). "The Pitch is In The Mail." *ComputerShopper,* June.

Platt, Charles (1999). "You've Got Smell." *Wired* 7(11).

Ransdell, Eric (1999). "Network Effects." *FastCompany*, September.

Rayport, Jeffrey (1999). "The Truth About Internet Business Models." *Strategy & Business,* Third Quarter.

Ryan, James (1999). "Your Online Shadow Knows." *Business2.0* June.

Somers, Asa (2000). "Battle of the Bots." *ComputerShopper,* May.

Weber, Thomas (2000). "Wireless Gadgets Will Help Firms Map Consumers Moves." *Wall Street Journal*, May 8.

Wildstrom, Stephen (1999). "Should Coffeepots Talk?" *Businessweek,* November 8.

Chapter 4

Pricing Strategies for Digital Books: Issues and Directions for Research

P.K. Kannan and Eva Guterres
University of Maryland, USA

Barbara Kline Pope
National Academy of Press, USA

While the World Wide Web has impacted many industries significantly, none of them have been affected as dramatically as the publishing industry. The ability to deliver electronic content online and to distribute it in various forms instantaneously using the Web have opened up technological possibilities and consumer expectations that have left the industry grappling for new business models. Most of those running publishing businesses have finally come to a consensus about the importance of the Web to the future of the industry and are embracing the new technologies but with little guidance on how to best use the medium. They are aware of the pressing need to adapt to the much speedier efficiencies, strategies, and requirements of the digital channel while balancing them with non-digital strategies that continue to work but are looking for some guidance on how to move forward. In this chapter, we first describe some of the key trends and challenges faced by book publishers with the emergence of the digital arena. We then focus on the issue of pricing electronic books distributed online, especially in conjunction with books distributed through traditional channels. We outline some of the possible strategies that book publishers could adopt and examine the pros and cons of the different strategies in light of the features of the product marketed and consumer segments targeted.

INTRODUCTION

The recent developments in Web technologies have created immense opportunities for the publishing industry, but at the same time the speed with which these changes have arrived has created much confusion among managers as to how best to take advantage of the opportunities. As the market transitions from one that is primarily based on providing print products to one that delivers content comprised of bits and bytes, there are many challenges with which the industry has to grapple. In this chapter, we focus on the book publishing industry, examining business models for book publishers in this transitional stage and concentrating primarily on pricing issues. We first describe some of the key trends in the market and challenges that the technological advancement creates. We then turn to the issue of pricing electronic books, especially in conjunction and in comparison with books distributed through traditional channels. We describe some of the possible strategies that book publishers could adopt and then examine the pros and cons of the different strategies in light of the product features and the targeted consumers.

KEY TRENDS AND CHALLENGES

The U.S. publishing industry consists of three distinct segments: daily newspaper, book, and magazine with expected gross sales of more than $125 billion by the year 2001. Although the three segments seem vastly different from a business model perspective, they have one significant thing in common – they are all evolving toward electronic media and they share many of the challenges that come with such a major change. While there is an immediate need for the publishing industry to adapt to the much speedier efficiencies of digital distribution and presentation, the benefits must be weighed in balance with the non-digital strategies that have worked for many decades and continue to work. For example, more than 95% of the books that are sold in the United States are still sold in printed form, and more than 70% of these books are sold through traditional retail outlets. Thus, any strategy that focuses on selling books in electronic form has to take into account consumer preferences and expectations regarding the many features of the books they purchase in print form. In addition, managers must do their best to predict what customers will want in the future regarding electronic content and not rely only on current consumer preferences (Christensen, 1997). Customers have trouble visualizing and communicating preferences about attributes or products that do not currently exist. And in this electronic age, new possibilities for innovative products and delivery systems arise daily, making long-term planning and building strategies for new business models even more daunting.

The book publishing world is characterized by a number of factors that have made moving to the digital world risky. Those responsible for the distribution systems for books for the general public have relied almost exclusively on the retail bookstore channel. If they were to start selling electronic content directly to consumers via the Web in this transitional phase, would the big chains of bricks-and-mortar stores that dominate the retail market retaliate by refusing to carry the printed book? What about security? How can these big publishing conglomerates make sure that their copyrights are protected in this electronic frontier? What level of security is necessary for publishers to feel comfortable distributing electronically?

On the positive side, digital distribution promises to alleviate some long-standing and thought-to-be intractable problems. The major two problems being physical inventory and returns—related evils that can cause the best publishers to falter and/or die. The online channel enabled by the Web has created opportunities for publishers to minimize the negative impact of both of these trouble spots. It provides publishers an opportunity to cut the costs of producing and distributing titles and to move away from the vagaries of supply-and-demand. No longer will publishers need to use the crystal ball approach to predict demand—the main cause of overprinting and inventory bloating. And, they will no longer be concerned about the high cost of keeping a book in print as demand lowers print runs, thereby increasing unit costs during the last years of the life of a book. No publisher-based printing will need to take place in an all-digital environment. Any printing will be pushed to the consumer. Many believe that on-demand printing at the publisher's or the publisher's printer's plant is the saving technology for the out-of-print issue—but it, too, can be costly and does not eliminate distribution costs as digital delivery does. In some ways, true print-on-demand (printing one book at a time under the control of the publisher) can actually increase distribution and back office costs.

Related to demand is the unique place that returns hold in the publishing industry. No other manufacturer takes goods back from their retailers in the volume that publishers do—if at all. Returns are the overt measure of an extremely inefficient distribution system. In the long run, it is the new electronic technology allowing delivery of content from the producer (publisher) directly to the consumer (reader) that holds the biggest promise for the industry. No longer will the publisher need to advance huge numbers of copies onto the retail shelves to look forward to having 50% of them returned and eventually pulped. But can publishers make it through the transition to bits and bytes? Most would say that they still need the bricks-and-mortar retailers today.

Digital publishing and distribution give rise to a number of issues. In the long run, e-publishing might be the norm, but in the short run, publishers have to manage the transition from printed books to e-books. That is, there will be a large segment of consumers who will want to buy printed books and there could be a significant segment of consumers who will prefer e-books. Given this reality, it is important to explore how books as products can be offered and priced both in print form and e-form.

DIGITAL BOOKS

It is useful to first understand the developments in the technology of digital books and their pricing practice thus far to fully appreciate the issues involved in pricing them. Currently digital books are made available in multiple formats and delivered in various ways. The major formats are (1) downloadable files that look like the page of the book (Adobe's PDF); (2) fully coded downloadable or readable files (HTML, XML); and (3) readable only on-screen in formats that exactly emulate the book page (image format). Each format brings with it different opportunities for business models and pricing with the first screaming for book-by-book and chapter-by-chapter pay-as-you-go pricing, the second best suited to either pay-as-you-go or subscription models, and the last for presentation of full-text browsable information to spur print format sales.

The most popular delivery mechanisms and those that are developing include (1) downloading to proprietary software (e.g., Microsoft's e-Reader with Clear Type) on a device that has the software and on proprietary hardware and software called e-book readers such as Rocket eBook or Softbook and (2) direct online access to content via the Web (such as aggregators like NetLibrary and budding businesses like iBook, Ebrary, and Questia).

The e-book reader is a handy portable device that can store several volumes in a compact space (shaped either like a paperback or a legal pad). There are several options that one can choose from to buy and download e-books onto these devices. One could plug a phone line into a build-in modem and get connected to an online bookstore, or one could download books via a cradle that plugs into a PC. The first e-books were introduced in late 1998. Examples are Rocket eBook from *NuvoMedia* and the SoftBook from *SoftBook Press*. The new Microsoft e-Reader with Clear Type will be on the market soon and will free the consumer from having to purchase a special device to read books. The software will run on any standard computer device that runs Microsoft Windows including the small pocket PCs and PDAs.

E-book readers and their related software transform electronic content in order to provide to consumers some of the positive features of printed books. Some of these printed-book-like features include portability and ease of handling. These e-book readers also offer attributes not found in printed books such as multiple type fonts and sizes and ample storage of content comparable to tens or thousands of printed books in a compact and lightweight package. E-book readers typically have two different pricing options: (1) pay-as-you-go pricing based on the specific books downloaded (the prices of which are similar to printed books) or (2) subscription-based pricing (usually a yearly contract) that allows a specific number of downloads per month with additional pay-as-you-buy pricing for book downloads that exceed the limit.

The second technology that allows reading of digital books is direct online access to content that cannot be downloaded to a PC or a printer. It is intended to be read online. Pricing options for online access to e-books range from free access that tends to encourage print format sales, free access funded by an advertising model, pay-as-you-go pricing, and subscription pricing.

ISSUES IN PRICING DIGITAL BOOKS

There are many factors that need to be considered in pricing digital books, especially in the transition phase when printed books are also produced and sold alongside digital content. We discuss some of these factors and their implication for pricing and business models.

Cost Structure of Print Versus Digital

The general approach to pricing printed books has been the cost-plus approach—balancing the need for cost recovery with an eye toward market pricing. To arrive at the price of a title in the cost-plus approach, the publisher takes into account the cost of content – advances and royalties paid to authors – together with the fixed cost of producing the title for the first time, and the variable cost of printing each copy (which itself depends on the length of the press run), discounts for wholesalers and retailers, inventory, warehouse and distribution costs, marketing and sales expenses, returns, plus a profit if applicable. The actual profit earned is a function of any combination of the variables above and, of course, of the number of units of the title ultimately sold.

Depending on the nature of the title (e.g., popular novel versus a scientific textbook), the ratio of fixed cost to variable cost can vary greatly for printed books. Thus, cost recovery in the case of printed books can be quite complex. In the case of digital content, the publishing costs are rather different. While the fixed cost of producing the first copy of the digital book is similar to the printed book, the cost of producing subsequent copies is very low compared to the printed version. This is because much of the variable costs that are associated with printed books quite simply disappears – e.g., printing, inventory, distribution, and returns. Thus, the marginal production and distribution costs can be quite close to zero. The only variable cost in the digital world is marketing costs that would vary depending on many factors including the number of digital copies one intends to sell. The lack of variable costs associated with selling digitally seems like such a major advantage that one would expect that all publishers would be jumping into this business immediately. But, with digital distribution also comes illegal copying and piracy. Just as these costs are low or nonexistent for the publisher, they are also likely to be quite insignificant for others, making the potential for illegal gains quite high. With significant piracy, the fixed cost recovery process becomes very difficult as all the costs are borne at the initial production stage. This helps to explain the significant effort that many publishers are expending to make the digital distribution process piracy-proof.

Consumers Expectations of Price and Quality

One of the important factors in setting prices for digital content is consumers' expectations of price and quality (the value) of digital books. The fact that the marginal cost of producing a digital copy is close to zero is well known. Similarly, the quality of digital books that are available now in terms of their interface and features are not yet sophisticated enough to match the quality of the printed book. Consumers factor these perceptions into account in building their expectations about digital quality and prices.

An obvious reference point for building such expectations is the printed book price. Hence, consumers tend to expect prices for digital books to be a fraction of the printed book price. This has important implications for setting printed book and digital book prices for new titles, when they are offered in both forms simultaneously. Thus, it might be fruitful to price digital books at a discount as compared to the printed book price. If a publisher charges the same price as the printed book price, then the digital form would need enhancements to the content to provide added value to consumers, given that the quality of digital books are generally seen as inferior. If digital content is priced at the same level as the printed book price without added enhancements, then the penetration levels of digital books are likely to remain quite small. With the rapid evolution of digital technologies, the true quality and the perceptions of the quality of digital books are likely to improve and this will have an obvious impact on consumers' willingness to pay higher prices for digital content. Thus, the implications of the evolving technologies on consumers' perceptions of quality and benefits of e-content vis-à-vis printed content have to be clearly evaluated for implementing an effective long-term pricing strategy.

Cannibalization of Print Books by Digital Content

To the extent that digital content is viewed as a direct substitute for the printed content, early on, publishers will have to contend with cannibalization of sales of printed books by distribution of digital content. The impact of cannibalization could be significant if digital content has to be sold at a lower price than printed books to match consumers' price expectations. This is not an issue if the net margin is not affected, but if the discounts are deep then it could lead to lower overall profits or losses. This is a serious concern that has impacted publishers' online strategy (or lack thereof) thus far.

The strategy that some publishers seem to follow to combat the short-term impact of cannibalization could actually be hurting the long-term viability of digital delivery. Many tend to price e-book content at or only slightly below printed book pricing. The net impact is that market penetration levels are not very high. Only a small segment of consumers who put a high value on the convenience of online content tend to purchase such "high-priced" digital products. In order to increase market penetration levels, it is most likely necessary to price digital content dramatically lower than the printed book in order to truly stimulate enough demand to make a difference in publishers' sales level—and get the industry moving faster in the direction of digital delivery.

But, having said that, the early cannibalization aspect of this strategy has to be considered, dealt with, and conquered, which will take time. To get through this transition period, publishers could be aggressive in pricing digital content at the expense of print content. This might be the price to pay for being the leader in the digital market. On the other hand, for most publishers, particularly those nonprofits looking for a break-even picture each and every year and with little capitalization, it is still too early to give up on printed content and concentrate only on selling digital content, no matter the level of cannibalization. Such a strategy could imperil short-term business health. Given this serious cannibalization issue, publishers clearly need a viable strategy to help them transition from the print world to the e-content environment. The following research questions are relevant in this context.

- Given the spectrum of printed content to value-added e-content and consumers' perceptions of their costs and benefits, how can publishers decide on what specific product to offer in a product line?
- How should the products in a product line be positioned, price and benefits wise, to minimize cannibalization?

Pricing Bundled/Unbundled Content

The nature of book content – ranging from novels and popular titles to reference material and manuals – has important implications for pricing. Popular titles – fiction and nonfiction (that we will call Type 1 content, for sake of convenience) – are crafted to be read from beginning to end. One does not typically dip in and out of a novel. However, there is a whole range of academic and scholarly books, scientific books, reference material and such (that we will call Type 2 content), the content of which is many times accessed by readers in chunks. These types of books can and should be unbundled and sold as separate pieces or chapters, which can have great value to consumers. The digital channel makes it very easy to unbundle content and sell those pieces individually.

In addition, content that is sold as separate printed books could be easily disaggregated and re-bundled as a package without much additional effort and cost. In the trade, this is typically called custom publishing. Many publishers of Type 2 content are excited about the possibility of offering custom publishing products in digital form in the hope that it may expand the overall market for Type 2 content. This might well be so, especially in cases where the printed versions are priced quite high and come in very aggregate form. The individual pieces could be sold for a fraction of the cost of the whole book but at a higher price than the exact fraction of the book price, leading to additional sales and to higher margins. For example, for a book with eight chapters that sells for $80, consumers would be willing to pay, say, $11.00 for each chapter—rather than the exact value fraction of $10. The market for these chunks would be those customers waging price resistance over the large, expensive scientific tome when they only need a section of the entire book. In this example, the customer saves $69 by not having to purchase the entire book and the publisher picks up a customer who would not have spent $80.

However, offering unbundled content has a potential trade-off—the possibility of unbundled content cannibalizing the sale of the whole books, whether in print and/or digital form. In offering such unbundled content, publishers will have to contend with many questions:

- Under what conditions can content be provided in unbundled disaggregate form (say, individual chapters) that will result in an overall market expansion and increased margins?
- Does the availability of disaggregated content diminish the value of the aggregate whole book from the consumers' perspective? Does this matter? And, if so, what steps can be taken to minimize this impact?

Degree of Free Content

Another important factor to consider in marketing digital content is the extent to which contents in a book be made available for readers for free for purposes of fully browsing the contents before purchasing the printed or e-book. There is little or no scientifically valid research on the issue of the impact of free browsing on overall sales. Some contend that it raises sales dramatically and others are quite skeptical of that claim. Both viewpoints are credible with the type of book most likely playing a key role in differences in sales—and the differences in opinion. For Type 1 book content, it is less important for customers to be able to browse the entire book to determine interest in purchasing the book. One can typically make a buying decision based on jacket copy and a peek at the first chapter. Allowing full browsing on Type 1 books might just encourage major cannibalization. For Type 2 book content, the customer is most likely searching for information rather than a good read. This aspect of Type 2 content leads to the conclusion that full-text browsing and searching probably attracts many more people to the content than would otherwise be aware of it at all. Most Type 2 books do not see the light of day in a bookstore. Therefore, before the Web, it was difficult for customers to know about these types of books. And, it was equally difficult and economically unfeasible for publishers to reach large groups of interested customers through promotional means given the low margin on Type 2 titles. So, while cannibalization could also be at work in Type 2 books, the overall effect on revenue is likely to be positive because of market expansion.

Some Type 2 content providers such as National Academy Press (NAP) (http://www.nap.edu) have been providing full-text books online free of charge for browsing to consumers visiting their Web site since 1995. Technically speaking, the content could also be downloaded and printed by consumers. However, the quality of such downloads are inferior to printed book quality (fax quality) and it takes quite a bit of time to download each page. NAP's sales have increased dramatically since putting content online for free browsing but whether the increase in sales can be solely attributed to free browsing is a subject of research. It is important to note that the quality of the product that is made available free online is significantly inferior to printed books, which could explain the lack of cannibalization of sales by free online content.

Research needs to be conducted on the issue of whether free samples of the digital content and unlimited browsing and full-text searching increases the sales of digital books or printed books or cannibalizes their sales. Another interesting issue for future research would be to examine the relationship between high quality content sales (print or electronic form) as a function of the quality and quantity of free online content. It can be conjectured that as the quality differential decreases, cannibalization effects will increase. However, it remains to be seen whether all Type 2 content is affected to the same extent. It is important for managers to understand from a consumer behavior viewpoint what the impact of free browsing is and how free browsing can be incorporated into a digital pricing strategy.

In the next section we discuss some of the possible strategies that publishers can follow in pricing digital content vis-à-vis print content that address several of the issues that we have raised above.

PRICING STRATEGIES

As discussed previously, the type of content that is sold online has important implications for its pricing. In discussing the possible pricing strategies we will differentiate between Type 1 content (e.g., fiction and nonfiction books intended to be read from beginning to end) and Type 2 content (e.g., academic and scholarly content, textbooks, and reference material). In suggesting these strategies we also point out the complexities involved in implementing them and further issues they raise that need resolution. These issues are identified as topics for further research.

Differential Pricing With Same Quality

Consumers vary in their willingness to pay for digital content. Some may assign great value for the convenience of purchasing and reading digital books and might be willing to pay more than others who have a lower reservation price for digital books. One option that many publishers of Type 1 content have been using is to price digital content at or slightly below the printed book price. In such a situation, cannibalization of margins or profits is not an issue. Those consumers who prefer the digital form buy digital content and those who prefer printed content buy printed books—at similar prices. Those who think the prices are too high stay out of the market (or check out the title from libraries).

This pricing strategy however does not take advantage of the fact that the marginal cost of production of digital books is close to zero. Thus, it is in the publishers' best interest to increase the market size by inducing those who stay out of the market for either digital or printed books due to lower reservation prices to enter the market. One such strategy that could be employed is differential pricing.

For content that is topical or is time-sensitive, publishers can use time-based (temporal) differential pricing schemes effectively to increase the market size. In this strategy, the digital content price is lowered over time in keeping with the demand for the digital product while quality remains the same. Thus, those consumers who need the book immediately and are willing to pay a higher price buy early—as soon as the digital content becomes available—while those who are willing to wait get the content at a lower price. The price variation itself could be made a function of digital demand. In order for this strategy to work, there would need to be as many early buyers of digital books as the later buyers to ensure no reduction in total revenue. However, given that the digital form attracts many early birds, revenue reduction is unlikely and an increase in overall revenue could occur. (This case is similar in nature to the traditional publishing model of introducing higher price hardcover versions first and then introducing lower price paperback versions later. The only difference is that in the case of printed books, quality is lowered a little, while the content is the same.) It is also possible that if the demand for content is very strong and if there are many consumers who are anxious to obtain the copies of the content early, a publisher could charge more for a prepublication version of books that is much lower quality than the later version. This strategy extracts the premium from consumers who are willing to pay to get the content early.

For content that is not time-sensitive, the differential pricing strategy could be implemented by segmenting the market on the basis of consumer characteristics, e.g., an individual versus a university or a business, or an individual versus a library.

In the case of temporal differential pricing, some consumers may anticipate the lowering of prices over time and will wait, especially if the prices come down quite fast. This would reduce the effectiveness of the differential price strategy. One way to counteract this is to announce the pricing policy ahead of time to consumers and stick with it rather than change it as the market develops. This takes the guesswork out of consumers' decision-making and helps to segment the market appropriately (Lilien, Kotlar, and Moorthy, 1992). The key to this strategy is estimating the demand for the book as a function of time. Thus, for some titles "later" could mean two to four months later, while for some others it could be more (six months to a year) as it depends on the subject material of the book.

Product Line Pricing Strategies

The issue of pricing digital books and printed books is essentially one of product line pricing. The two forms – digital and print – can be viewed as partial substitutes and thus the issue of cannibalization is relevant. One way to minimize cannibalization is to vary the quality and features associated with each form and make the products as different as possible. This may result in each of them appealing to two entirely different segments of buyers. For example, while the printed book has its usual quality, the digital form may be read only on the screen and thus have a lower price. Or, there could be two digital forms – one read only on a PC screen in hard-to-read type while sitting upright in a chair and the other in an e-book form compatible with convenient handheld readers. The first digital format could be offered at a lower price while the second digital format could be priced at the same level as printed books. The important insight here is that a quality differential between products in a product line can be strategically controlled to ensure that cannibalization effects are minimized. This also ensures that consumers with lower reservation prices are able to buy the inferior quality product, while consumers with higher reservation prices "self-select" themselves to the printed version or the hand-held e-book version depending on their preferences.

If the preferences of consumers are well known, then it is possible for the publisher to craft the low quality e-content and its price in such a way that consumers who generally prefer higher quality e-content and/or printed books have no incentive to buy the low quality product. In a similar way, the higher quality products could be so designed and priced that the consumers with low-price preference will have no incentive to purchase the higher quality—and higher priced products. Such a pricing scheme is called incentive compatible pricing strategy (Choi, Stahl and Whinston 1997, p. 356).

Maintaining a quality differential between digital books of various forms and printed books also helps to combat the problem of consumers' expectations about digital prices based on their knowledge of printed book prices. When the features of the products are very different and they are not comparable, or even if comparable the utilities provided them are very different in nature, then the issue of price comparison between forms is minimized. Thus, in the long run, printed book prices may not turn out to be a reference point for the digital book, thereby allowing the publisher to charge a higher price for digital content than otherwise.

If cannibalization is still a problem, some brave publishers might choose to only offer the digital version and forego the printed version altogether. Or they might first introduce the digital product, priced at a level justified by cost recovery, and then introduce the printed version at a higher price, that could be targeted at a different segment such as institutions. This sequential introduction of products, digital followed by print, could allow higher prices for printed books as warranted by shorter print runs and therefore higher production costs. This pricing strategy also has the potential for higher profits than a simultaneous introduction of e-content and print. By introducing e-content first, one could charge relatively high prices and still attract those consumers who typically opt for lower quality (and thus extracting higher profits than otherwise) and then introduce higher quality products with even higher prices later. This strategy assumes however that the digital book market is well developed and a substantial percentage of the consumers are online. This may not be true for quite some time as the digital market develops.

The implementation of such product line pricing is complex. First, it is necessary to estimate, however crudely, the reservation prices of consumers preferring various types of digital and printed content. These are not easy tasks as self-reported reservation prices are not very reliable. Second, digital book technology is still under development and hence consumers may not have clear ideas about its quality and features vis-à-vis printed books. This makes the task of reliably estimating consumers' willingness to pay measures quite difficult. However, providing different types of content to different segments of consumers could be the best strategy for publishers to follow in the transition period of moving from the print environment to the digital environment.

Pricing of Bundled/Unbundled Content

When Type 2 content is produced, one can generally view it as consisting of several distinct sections, chapters, or pages, each possibly having a differing demand level among different consumer segments. In traditional publishing, these chapters are bundled together and the whole printed book is priced to sell a significant number of copies within the targeted group. Producing a printed book consisting of chapters is usually cheaper per unit than making each chapter a separate printed book, and if priced and bundled appropriately, a significant number of copies can be sold. When consumers buy such books, it is possible that some of them value some chapters very highly and the other chapters not so highly; whereas, some other consumers may value these chapters in reverse order. Such negative correlation in valuation of these chapters helps in bundling them together and pricing it in such a way to sell copies of the whole book to each of those very different consumers. There could be consumers in the market who might value some chapters highly, but if those valuations are not higher than the printed book's price, they will not buy the book. Thus, there could be unmet demand for certain chapters in the consumer population, but producing separate print chapters for such consumers may be uneconomical from a printed book production standpoint. Hence, in the print world, such demand usually remains unmet and those consumers either borrow the book from the library or from friends, or forego reading the chapter.

With the advent of e-content, the situation changes rather drastically from the standpoint of production costs. It is now possible to produce these chapters in unbundled form and sell them individually to consumers at almost zero marginal cost. The question is whether there is cannibalization at work or not.

When products are sold in bundled form as well as in unbundled form, such a strategy is called a mixed bundling strategy. Researchers have shown (e.g., McAfee et al., 1989) that under very general conditions, mixed bundling strategy almost always increases sellers' profits when compared to selling products purely bundled or purely unbundled. Based on this research finding, it seems that it is in the publishers' best interest to offer both whole books and individual chapters at the same time. It can be shown that under general distributions of consumer valuations of individual chapters and positive correlation of these valuations that market expansion due to the sale of individual chapters more than compensates for the cannibalization of whole book sales by the sale of individual chapters (Choi, Stahl and Whinston, 1997, p. 358). If the market size is large enough and the production costs low enough, it is also possible to price the bundled product low to stimulate significant market penetration and generate profits. However, if consumers derive negative externality in obtaining the other chapters (that is, having the extra chapters actually decreases their overall utility – extra space occupied by the chapters on the shelf or the hard drive, additional searching, and so forth), then the unbundled strategy would be better off than the bundled strategy. These alternate strategies, therefore, depend on the market size, production costs, and distribution of consumer valuations for the chapters that make up the bundle.

Sale of unbundled products could also have positive impact on sales of the whole book as it acts as a sample of the bundled product and reduces, from the consumers' viewpoint, the product's performance risk that the consumer will have to bear. Thus, if the book is of very high quality and consumers get the chance to sample it by buying a portion of it, they are more likely to buy the whole book. If the book is of poor quality, then this situation could, however, adversely affect the sale of the whole book.

This discussion leads us to the related issue, discussed in detail above, of whether content (either portions of books or the whole book) should be provided *free* for browsing purposes. The issue is whether such a strategy helps in increasing the sale of books, print or otherwise.

CONCLUSIONS

In the world of disseminating ideas, the World Wide Web has created an opportunity never before and probably never hence equaled. But, it is currently a world where—like a desert landscape experiencing a downpour—book publishing professionals can barely deal with the flood of ideas, with the chaotic flow of conflicting stories presented at conferences with no scientific data to support the assertions, and with a general feeling that the publishing environment as they know it is coming to an end and that they are being swept away in the current to a place filled with new and hidden enemies and risks.

There is no question that the risks are high; that the issues to be addressed, are indeed, complex. But they are not insurmountable. Serious research needs to be done. The complexity of positioning and pricing digital books vis-à-vis printed books is clear. Exactly how to reduce that complexity is not. Drawing information from the general pricing literature as we have done here is certainly helpful, but the real strides in understanding all the implications of positioning, pricing, and distributing bits and bytes rather than paper and ink will not be truly understood until much more research has been funded and completed.

This chapter has raised many more questions than it has answered. And, while those questions are some of the most complex ones facing today's managers of publishing programs, it is the subsequent research that we hope will abound that will provide much needed direction in this new, exciting realm of electronic publishing and distribution.

REFERENCES

Boyce, Peter and Heather Dalterio (1996). "Electronic Publishing of Scientific Journals," *Physics Today*, January.

Choi, Soon-Yong, Dale O. Stahl, and Andrew B. Whinston (1997). *The Economics of Electronic Commerce*, Macmillan Technical Publishing, Indianapolis, IN.

Christiansen, Clayton (1997). *The Innovator's Dilemma,* Harvard Business School Press, Cambridge, MA.

Dataquest (1998). "The Publishing Industry in the Digital Age," *Vertical Market Opportunities North America Market Analysis,* May 18.

Lilien, Gary, Philip Kotler, and K. Sridhar Moorthy (1992). *Marketing Models,* Prentice-Hall Inc, Englewood Cliffs, NJ.

McAfee, R. P., J. McMillan, and M. D. Whinston (1989). "Multiproduct Monopoly, Commodity Bundling, and Correlation of Values," *Quarterly Journal of Economics*, 93:371-383.

Varian, Hal (1996). *"Pricing Electronic Journals,"* D-Lib Magazine, June.

Chapter 5

Factors Influencing Marketing Performance on the Web

Ashok Ranchhod, Julie Tinson, and Fan Zhou
Southampton Business School, UK

Despite the current development of Internet marketing, understanding the effective use of the Internet still poses problems for academic researchers and marketers (Kassaye, 1999). This research attempts to empirically explore some aspects of the factors influencing commercial company Internet and Web development. The key factors considered for company Internet and Web site development are technology capacity, the use of different developers, company on-line measurement patterns and marketing executives' Web site knowledge. As a result of a cross-sectional comparative study of 'effective' and 'ineffective' companies, the findings indicate that companies with better performance from Web sites tend to possess higher technological capabilities for Internet-based marketing. It seems that their marketing executives have more knowledge of technical aspects of Web site development. They tend to be early Internet adopters using a multiple approach to measure their on-line performance. These results help to improve general understanding of company effectiveness in developing on-line marketing strategies.

INTRODUCTION

As the Internet and the World Wide Web are dramatically changing the landscape of business, the effective utilization of this new media, for marketing in particular, has become a major concern to marketing practitioners as well as marketing scholars (Berthon, 1998, Herbig and Hale, 1997; Kassaye, 1997). Despite the often hyped strategic advantages of effective Internet marketing (O'Connor and Galvin, 1998; Rohner, 1998; Morris, et al., 1997; Hamill and Karl, 1997; Ellsworth and Ellsworth, 1996; Quelch and Klein, 1996; Hoffman and Novak, 1996), there have been few empirical studies focused on understanding the factors affecting Internet marketing. Current research in this field is largely unbalanced. Researchers tend to focus primarily on marketing management issues such as company Internet usage patterns (Haynes, et al., 1998; Lymer, et al., 1998; Soh, et al., 1997), company Internet marketing and globalization strategies (Bennett, 1998), and Internet and Web marketing applications (Dixon and Tim, 1998, Feher and Towel, 1997). Although this knowledge of on-line marketing is helpful, a gap remains in the understanding of the technical aspects of company Web development and its impact on performance as related to issues such as ease of access, traffic flow, improvement of customer relationship and enhancement of company image. The multidimensional and multi-functional features of Internet marketing mean that both hardware technology and the level and sophistication of the software used have an important role to play in developing effective on-line marketing. In addition to this, issues surrounding the management of the technology may have an even greater impact on on-line marketing effectiveness.

According to Porter (1985), the development of a proper level of technological resource and capability by a firm is essential for achieving sustainable competitive advantage. For a firm, the major part of cybermarketing relies heavily on the deployment of the latest technology. The resources available in this area must surely offer strategic advantages. At the same time, the effective use of the resources for marketing activities depends not only on a well-developed marketing intelligence, but, more importantly, a proper understanding and awareness of technological capability. This capability is one of the critical prerequisites for Internet based marketing. In a recent article on Web advertising, Kassaye (1999) points out that the mismatching between marketing objectives and Internet technology has become a primary problem for effective on-line marketing. A research study also reveals that information technology managers often fail to properly evaluate the business use of the Internet (Feher and Towell, 1997). This gap becomes serious, with more and more marketing practitioners beginning to doubt the increasingly complex Web site statistics and the often poor on-line marketing performance (Murray, 1997). These findings indicate the urgency to empirically examine some technical and managerial aspects of Internet marketing.

Based on the arguments made above, a randomly selected sample of 600 UK companies resulted in a response from 122 companies. The questionnaire was designed to test the effective use of the Internet and the Web for marketing, marketing communications and the understanding and management of Web sites. Given that the majority of UK companies have already established on-line presence and many European companies are turning to the UK for technical assistance (O'Connor and Galvin, 1998), this national investigation was considered to be important and necessary. In order to understand the marketing use of the Internet and the Web, all survey questionnaires were addressed to marketing or brand managers. Existing company Internet technology levels and Web site capabilities were measured using the methods developed by Vorhies (1998). Company on-line performance was also measured. Responding companies were grouped into 'effective' and 'ineffective'. This study intended to explore the role and impact of the following factors:

1. Company Internet capabilities
2. Internet and Web marketing developers
3. Marketing knowledge on the effective use of the Internet.
4. Current pattern of on-line performance measurement.

The rest of the chapter focuses on a discussion of the technological dependency of Internet marketing followed by a description of the research model and research hypotheses. Data collected from the company survey is then statistically analyzed and discussed. Finally an improved model is proposed for understanding the effectiveness of company on-line marketing.

THE INTERNET AND CYBERMARKETING

O'Connor and Galvin (1998) define the Internet as a collection of interrelated networks that allow users with PCs and necessary software to communicate with each other locally and globally. As a marketing tool, the Internet, and particularly the World Wide Web, open up tremendous possibilities to organizations of all types (Ellsworth and Ellsworth, 1996; Quelch and Klein, 1996; Hoffman and Novak, 1996). Its applications in different marketing functions such as market research, advertising and branding, customer relations, and direct selling have been continuously explored and discussed. Scholarly predictions indicates that the business world is rapidly developing into the age of cyber marketing.

According to the definition given by Keeler (1995), cybermarketing is the type of marketing that is carried out through computers and telecommunications networks. The Internet and its multimedia presentation, the Web, provide a unique environment for cybermarketing. The core features of Internet based marketing include interactivity, multimedia usage, on-line control and global reach (Hoffman and Novak, 1996). The performance of on-line marketing depends very much on the performance of many Internet and Web-based applications such as on-line database, animation, virtual reality, and CD writers (O'Connor and Galvin, 1998).

Based on the discussion of Internet technology capabilities (Keeler, 1995; O'Connor and Galvin, 1998), a matrix of Internet and Web marketing technology dependency is shown in Table 1.

This matrix, though not perfect, illustrates the technological dependence of on-line marketing activities. These marketing activities include marketing research, advertising and branding, customer relations (public relations), and selling and distribution.

Table 1: The matrix of Internet and Web-based marketing and its technology dependence

	Searching, browsing capabilities	Posting, hosting, presentation capabilities	Communication capabilities	Transaction, security, and monitoring capabilities
Marketing Research	Highly dependent			
Advertising, Branding		Highly dependent		
Customer relations, Public relations			Highly dependent	
Selling, Distribution				Highly dependent

- *Marketing research*
  Web technology allows easier development of customer-opinion surveys. These could be product-interest, market reaction research, on-line interviews, focus group discussions and market testing. On the other hand, effective on-line marketing research depends very much on the reliability and performance of many Web-based applications. Companies need to use these tools to efficiently access, collect, analyse and present marketing research.
- *Advertising and branding*
  The capabilities of the Web provide powerful tools for effective information posting, hosting and presentation. Product or service information can be presented in a colorful and graphical multimedia format. Advertisements can be posted in the form of banners, pop-up screens, live cyber radio broadcasting, virtual games, even movies and video clips (Ranchhod, 1998). Advertising can not only have the potential to reach more people, but also in a more effective way. The best utilization of all these effects comes only through the proper use of technology.
- *Customer relations*
  Web technology, particular database and on-line intelligent technology, can allow companies to gather information about their customers and to strengthen the relationships with them. Powerful software programs can track and search for potential on-line users, collect and analyze necessary profile data, and provide important methods for forging long-term customer relations based on this information.
- *Direct sales*
  With the improvement in Web security systems for payment and on-line transactions, the use of the Internet for distribution and direct on-line selling becomes a reality. Software programs can be used to process on-line orders,

stock check, distribution arrangement and payment arrangement. This improvement in technology indicates the potential and the future use of e-commerce.

The matrix indicates that the development of Internet and Web marketing is heavily dependent on Internet technology capacity. To use the Internet effectively, companies have to properly evaluate the impact of the Internet technology on their existing business and develop an appropriate strategy to maximize its potential.

RESEARCH MODEL AND HYPOTHESES

To critically examine organizational IT systems development, Sauer (1993) proposes a model of triangle dependencies. According to this model, the success of an information system depends on the interrelationships between its developers, its supporters (those who require the information system) and its performance. Its supporters need a system that can fulfill their requirements and they need feedback from the system. Its developers need to create a system that can serve the needs and interests of its supporters. There is a strong dependency between each area of the system. This approach has been used to examine the development of company Internet and Web marketing. The modified research model is shown in Figure 1.

Development Processes

This model shows the three major components of company Web marketing development, indicating the processes needed for effective site formulation. The development of the company Web site is dependent on the needs of the marketing, sales and distribution functions. Specific system requirements, once they are approved, need to be sent to the developer(s). The developer(s) can be the company IT department, Internet specialists, advertising agencies, etc. depending on internal company resources and capabilities. The developer(s) then design and implement

Figure 1. Model for organization Internet and Web marketing development

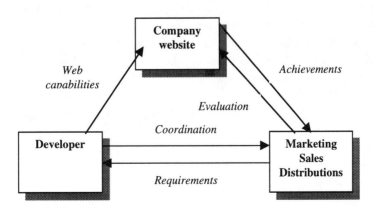

the company Web site. The Web site needs to serve the requirements of its proposers and produce expected results. Hence, the performance evaluation of sites is of major concern to the proposers.

Relationships

Based on this model three sets of relationships have been identified with arrows indicating their directions. They are: Proposer(s) $\leftrightarrow$ Developer(s); Developer(s) $\rightarrow$ Web site; Proposer(s) $\leftrightarrow$ Web site.

1) Proposers and Web marketing developers

The relationships between Web marketing proposers and its developers are twofold. Proposers should ascertain that the requirements of a Website are thoroughly understood and the developers need to provide necessary assistance and coordination. The Internet and the Web dramatically change the conventional process of marketing development and management. Multimedia, interactivity, user control and 24 hour global access (Berthon, 1998; Herbig and Hale, 1997) mean that conventional marketing strategies are not easily applicable. This means that on-line marketing effectiveness relies heavily on the developers for site management and control. O'Connor and Galvin (1998) point out that company Web sites are often designed and created by IT departments or Internet specialists, rather than marketing departments. Often, the marketing message on the Web may not necessarily complement the marketing message or approach that is being adopted by the company in conventional marketing channels. This inconsistency may result in ineffective and poor performance of on-line marketing activities.

2) Developer(s) and Web development

Information technology has long been recognized as having a positive connection with business performance (Parker, 2000; Rai, et al., 1997). The important issue here is that developers have to decide the requirements of Web site and match that to the level of Web site capabilities. Early Internet research and practice clearly show that the capability of a Web site can influence user on-line experience and return rate (O'Connor and Galvin, 1998). As mentioned before, the research study carried out by Feher and Towell (1997) indicates that most IT managers fail to appreciate the significance of using the Internet and the Web for business purposes. As a result, an inadequately developed Web site may result in poor on-line marketing performance.

3) Proposers and Web performance

A company Web site must serve the needs and requirements of its proposer(s). It has to perform well and produce results, in terms of sales or inquiries. Failure to produce results affects the dependency triangle portrayed in Figure 1. Marketing executive knowledge of company Web sites, company on-line marketing experience and the approach for measuring on-line performance are important factors that feed into the triangle.

The contemporary development and change in new technology alter the traditional role, responsibilities and requirements of managerial positions (Boddy, 1986). On the one hand, the capabilities of the Internet and the Web open up many new possibilities and opportunities, on the other hand, the multifunction and multidimensional nature of this new medium requires multiskilled marketing executives. In order to use this new medium effectively, some essential knowledge of a company Web site and the Internet market is important and necessary. An understanding of basic technical aspects and processes of company Web site operation, in particular their capacities and limitations for marketing use, should be basic knowledge for all marketers. In addition to this, they should be constantly learning and gaining insights into the increasingly fragmented Internet market.

The last part of the relationship requires a proper performance measurement. Normally, the effectiveness of on-line performance is measured by developers and evaluated by its proposers. There is still no universal standard to measure the performance of on-line effectiveness. Companies have different purposes and approaches when using the Internet. They tend to measure on-line performance according to these objectives and expectations. Current research in marketing and information system measurement suggests the application of a multiple measurement approach (Thomas, 1998).

Research Design

Based on the above discussion, the objective of this study is to examine the relationship between company Internet marketing capability and on-line performance. Therefore if company on-line marketing efforts are grouped into effective (with higher management satisfactory level), and noneffective (with lower management satisfactory level) ones, the following hypotheses are developed:

H1. A significant difference exists between the two groups in the use of IT or Internet specialists for Web development.

H2. There is a significant difference in Web capabilities between the two groups

H3. There is a significant difference between the groups in the length of time that the Internet and the Web have been used.

H4. There is a significant difference between the two groups in the Web knowledge base of the marketing managers.

H5. There is a significant difference in the sophistication of Web performance measurements between the two groups.

RESEARCH METHODOLOGY

The Sample

The sample for this study consists of a cross-section of 600 UK companies randomly selected from various Internet sources. Based on O'Connor and Galvin (1998), the majority of UK companies already have an on-line presence. Currently the UK is regarded to be at the forefront of Internet development in Europe.

The survey was conducted between November 1999 and January 2000. Printed questionnaires were mailed to a sample of 600 UK-based organizations, preceded by a pilot study of 50 companies. The selection of sample covered a cross-section of UK companies. The sample was randomly selected from the following sources: major UK company directory (1998), UK on-line company database, and Yell (UK on-line directory). Companies from manufacturing, retailing, transportation, travel, entertainment, media, construction, finance and computing were included in the sample. Also careful considerations were taken to cover small, medium and large size companies. The selection enables the identification of the major Internet usage patterns in various UK companies. It also facilitates the generation of useful insights and strategies that are applicable to the Internet marketing industry as a whole.

The questionnaire was sent to the marketing director or brand manager (by name if known) of the organization. Fifteen questionnaires were returned because the companies had ceased trading. One company rejected the questionnaire as a result of company policy. A usable sample of 122 responses was received from the 600 questionnaires (including the pilot study), achieving a response rate of 20%. However, out of these only 83 had a Web presence. The other respondents were considering the development of an on-line marketing strategy. The response rate was considered to be acceptable, especially considering the fact soliciting survey answers from large companies is notoriously difficult, owing to restrictive company policies (Leverick, et al., 1998). In some cases, as Internet marketing is often a cross department or function project, marketing managers may have been discouraged by parts of the questionnaire specific to Internet and Web technology.

MEASUREMENTS

On-line Marketing Development

This is mainly designed to understand the differences in involving the marketing department, IT department and Internet specialists in on-line marketing development. It is measured at the ordinal level with higher scores representing the fact that more parties are involved in the development of the Web site. However this measure does not indicate efficiency or coordination factors.

Web Technology Capabilities for On-line Marketing

Four aspects of Internet and Web technology capabilities are also measured at ordinal level. Respondents were asked to rate the capacities of their company Web server on a five-point Likert scale. They included the capacity to host Web content, the capacity to control site traffic and flow and the capacity to use multimedia techniques. As previously mentioned. all of these are necessary for developing and managing Internet and Web advertising.

The Length of Time on the Internet

Respondents were asked to choose the length of time they had been on the Internet from five categories
  a) Less than 6 months,
  b) from 6 months to 1 years,
  c) 1-3 years,
  d) 3-5 years and
  e) over 5 years.

Knowledge of Internet and Web technology

Respondents were questioned about their knowledge of the kind of Web technology being used for Web marketing development within their organizations. This included aspects of Web site design, development and maintenance. Within this there was a 'don't know' category.

On-line measurement

This was designed to measure the sophistication of company on-line performance measurement. Specifically, companies adopting more on-line measurement methods were regarded as being more sophisticated. Again this data was recorded at an ordinal level.

On-line Performance

According to the criteria, on-line effectiveness represents the difference between the on-line results and management expectations. Four aspects of performance were measured which included effectiveness in broadcasting to a large number of on-line audiences, in attracting target on-line customers, in improving company image and on-line customer relations. A 5 Likert scale was used to collect this information. 'Effective' and 'Non-Effective' companies were grouped on this self-described level of Web site performance by marketing managers.

Data Validation

To ensure the accuracy of measures, a small-scale t-test was used to compare the company characteristics of early respondents and late respondents. As a result no significant differences were found between the two.

Data Analysis

General description data were analyzed using SPSS. The testing of Hypotheses 1 to 5 required a statistical testing of the difference between two sets of ordinal data. The non-parametric Mann-Whitney Test was used.

RESULTS

Profile of respondents

Table 2 provides some details of the research sample.

As previously mentioned, the respondents were asked to provide some basic information about their company. Thirty-two percent of the companies were from the manufacturing sector, while 18.9% were from the computer-related business sector. Companies involved in media and news, and entertainment took up 12.3 %, while 9.8% were from travel and transportation sectors. However, the majority of the responding companies have less than 500 employees, while only less than 9% of the companies have over 5,000 employees. Although, the figure is on the small side, it is acceptable, taking into consideration the factor that large companies are more reluctant to take part in surveys of all kinds because of company policy, considering and large amount of surveys aimed at them each year (Leverick et al., 1998). 48.4% of the companies have been on the Internet for 1-3 years, while 27.9 % and 13.9% of the companies have been on the Internet for 3-5 years and over 5 years respectively. Only less than 10% of the companies have been on-line for less than one year. Obviously, our sample reflects more of those companies that have been using the Internet for several years. The majority of the companies report to have IT support within the organization (59.8%), and have a formal Internet policy (57.4%).

Hypotheses Tests

Table 3 displays the results of hypothesis tests. Hypothesis 1, the differences in using different Web development parties, is not supported by the data ($p > 0.05$) indicating that the difference is not significant. Hypothesis 2 shows the differences in Web capability. The results of SPSS analysis strongly indicate that there is a

Table 2: Respondent sample details (N = 122)

Business Sector	Percentage	Company size	Percentage
Computer –related	18.9%		
Entertainment	2.5%		
Finance and banking	4.9%	Less than 100	52.5%
Media and news	9.8%	100 to 499	29.5%
Travel and transportation	9.8%	500 to 4,999	9.8%
Retailing	5.7%	5,000 to 10,000	5.7%
Manufacturing	32.0%	Over 10,000	2.5%
Other (construction, consultant, business services etc.)	16.6%		

significant difference in the technology capabilities between effective and non-effective companies ($p < 0.05$). A further look at the data indicates that companies reporting satisfactory on-line performance tend to have higher level of technology capabilities. Hypothesis 3 shows the differences in the length of time using the Internet for marketing. Strong support for this hypothesis is found from the data ($p < 0.05$). It is obvious that 'effective' companies are on-line longer than those 'ineffective' ones. The result also supports Hypothesis 4 that there is a significant difference between the knowledge of marketing managers ($p < 0.05$). Marketing managers from 'effective' companies know more about the technological aspects of the Web. Strong statistical evidence also suggest that the difference in performance measurement is significant ($p < 0.05$). Therefore Hypothesis 5 is supported by the data.

DISCUSSION

Four research hypotheses are strongly supported by the empirical data. Statistical evidence shows that the development of a highly capable Internet Web site, a proper understanding of its function, and a multiple measurement of on-line activities can positively affect its on-line performance. Besides, for most compa-

Table 3: Hypotheses tests results

Hypothesis	Effective companies (Mean Rank) N = 35	Non-effective companies (Mean Rank) N = 48	Mann-Whitney U	Significance (2 –tailed , 0.05 level*)	Con-clusions
H1. Difference in involving IT or Internet specialists in developing on-line marketing.	46.64	38.61	677.500	0.090	NS
H2. Difference in Web capacities for on-line marketing.	31.08	19.16	154.000	0.002*	S
H3. Difference in the length of time using the Internet.	50.87	35.53	529.500	0.002*	S
H4. Difference between market-ing managers' Web knowledge	52.89	34.06	459.000	0.000*	S
H5. Difference in using on-line measurement methods	52.99	33.99	455.500	0.000*	S

nies, on-line marketing could be a learning process. Companies can achieve effectiveness in the long run. This evidence strongly supports the scholarly assumptions that on-line disadvantages and ineffectiveness may result from factors such as incapability of using the Internet for marketing (Haynes et al., 1998), potential gap between marketing applications and proper measurement (Kassaye, 1999). However no significant difference was found in using various Internet marketing developers. Based on these findings, an initial model for understanding these relationships is constructed (see Figure 2).

As shown in the diagram, to properly understand and achieve on-line marketing effectiveness, companies have to go through the following critical management stages:

    a) cooperation with Internet developers,
    b) integration of Internet marketing perceptions with technology capabilities,
    c) building experience and knowledge of Internet marketing and on-line market, and
    d) a proper approach to performance measurement.

H1. A significant difference exists between the two groups in the use of IT or Internet specialists for Web development.

The hypothesis was not supported by the empirical data. The survey indicates that the use of different Internet marketing developers appears to have little difference between effective and ineffective companies. It implies that the use of a company IT department, Internet specialists or advertising agents can equally contribute to effective company Web development. Thus once a Web objective is established, a company could choose different parties for Web marketing development. If this is the case, further research should focus on issues surrounding coordination and cooperation.

Figure 2. An improved model to understand company on-line marketing effectiveness

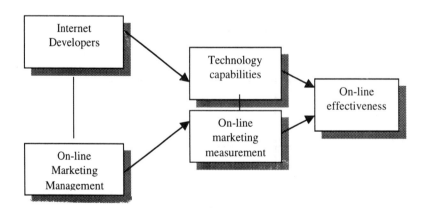

H2. There is a significant difference in Web capabilities between the two groups.

The significant difference between the knowledge of marketing managers strongly suggests that the effectiveness of on-line marketing depends very much on a thorough understanding of the core features and functions of the Internet medium. Different from conventional marketing media, the Internet provides users with more opportunities and controls (Hoffman and Novak, 1996). However, the effective use of this medium depends very much on a level of Internet knowledge, discussed previously. Cybermarketing relies heavily on the deployment of modern technology. It strongly suggests that the new marketing paradigm alters the conventional requirements for a marketing managerial position. It puts the issue of continuous learning on the company Internet marketing agenda.

H3. There is a significant difference between the groups in the length of time that the Internet and the Web have been used.

Experience and knowledge of the Internet and Internet market are critical. Companies have to allow for knowledge acquisition and experiential learning. As many companies aim at achieving immediate profits from on-line marketing, this finding may have some implications regarding the level of competencies required. Most companies need to prepare for a learning and testing period. As mentioned earlier, Internet marketing and Internet markets differ greatly from traditional marketing and markets. Companies should devote time and efforts to understand the new features, to forge close relationships with on-line users and to develop proper on-line marketing strategies. As reflected in the survey, Internet marketing should be a long-term company strategy, the more experience and knowledge gained, the better the on-line performance.

H4. There is a significant difference between the two groups in the Web knowledge base of the marketing managers.

The importance of the technological capabilities of company Websites can not be ignored. It is often regarded as the responsibility of IT managers. As mentioned before, many information technology (IT) managers are unable to properly evaluate the business contribution of company Internet technology (Feher and Towell, 1997). The results of this survey underline the importance on-line technology and its contribution to effective on-line marketing. Marketers and developers need to work together and make considerable effort to ensure that a company Web site can fulfill internal and external expectations.

H5. There is a significant difference in the sophistication of Web performance measurements between the two groups.

Last but not least, performance of on-line measurement is multidimensional. It is not surprising that the survey results strongly suggest that a single measure of on-line effectiveness is no longer appropriate for understanding the performance of a company Web site. Effectiveness, as mentioned by Thomas (1998), is the measurement of on-line results with management expectations. For sensible on-line marketing performance measurement, it is necessary to adopt a multiple approach to understand what is being achieved. Early discussion reveals that there are two dimensions of 'tangible ' and 'intangible' measures (Thomas, 1998). This survey indicates that most 'effective' companies adopt both types of measurement to assess their on-line performance.

CONCLUSION

Boddy (1986) points out that the rapidity of contemporary technology development has put increased pressure on organizations. In order to stay competitive, organizations have to develop proper strategies to respond appropriately, to adopt new technology as quickly as their competitors, and to ensure that applications are introduced smoothly and used effectively. The current development of the Internet and cybermarketing positively echoes this argument. The Internet and the Web can not only provide companies with great business potentials, but also place considerable challenges on its development and management.

This study addresses several important issues concerning the effective use and management of company on-line marketing. In particular, it explores the role of Internet developer, the importance of the management of knowledge and learning, the impact of on-line technological capabilities and proper measurement. The implications of these findings are twofold; first Internet marketing can no longer be regarded as traditional marketing. It is a multidimensional development demanding requisite skills. Its success depends very much on the level of technology and knowledge. Secondly, Internet marketing is a cross-functional operation. For many organizations, this may require internal integration and reengineering.

CURRENT LIMITATIONS

This is a part of a research project carried out by the authors. In the future, research efforts will be focus on three areas:

a) exploring other potential factors that could have impact on the performance of company on-line marketing. For example, whether the use of different on-line marketing strategies can make a difference in effectiveness;

b) connecting the company survey with the content analysis of company websites. It is important to relate the survey results with an investigation of the information content of company websites. This cross-examination may generate some important insights into the understanding of what types of different interface design and development improve on-line performance. This would also provide an independent assessment of the site; and

c) connecting the company survey with an on-line consumer behavior study and empirically investigating Internet user perceptions of different company Web marketing sites.

REFERENCES

Barnatt, C. (1998). 'Virtual Communities and Financial Services: On-line Business Potentials and Strategic Choice,' *International Journal of Bank Marketing.* 16(4), 161-169.

Bennett, R. (1998). 'Using the World Wide Web for International Marketing: Internet Use and Perceptions of Expert Barriers Among German and British Businesses,' *Journal of Marketing Communications,* 4, 27-23.

Berthon, P. et al. (1998). 'The World Wide Web as an Industrial Marketing Communication Tool: Models for the Identification and Assessment of Opportunities.' *Journal of Marketing Management,* 14, 691-704.

Boddy, D. (1986). *Managing New Technology.* Oxford: Blackwell.

Day, G.S. (1994). The Capabilities of Market-Driven Organizations. *Journal of Marketing* 58, 37-51.

Ellsworth, J.H. and Ellsworth, M.V. (1996). *Marketing on the Internet - Multimedia Strategies for the World Wide Web,* New York: John Wiley.

Feher, A. and Towell, E. (1997). 'Business Use of the Internet.' *Internet Research: Electronic Networking Applications and Policy. 7(3), 195-200.*

Hamill, J. and Gregory, K. (1997). 'Internet Marketing in the Internationalization of UK SMEs,' *Journal of Marketing Management,* 13, 9-28.

Haynes, P.J., et al. (1998). 'Small and Mid-sized Businesses and Internet Use: Unrealized Potential?' *Internet Research: Electronic Networking Applications and Policy.* 8 (3), 229-235.

Herbig, P. and Hale, B. (1997). *'Internet: the Marketing Challenge of the Twentieth Century',* 7(2), 95-100.

Hoffman, D.L. and Novak, T.P. (1996). 'A New Marketing Paradigm for Electronic Commerce,' http://www2000.ogsm.vanderbilt.edu/

Kassaye, WW. (1997). 'Global Advertising and the World Wide Web,' *Business Horizons,* 40(3), 33.

Kassaye, W.W. (1999). 'Sorting out the Practical Concerns in World Wide Web Advertising,' *International Journal of Advertising,* 18, 339-361.

Keeler, L. (1995). *Cybermarketing.* New York: Amacon.

Kiani, R.G. (1998). 'Marketing Opportunities in the Digital World,' *Internet Research: Electronic Networking Applications and Policy.* 8(2), 185-194.

Leverick, F. et al. (1998). 'Using Information Technology Effectively: A Study of Marketing Installations,' *Journal of Marketing Management,* 14, 927-962.

Morris, M.H. et al. (1997). 'Is the Web World Wide? Marketing in an Emerging Market,' *Journal of Strategic Marketing* 5, 211-231.

Murray, M. (1997). 'Evaluating Web Impact: The Death of the Highway Metaphor,' *Direct Marketing,* Jan.

O' Connor, J and Galvin, E. (1998). *Marketing and Information Technology,* London: Pitman.

Parker, A.R. (2000). 'Impact on the Organizational Performance of the Strategy-Technology Policy Interaction.' *Journal of Business Research.* 47, 55-64.

Poon, S. and Strom, J. (1997). 'Small Businesses' Use of the Internet: Some Realities,' http://World Wide Web.isoc.org/inet97/proceeding/.

Porter, M.E. (1985). *Competitive Advantage*. Free Press: New York.

Quelch, J.A. and Klein, L.R. (1996). 'The Internet and International Marketing,' *Sloan Management Review*, Spring, 60-75.

Rai, A. et al (1997). 'Technology Investment and Business Performance.' *Communications of the ACM*. 40(7).

Ranchhod, A. (1998). Advertising into the next millennium, *International Journal of Advertising*, 17(4) , 427-446.

Sahay, A. Gould, J. and Barwise, P. (1998). 'New Interactive Media: Experts' Perceptions of Opportunities and Threats for Existing Businesses,' *European Journal of Marketing,* 32, (7/8), 616-628.

Sauer, C. (1993). *Why Information Systems Fail: A Case Study Approach*. Henley-On-Thames: Alfred Waller.

Soh, C. et al. (1997). 'The Use of the Internet for Business: the Experiences of Early Adopters in Singapore,' *Internet Research: Electronic Networking Applications and Policy* 7 (3), 217-228.

Thomas, M.J. (1998). 'Measuring Marketing Performance,' *Journal of Targeting, Measurement and Analysis for Marketing, 6(3),* 233-246.

Vorhies, D.W. (1998). 'An Investigation of the Factors Leading to the Development of Marketing Capabilities and Organizational Effectiveness,' *Journal of Strategic Marketing, 6,* 3-23.

Weiber and Kollman, (1998). 'Competitive Advantages in Virtual Markets—Perspectives and Information-Based Marketing in Cyberspace,' *European Journal of Marketing*, 32(7/8), 603-615.

Chapter 6

Positioning in Cyberspace: Evaluating Telecom Web Sites Using Correspondence Analysis

Pierre Berthon
University of Bath, UK

Leyland Pitt, Michael Ewing, Nimal Jayaratna, and B. Ramaseshan
Curtin University of Technology, Western Australia

The growth of presence in the marketspace of the Web has been exponential, both in general and within specific industries. While the academic literature on the phenomena is still in its infancy, there exists a pressing need to establish methodologies to evaluate and map Web sites within and between industries. With the exception of a few notable papers little or no theoretical, descriptive, or normative research has been conducted into the evaluation of Web site market positioning. This chapter goes a little towards addressing this lacuna. Specifically, Web sites from the telecom industry are evaluated and mapped using correspondence analysis. The technique of correspondence analysis and the interpretation of the maps produced are described in detail. The implications for management are discussed.

INTRODUCTION

The Internet is possibly the most prominent manifestation of what Rayport and Sviokla (1994) term the marketspace—the virtual equivalent of the traditional physical marketplace. Web sites have seen explosive growth in the last few years (e.g., Kehoe, 1996). Amongst most major and minor organisations (both for profit, not-for-profit, and governmental), there has been some experimenting with Web sites ranging from simple presence to sophisticated virtual organisations. While the academic literature on the phenomenon is still inchoate, there exists an exigent need to develop methodologies to map and evaluate the marketing impact of Web sites in and between industries (Jayaratna 1999). With the exception of a few papers (e.g., Berthon, Pitt and Watson, 1996; Berthon, Pitt and Prendergast, 1997; Peterson, Balasubramanian and Bronnenberg, 1997), little or no theoretical, descriptive, or normative research has been conducted on the evaluation of Web sites. This chapter is offered as a step towards addressing this deficiency. The technique of correspondence analysis and the interpretation of the maps produced are described in detail, with the international telecommunications industry as a focus. The implications for management are discussed.

WEBBING THE NET

The Internet is the name given to a vast global collection of interconnected computer networks. It comprises many separate networks, belonging to disparate organisations such as universities, business and Internet service providers, joined together in a haphazard way. The Web or World Wide Web can be thought of as a platform that rides on the Internet: a hypermedia information system that links computer-based resources around the world. Browser software allows hyperlinked words or icons to display a multitude of spatially dispersed media sources—comprising text, video, graphics, and sound - on a local computer screen. Characteristics of the Web that are important from a strategic marketing perspective include:

- *Interactivity*: the ability to interact both with and through the medium.
- *Availability*: 24-hour-a-day presence.
- *Facilitation and flexibility*: advertising, informing, full-colour virtual catalogues, on-line transactions, on-line customer support, distribution of certain products and services, and the eliciting of customer feedback.
- *Non-intrusiveness*: The customer generally has to find the marketer rather than vice versa, to a greater extent than is the case with most other media (e.g., Anderson, 1995). This renders the medium unique from a marketing perspective.
- *Cost*: (In most cases) initial presence on the medium is relatively easy and inexpensive to establish.
- *International reach*: Any business or organization that has a Web presence is international by definition.

- *Equality*: Compared to other media, the Web provides a more or less level playing field for all participants—access opportunities are essentially equal for all players, regardless of size.
- *Intermediaries*: Permits a lot of intermediaries to operate without the customer becoming aware of it.

Given the characteristics of the new medium, it is perhaps unsurprising that the Web has achieved such a phenomenal growth rate. However, while many companies are simply attempting to establish a beachhead in marketspace, others view it as their lifeblood. What is certain is that the issue of the effective use of the new medium will escalate rapidly in importance, as the growing number of managerial 'how to' books on the subject attests (e.g., Cronin, 1994). Therefore the issue of evaluation and comparatively mapping Web sites—both within and between industries will continue to become a significant issue for marketeers.

EXTANT LITERATURE

Research into the evaluation of Web sites as a marketing medium is still in its infancy. Berthon, Pitt and Watson (1996) and Berthon, Pitt and Prendergast (1997) developed and refined a series of metrics for the objective measurement of Web site effectiveness. Peterson, Balasubramanian, and Bronnenberg (1997) go some way toward trying to understand what types of products and services are likely to sell effectively through Web sites, while Ainscough and Luckett (1996) explore the elements of effective consumer marketing on the Web. Other research has begun to lay the conceptual foundations of marketing on the Web (e.g., Deighton, 1997; Hoffman and Novak, 1996), but little or no attention has been paid to empirical research into evaluation, comparing and positioning of Web sites.

A BRIEF INTRODUCTION
TO POSITIONING STRATEGY

The term positioning is widely used in marketing strategy and management. The term itself was popularised by two advertising executives (Ries and Trout, 1982). Ries and Trout had been fascinated by the spectacular failures of many organisations that had attempted to combat opposition head on. They pointed to the sensational flops of companies such as General Electric and RCA in the 1960s in their attempts to enter the mainframe computer market in direct opposition to an entrenched company such as IBM. Ries and Trout explained the failure of these strategies by saying that it was very difficult to disenthrone an entrenched competitor from a market, because that competitor was firmly 'positioned' in the minds of prospects. Thus for one to say that your firm would also be a successful very large manufacturer of mainframe computers was simply an imitation strategy - for the customer knew who the real champion was. It was IBM.

It would be far more effective, said Trout and Ries, to position products by looking for 'gaps' in the minds of customers. Thus for Avis it made more sense to reinforce the objective knowledge that consumers already had (that Hertz was the largest car rental company) and to position itself against Hertz, not as an equally large or very large competitor, but as 'number two.' The consumer could accept this —he or she knew that Avis was indeed the second largest competitor in the market. This position against the entrenched competitor enabled Avis to further pursue the strategy by saying that because it was number two it would have to try harder. The 'We Try Harder' campaign became one of the most successful advertising and indeed positioning strategies of all time.

Thus we see that positioning has both an objective and a subjective element. Positioning is something that occurs in the minds of a customer and which marketers actively seek to influence by framing (direct and indirect) objective knowledge in new ways. A product must match or fulfil the communicated message or the customer will rapidly become disappointed – as the disconfirmation paradigm argues (Oliver, 1980). Positioning maps have a number of important uses:

- First they enables the marketer to see where his or her product or brand (a Web site in this instance) is positioned compared to others in the marketplace. Thus the marketer can see where their brand is relative to a brand leader.
- The marketer can also use maps to determine the effectiveness or otherwise of marketing strategy, particularly marketing communication strategy.
- Maps can also be useful to marketers who wish to 'identify a gap in the market'. Thus there may be a market for brands for which there is no position or closely associated position occupied at the present time. However just as one inquires 'It there a gap in the market?' one should also always ask the question 'Is there a market in the gap?' Indeed there may be gaps in a particular market because there are no customers there.
- Naturally the construction of maps can be used to track the perceptions of a market over time.

THE TECHNOLOGY OF MAPPING – MULTIDIMENSIONAL SCALING

The Web provides multidimensional influences that need to be captured and multidimensional scaling is an ideal research analysis method for mapping multi variables. It includes a number of related techniques for mapping data onto a single scaled dimension (the origin of the 'scaling' in the name) or into a multidimensional space (e.g., Davison, 1992; Green, Carmone and Smith, 1989). Some methods take symmetrical matrices of similarity or dissimilarity data; others take rectangular matrices of ratings or rankings of objects, while yet others handle multiple similarity or dissimilarity matrices which might arise when a number of judges are asked to compare different things. The scaling methods can take a variety of approaches based on the presumed nature of the data and the measurement (ratio, interval, ordinal, nominal) and rely on multiple methods for handling ties in both the data and the mappings. One of the oldest methods, known as "classical scaling" or "principal coordinate analysis," is conceptually and mathematically closely related to principal component analysis; however other MDS methods are computationally more complicated. The mapping technique used in the current research is correspondence analysis. Correspondence analysis is the analysis of cross-classified frequency data to display pattern of association among row and column objects (e.g., Greenacre, 1984). The technique is essentially as an MDS procedure for the displaying of categorical data. More formally, Hoffman and Franke (1986) describe correspondence analysis as a multidimensional scaling technique for spatially portraying categorical data, where data is represented in a joint space in which the squared interpoint distance can be related to a chi-squared.

POSITIONING AND THE WEB

The Web offers some interesting challenges to marketers in terms of positioning. First, the Web is much more than just another marketing communications channel —Web sites have the potential to provide customised services and deliver products on a one-to-one basis: The Web is as much a *marketplace* as a *communication medium*. Thus the Web is a medium through which marketers attempt to communicate with customers to position products, and the Web is also the market place in which products and services are experienced and bought. Second and concomitantly, objective and subjective knowledge are closely intertwined on the Web. For the Web is quintessentially an information medium where the experience of interaction with a Web site is as important as is the content the Web site provides. Third, interaction with a Web site has many of the characteristics of services, namely, intangibility, simultaneity, heterogeneity, and perishability. Fourth, many of the research data of products and services that used to be assessed in a subjective form can now be quantified with objective data. For example, generally the time spent reading a magazine page had to be based on readers' perceptions; whereas, on the Web this can be precisely measured in time units. Similarly, questions such has "How do you rate the promptness of our service?" can be precisely quantified on the Web.

THE RESEARCH

The current research comprised a number of stages. First, relevant facets of the focal population of telecom companies on the Web are described, along with sampling issues. Second, dimensions of Web site effectiveness are outlined, and the process of evaluating each site described. Third, the technique of correspondence analysis is described. Finally, the data gathered on the telecommunications industry is analysed, plotted and discussed.

THE TELECOMMUNICATIONS INDUSTRY

The industry chosen for the research was that of telecoms industry. The telecoms industry was selected for a number of reasons. These included:

- Telecoms companies provide much of the direct and indirect infrastructure of the Internet and thus are pivotal players in the development of the Web.
- Telecommunications is an information-rich service, with information prior to, at the point of sale and during all subsequent usage having a major influence on the purchasing decision and usage patterns.
- The Web appears to be a "natural" medium for the telecoms industry. The industry recently has increasingly come to depend on creating and nurturing one-to-one customer relationships. Moreover these relationships involve a complex interactive dialogue between telecom companies and their customers. Thus the Web, which excels in the areas of interactivity and mass-customisation (Berthon, Pitt and Watson, 1996), has great potential to add value to the services that companies supply to their customers.

SAMPLE FRAME AND SAMPLE

The population was telecom companies with a presence on the Web. The sample frame was the Yahoo search engine directory of telecom companies. From this sample frame, a selection of 15 companies was made, taking into consideration company size, geographical location, business type, and brand recognition. The list of companies appears in Table 1, along with the Web site URL.

Table 1: The sample

Telecom Company	URL
Ameritech	www.ameritech.com
AT&T	www.att.com
Bell Atlantic	www.bell-atl.com
BT	www.bt.com
Deutsche Telecom	www.dtag.de
France Telecom	www.francetelecom.fr
KDD Japan	www.kdd.co.jp
MCI	www.mci.com
Mercury	www.mercury.co.uk
Sprint	www.sprint.com
Swiss Telecom	www.swisscom.com
Telecom Italia	www.telecomitalia.interbusiness.it
TeleDanmark	www.teledanmark.dk
Vodaphone	www.vodafone.co.uk
Worldcom	www.wcom.com

DIMENSIONS OF WEB SITE EVALUATION

As a first stage of the research semi-structured interviews were conducted with telecomm customers which regularly used the Web and who had some experience of telecomm Web sites. This study of customers' experience of interacting with telecom Web sites elicited three quite separate sets of criteria. The first comprised Web site basics, such as ease of finding the site, speed of the site, and extensiveness of the site. The second set concerned whether people liked the site, found it interesting and useful enough to revisit, and on revisit whether the content was up-to-date. There was a third group of criteria that are not directly pertinent to the present study, and comprised elements of product and service quality.

In more detail, the criteria we focus on in this chapter, comprise Web site basics - those considered critical in determining whether a person returns to a site or not. The first of these was speed of the site – customers don't like long waits, and alternative sites are only a mouse click away. Second, freshness of the sites' contents – out-of-date material negates one critical reason why people use the Web – to be availed of the latest, up to the minute information. Moreover, regularly updated sites give customers a reason to return. Third, content – extent and depth of content provide added value to the customer–interviewees were unimpressed by a few pages of "window dressing." These criteria are consistent with the extant literature on what makes Web sites effective (e.g., Christopher, Payne and Ballantyne, 1991; Ellsworth and Ellsworth, 1995; Raisch, 1996; Waltner, 1996; Peterson, 1997; Peterson, Balasubramanian and Bronnenberg, 1997). The full set of criteria, their scoring process and definitions are outlined in Table 2. Each Web site was evaluated on the outlined criteria. Information on each site was obtained from the Web database supplied by the Internet organisation Alexa (www.alexa.com) and is a mixture of objective and subjective data.

CORRESPONDENCE ANALYSIS:
AN INTRODUCTION

Benzecri (1969) first developed correspondence analysis in France, while its popularization to the English-speaking world is, to a large extent, due to Greenacre (1984). In addition the work of Hoffman and Franke (1986) has been influential to its introduction in the marketing area. Two lesser-known works (Underhill and Peisach, 1985, and Bendixen, 1991) provide excellent examples of applications of correspondence analysis. These papers have strongly influenced the manner in which the output from the correspondence analysis computer program, used for this study, is presented and interpreted.

Correspondence analysis is a multivariate analysis technique that can be used to analyze and interpret cross-tabulations of categorical data. More specifically it can be used to determine the nature and dependency between the r-1 rows and the c-1 columns of the contingency table resulting from the cross-tabulation. The main output from a correspondence analysis is a graphical display that is a simultaneous

Table 2: Web site evaluation criteria

Attribute	Scoring	Definition & notes
Traffic	A score out of 5, where 5 is high and 1 low. 5 = Site is among the Top 10 for Web traffic 3 = Top 1,000 1 = Top 100,000	This rating illustrates the amount of traffic to a particular site. It is based on hit counts recorded from various caches on the Internet backbone by ALL Web users.
%like	This is a percentage score of people who liked a particular site to the total number of people who expressed an opinion about the site	Tally of Alexa users who voted on a particular site. Users choose either "I like this site" or "I dis-like this site" for their vote. Alexa users can only vote once. Votes are specifically tallied at the site level, and not the page level.
Visits	Visits and revisits by Alexa users	This is the total number of Alexa users' visits and revisits to a particular site. This gives an indication of a site's popular-ity to Alexa users.
Connectivity	No of "backpointers"	"Backpointers" is the number of different Web pages that link to a particular Web site. This is a measure of the sites intercon-nectivity on the Web.
Speed	3 = Fast (@50 kB/s) 2 = Average (@28.8 kB/s) 1 = Slow (@14.4 kB/s)	"Speed" is the average amount of time it takes to display a page from a particular site. Speed data is based on a periodic update to Alexa's archive of the Web.
Freshness	5 = Less than 1 week old 4 = Less than 3 months old 3 = Less than 6 months old 2 = Less than 24 months old 1 = More than 24 months old	Freshness is determined by analyzing the dates of pages found during Alexa's periodic crawls of the Internet. The "freshest" 5% of all pages on the site are evaluated to deter-mine their average age.
Size	Total number of pages	"Pages" is the number of Web pages on a particular site. Num-ber of pages is based on a peri-odic update to Alexa's archive of the Web and is a measure of the extent of the content pro-vided by a particular site.

plot of the rows and columns of a contingency table in a space of two or more dimensions. Those rows with similar profiles are plotted 'close' together; similarly for columns with similar profiles. The number of dimensions needed for a *perfect* representation of a contingency table is given by the minimum of (r-1) and (c-1), which for a large contingency table will clearly not be helpful. The idea underlying correspondence analysis is to find a lower dimensional representation of the table, preferably two or at the most three dimensions, which will provide an 'adequate' summary of the results. The decision concerning the number of dimensions to retain for interpretation purposes is made on the basis of the variation or inertia, as it is more likely to be called, that the retained dimensions explain. In practice the focus is usually on the two primary dimensions.

CORRESPONDENCE ANALYSIS OF TELECOM WEB SITES: RESULTS

In Table 3 appears the data in the form of a contingency table. It portrays the each telecom site's score on the various chosen attributes. This contingency table, with a few exceptions outlined below, formed the basis of the data for the correspondence analysis. As can be seen from the table, all telecom sites scored a maximum of 5 for freshness. Thus freshness was excluded from the analysis as it did not differentiate between sites. Furthermore, KDD Japan, Mercury and Vodaphone were excluded because of missing data. These exclusions yielded a core sample of 12 sites that appear on the correspondence analysis plot.

Table 3: Telecom sites and attributes

Company	Traffic (rating*2)	%like	Visits (*100)	Connect-ivity(*100)	Speed	Fresh-ness	Size (*100)
Ameritech	3	50	39	41	1	5	10
AT&T	5	80	215	176	1	5	10
Bell_Atlantic	2	100	7	16	2	5	10
BT	4	90	27	42	2	5	10
Deutsche_Telecom	3	40	26	29	1	5	7
France_Telecom	2	50	9	10	1	5	6
KDD_Japan	2	50	3	7	2	5	10
MCI	4	80	123	55	2	5	10
Mercury	2	50	3	1	1	5	3
Sprint	4	70	97	49	1	5	10
Swiss_Telecom	2	50	44	3	2	5	6
Telecom_Italia	2	50	24	24	1	5	10
TeleDanmark	3	70	17	9	1	5	7
Vodaphone	2	50	6	5	2	5	8
Worldcom	7	100	18	12	2	5	5

The data was analyzed using the SAS JMP package. The results appear in Table 4, Table 5a, Table 5b, Table 5c and a two-dimensional plot, Figure 1. The interpretation of this output follows.

Table 4: Chi squared analysis and related statistics

Test	ChiSquare	Prob>ChiSq
Likelihood Ratio	224.967	<.0001
Pearson	233.202	<.0001

Source	DF	LogLikelihood	RSquare (U)
Model	55	112.4837	0.0667
Error	1294	1574.3255	
C Total	1349	1686.8092	
Total Count	1354		

Table 5a: Dimensional inertia

Dimension	Singular Value	Inertia	Portion
1	0.33992	0.11554	0.6709
2	0.20562	0.04228	0.2455
3	0.10539	0.01111	0.0645
4	0.04963	0.00246	0.0143
5	0.02898	0.00084	0.0049

Table 5b: Company coordinates

Company	c1	c2	c3
AT&T	-0.2976	-0.1154	0.03875
Ameritech	0.05185	-0.1739	-0.0516
BT	0.28158	-0.2614	0.02761
Bell_Atlantic	0.92173	-0.1583	-0.175
Deutsche_Telecom	0.11458	-0.175	0.00753
France_Telecom	0.65299	-0.0353	-0.0802
MCI	-0.191	0.18652	-0.0185
Sprint	-0.1543	0.13236	-0.0193
Swiss_Telecom	0.06098	0.62369	-0.1139
TeleDanmark	0.57798	0.19306	-0.0168
Telecom_Italia	0.24775	-0.117	-0.1695
Worldcom	0.70310	0.20686	0.42117

Table 5c: Attribute coordinates

Attribute	c1	c2	c3
%like	0.82817	0.10358	0.06549
Connectivity	-0.0766	-0.275	0.02057
Size	0.61887	-0.0183	-0.263
Speed	0.82130	0.25851	-0.0047
Traffic	0.65861	0.14943	0.42610
Visits	-0.2113	0.17163	-0.009

Figure 1. Correspondence analysis

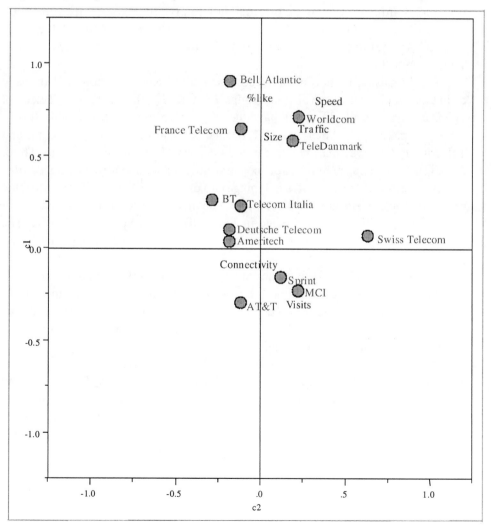

The first step is to establish whether there is dependency between the rows (telecom companies) and the columns (attributes). Table 4 provides the results from a Chi-square analysis of the data, which confirms evidence of strong dependency (P< 0.001). The second step is to decide upon the number of dimensions to retain for further analysis. Table 5a provides the inertia report needed for this decision. The first and second dimensions account for 67.09% and 24.55% of the inertia respectively. Together they account for 91.64% of the inertia. Thus a two dimensional solution should provide an 'accurate' description of the data.

The third step involves interpreting the retained dimensions. This involves studying the absolute magnitudes and the signs of the coordinates for the attributes and the telecom companies that are to be found in Tables 5b & c . Those with large coordinates, positive or negative, play a significant role in determining the dimension and thus its interpretation (see Underhill and Peisach, 1985, 53). The dimensions are purely numerical scales that are produced to show relative distance from the centroid in a graphical way. The dimensions can be thought of as artificial variables synthesized from the original data to give the maximum explanation of the differences and similarities between the originally observed values. It is up to the analyst to attribute meaning to the dimensions (Remenyi, Money and Twite, 1995, 143).

For dimension 1, analysis of the company coordinates (see column Company c1 in table 5b) reveals three distinct groups. First, Bell_Atlantic, France_Telecom, TeleDanmark, and Worldcom all have 'large' positive coordinates and thus form a clear group. Second, Ameritech, BT, Deutsche_Telecom, Swiss_Telecom, and Telecom_Italia have small positive coordinates and form a second group. Third, AT&T, MCI, and Sprint have 'large' negative coordinates and form another distinct group. In terms of the attributes mapping onto dimension 1 (see column Attribute c1 in Table 5c), two groups are discernible. The first group comprises attributes that have a large positive coordinate and include %like, Size, Speed and Traffic. The second group has negative coordinates on dimension 1 and comprise Connectivity and Visits.

For dimension 2, analysis of the company coordinates (see column Companies c2 in table 5b) reveals that this dimension does less well in differentiating the various telecom companies. Nevertheless distinct groups can once again be discerned. The first group comprises Bell_Atlantic, France_Telecom, BT, Telecom_Italia, Deutsche_Telecom, Ameritech, and AT&T, which all have negative coordinates on dimension 2. In contrast, a second group, TeleDanmark Worldcom, MCI, and Sprint all have positive coordinates on the second dimension, with Swiss_Telecom having a relatively large positive score and effectively forming a group-of-one on its own. In terms of the attributes mapping onto dimension 2 (see column Attribute c2 in table 5c), the second axis essentially differentiates between Connectivity and Size which have negative scores, and %like, Speed, Traffic and Visits, which have positive scores.

Combining the two dimensions (see Figure 1) reveals further insights. Telecom companies that are positioned close to one another have similar profiles with respect to the six attributes. The plot suggests that BT, Deutsche_Telecom, Ameritech, and Telecom_Italia cluster together forming a distinct group (Companies Group1), and Bell_Atlantic, France_Telecom, TeleDanmark, and Worldcom form a second (Companies Group 2). AT&T, Sprint and MCI form a third distinct group (Companies Group 3), while Swiss_Telecom is an anomaly, having less in common with the other companies. These groupings are outlined in Figure 2.

The Web site attributes form three groupings for the telecom companies in the sample. First, Connectivity is a unique attribute in and of itself and independent of the other attributes (Connectivity loads negatively on both c1 and c2). Second, Visits, like Connectivity, is a unique and independent attribute (Visits loads negatively on c2 and positively on c1). Third, Size, Speed, Traffic and %like form a relatively tight group, all with large scores on c1 and small positive scores on c2 (with the exception of Size, which only just achieves a negative score).

Figure 2. Correspondence analysis showing telecom company groupings

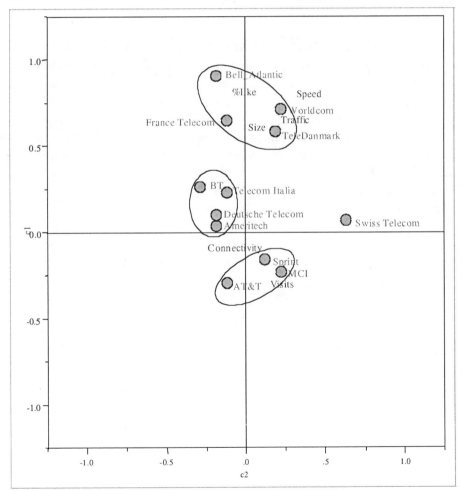

It is interesting to observe that a Web site's size and speed are related to the degree of overall traffic a site receives and also to the percentage of people who like the site. It would be insightful to perform a conjoint analysis to see how people trade off these attributes and whether there are critical "break points" in terms of speed and size that detrimentally affect traffic and the percentage of people who like a particular site.

Further examination of Figure 1 shows which telecom companies are associated with which attributes. Again, telecom companies that are positioned close to one another have fairly similar profiles with respect to the various attributes. Thus companies in Group 1 (BT, Deutsche_Telecom, Ameritech, and Telecom_Italia) sit relatively equidistant between the various attributes, but *differentially* place slightly more emphasis on Connectivity and Visits than on Speed, Size, Traffic and %like. In contrast companies in Group 2 (Bell_Atlantic, France_Telecom, TeleDanmark, and Worldcom) tend to place *relatively*[1] more emphasis on size, speed, traffic and %like than Connectivity and Visits. Finally Group 3 (AT&T, Sprint and MCI) appears to be the opposite of Group 2, placing *relatively* more emphasis on connectivity and visits, than size, speed, traffic and %like.

DISCUSSION AND CONCLUSION

In this chapter we employ correspondence analysis to inspect how different telecom companies on the Web are relatively positioned with respect to key dimensions of effective Web sites.

The technique could be extended to other types of Web sites, offering different products and services. This type of analysis could be of help to a number of different parties. First, to new telecom companies preparing to establish a Web presence – such an analysis could help position their site vis-à-vis extant offerings.

Second, to telecom companies wishing to compare their sites to those of competitors – this would provide insight into whom they 'cluster' with, and areas for improvement. Third, to companies wishing to benchmark their sites with those of 'best practice' in other industries. Indeed it would be informative to compare a group of similar telecom company Web sites with best practice web sites from other service industries.

Finally, the method described in this chapter gets away from simplistic "more will always be better" prognostications. Web site design, like much of strategic marketing, involves complex positioning decisions. A company's Web site design must be fully integrated with its strategic goals.

REFERENCES

Ainscough, T.L. and Luckett, M.G. (1996). The Internet for the Rest of Us: Marketing on the World Wide Web. *Journal of Consumer Marketing.* 13 (September): 36-47.

Anderson, C. (1995). Computer as audience. In *Interactive Marketing: The Future Present*, edited by E. Forrest and R. Mizerski. Lincolnwood, IL: NTC Business

Books and American Marketing Association.

Bendixen, M. T. (1991). Correspondence Analysis, Working Paper, Graduate School of Business Administration, University of Witwatersrand, South Africa.

Benzecri, J. P. (1969). *Statistical Analysis as a Tool to Make Patterns Emerge from Data: Methodologies of Pattern Recognition.* New York: Academic Press.

Berthon, P., Pitt, L. and Prendergast, G. (1997). Visits, Hits, Caching and Counting on the World Wide Web: Old Wine in New Bottles? *Internet Research,* 7(1). 5-8.

Berthon, P., Pitt, L. and Watson, R. (1996). The World Wide Web as an Advertising Medium: Towards an Understanding of Conversion Efficiency. *Journal of Advertising Research,* 60(1): 43-54.

Christopher, M., Payne, A. and Ballantyne, B. (1991). *Relationship Marketing.* Oxford: Butterworth-Heinemann.

Cronin, M J (1994). *Doing Business On The Internet.* New York, NY: Van Nostrand Reinhold.

Davison, M.L. (1992). *Multidimensional Scaling.* Malabar, CA: Krieger Publishing.

Deighton, J. (1997). Commentary on "Exploring the Implications of the Internet for Consumer Marketing. *Journal of the Academy of Marketing Science,* 25 (4, Fall): 347-351.

Ellsworth J., Ellsworth E. (1995). *Marketing on the Internet: Multimedia Strategies for World Wide Web Businesses.* New York, NY: John Wiley & Sons.

Green, P.E., Carmore, F.J. and Smith, S.M. (1989*). Multidimensional Scaling: Concepts and Applications.* Boston: Allyn and Bacon.

Greenacre, M. J. (1984). *Theory and Applications of Correspondence Analysis,* London: Academic Press.

Hoffman, D L & Novak, T P (1996). "Marketing In Hypermedia Computer-Mediated Environments: Conceptual Foundations, *Journal Of Marketing,* 60 (July), 50-68.

Hoffman, D. L. and Franke, G. R. (1986). Correspondence Analysis: Graphical Representation of Categorical Data in Marketing Research, *Journal of Marketing Research,* 23: 213-227.

Jayaratna, N. (1999). Understanding and Evaluating Methodologies: NIMSAD Framework. McGraw-Hill, UK.

Kehoe L (1996). "Ahead Of The Pack On The Information Superhighway," *Financial Times IT Supplement,* 3rd July 1996.

Oliver, R. L. (1980). A Cognitive Model of the Antecedents and Consequences of Satisfaction Decisions, *Journal of Marketing Research,* 47(Winter), 68-78.

Peterson R. A. (1997). Electronic Marketing: Visions, Definitions, and Implications. *Electronic Marketing and Consumer,* 2(1): 1-16.

Peterson, R.A., Balasubramanian, S. and Bronnenberg, B.J. (1997). Exploring the Implications of the Internet for Consumer Marketing. *Journal of the Academy of Marketing Science,* 25(4): 329-346.

Pitt, L., Berthon, P., and Watson, R. (1996). Conversion Efficiency on the World Wide Web: What Marketing Managers Might Want to Know. *Journal of General*

Management, 22(1, Autumn): 1-13.

Rayport, J.F. and Sviokla, J.J. (1994). Managing in the Marketspace. *Harvard Business Review*, November-December, 141-150.

Raisch R. (1996). Easier For A Camel To Go Through A Needle's Eye: Advertising Exposures and Clickthroughs. *The Internet Company*, August 6, http://www.Internet.com.

Remenyi, D. Money, A. H. and Twite, A. (1995). *Effective Measurement & Management of IT Costs and Benefits*. London: Butterworth Heinemann.

Ries, Al, and Jack Trout (1982). *Positioning: The Battle for Your Mind*. New York, NY: Warner Books.

Underhill, L. G. and Peisach, M. (1985). Correspondence Analysis and Its Application in Multielemental Trace Analysis. *Trace and Microprobe Techniques*, 3 (1&2): 41-65.

Waltner C. (1996). Going Beyond The Banner With Web Ads. *Advertising Age*, 67(10), March 4, 22.

ENDNOTE

1 It is important to remember that in correspondence analysis, positions are always relative. Thus, a company (X) can appear close to a particular attribute (A) even when in absolute scoring another company (Y) may achieve a higher score on the attribute. This is because company X scores higher on that particular attribute *relative* to its scoring on the other attributes in the focal attribute set.

Chapter 7

Investigating Social Motivations for Internet Use

Thomas F. Stafford
Texas Woman's University, USA

Marla Royne Stafford
University of North Texas, USA

The uses and gratifications theoretical framework has continued to prove useful in the study of new and emerging media. This chapter utilizes the uses and gratifications perspective to better understand the factors motivating commercial Web site use. Through the cooperation of two major on-line companies, this research reports the results of a two-part study that begins with the identification of 179 motivations for Web use and subsequently reduces those to five primary underlying factors. These factors are discussed and related to three key indicators: frequency of Web use, frequency of computer use, and affinity with the computer. Implications for a third general media gratification beyond the basic gratifications of content and process are discussed, and directions for future research are proposed.

INTRODUCTION

Information forms the underpinnings of modern society (Ball-Rokeach & Reardon, 1988; Rogers, 1986), and since media are required for the transmission of information at any level other than the interpersonal, the new medium represented by the World Wide Web might be considered the vanguard of the information society (Stafford & Stafford, 1998). The marketing strategies of industry are evolving into a mediated process that will support the commercial viability of "segments of one" in the form of direct-to-consumer commerce over computer networks (Rogers, 1986; Sheth, 1992). As this evolution takes place, the marketing communications flows that support commercial activity are reversing from marketer-consumer to consumer-marketer (Sheth, 1992); consumers are beginning to seek out the companies and products that interest them rather than relying on traditional mass marketing activities to inform and persuade them about opportunities.

As this idea of the segment of one develops in practice, it seems clear that the World Wide Web will present potent capabilities for reaching and commercially serving consumers (Drèze & Zufryden, 1997). However, throughout this evolutionary process, it also seems clear that marketers must begin asking questions about the unique characteristics of this new commercial medium; one critical question will concern the nature of motivations which bring consumers to *utilize* this new medium for commercial purposes (Stafford & Stafford, 1998). This consideration implies not only a need to understand what might motivate consumers to attend to marketing efforts on the Web, but also what might motivate them to use commercial Web sites, in general. In short, what are consumers' uses for, and associated gratifications in use of, commercial Web sites?

The Internet is experiencing phenomenal growth; it is growing so fast that researchers have a hard time simply keeping up with its current size and likely future growth. In previous years, the growth rate was estimated at between ten percent (Rubinstein, 1995) and twenty percent *per month* (Thomsen, 1997), with early estimates of the Internet audience suggesting that there were between 30 and 50 million users (Fox, 1995; Kambil, 1995). Audience size was expected to be near 150 million by the millennium (Barker & Groenne, 1997), but more current reports (Applegate, McFarlan & McKenney, 1999) placed 1995 audience levels at 40 million, with 100 million consumers logged on in 1998 and estimates of one billion Internet users by 2005. Presently, at least one home in four in the U.S. has Internet access (Clark, 1999), and the number of registered Internet commerce sites nearly tripled, from 600,000 to 1.7 million, in a one-year period monitored between 1996 and 1997 (Applegate et al.., 1999).

This combined pattern of growth among both consumers and businesses in the use of the Internet underscores its obvious utility for making connections between buyers and sellers. The Web promises to be a potent marketing vehicle, combining the power of promotional communications with the instant gratification of on-line purchases. A better understanding of the motivations which bring consumers to specific sites and the uses consumers might make of those sites can assist marketers in the design of more effective and compelling offerings in the new Internet medium. Consequently, the overall purpose of this chapter is to report a study that examines consumer motivations that drive Web site use.

Motivations for Web Use

Previous research suggests that motivations for the use of media, in general, tend to be dichotomous, split between the preference for media content versus enjoying the experience of media usage (e.g., Stafford & Stafford, 1996). Correspondingly, some people may prefer to randomly browse the Web for enjoyment (Hoffman & Novak, 1996), while others may prefer to seek out and use specific Internet sites primarily to access site-related information (Stafford & Stafford, 1998). These are the modern analogs of process and content gratifications in the new Internet medium.

In the formative days of uses and gratifications research, McGuire (1974) noted that it seemed less important to know how a user came *to* a medium than to understand how the medium could *hold* a user once browsing had its intended effect, and Internet scholars voice this same concern with regard to the "holding power" of Web site content (Barker & Groenne, 1997). Hence, while browsing might be considered a general motivation for Internet use, what a commercial Web site specifically offers in terms of content appears to be a key factor that will determine if that site has influence with potential consumers.

USES AND GRATIFICATIONS FOR WEB SITES

In the Internet marketplace, understanding the motivations which bring consumers to a site can be a success characteristic, since the "segment of one" approach can only be profitable if a marketer can reliably attract and serve *numerous* individual customers (Stafford & Stafford, 1998). Hence, knowledge of what consumers desire and benefit from in accessing commercial Web sites will provide Internet marketers with the ability to better, more profitably, serve their audiences. To that end, uses and gratifications theory can be diagnostic in understanding consumer motivations for using the Web (Newhagen & Rafaeli, 1996; Rafaeli, 1988).

Some say that the Web will simply serve as an additional tool to be integrated with traditional advertising and marketing processes (Peterson, Balasubramanian & Bronnenberg, 1997; Philport & Arbittier, 1997). Others consider the Internet to be a genuinely new medium for communication between buyers and sellers, and suggest that the uses and gratifications approach (U&G) will be useful for examining emerging trends in the commercial use of the Web (Eighmey, 1997b; Newhagen & Rafaeli, 1996). U&G theory has already been demonstrated in business-to-business Internet applications (Eighmey, 1997a; 1997b), and preliminary U&G work on consumer Web site applications has shown much promise (e.g., Stafford & Stafford, 1998).

USES AND GRATIFICATIONS FOR MEDIA

The basic premise of the U&G paradigm focuses on what people do *with* the mass media (Klapper, 1963). It has long been known that individuals have particular motives for media use (Katz, 1959), and that individuals' media choices are motivated by particular self-defined uses and goals (Lin, 1977). In the case of the Internet, U&G provides the theoretical framework for understanding motivations that drive Web use.

The Active Audience

A basic tenet of uses and gratifications theory is the active audience (Katz, Blumler & Gurevitch, 1974; Rubin, 1981), and this concept of active involvement is particularly important when investigating the emerging Internet medium, where communication is best conceptualized as a *reversed* flow, and the individual user controls the process by simple virtue of initiating access (Stafford & Stafford, 1998). To paraphrase Klapper, what people do with the Web is to use it to their own *personal* ends.

Active audiences are selective and make their own choices (Levy & Windahl, 1984), so understanding the activities prized by audience members is critical, since these activities are representative of the underlying motivations which influence selective and individual media access. Hence, the Web site marketer is best served by a clear understanding of those activities and motivations which influence audience members who electronically access and use Internet resources. Audience activity is axiomatic in emerging Internet media — Web sites are *designed* for active use, since undirected viewing does not engage search engines or access information packets (Stafford & Stafford, 1998).

Content and Process Gratifications

As noted previously, motivations to access media are generally considered to be either content related or process related; content gratification includes *use* of the messages carried by the medium, and process gratification relates to enjoyment of the *act* of using the medium, as opposed to interest in its content (Cutler & Danowski, 1980). While it has been posited that the mere act of Web surfing, itself, is inherently gratifying (Hoffman & Novak, 1996), there currently is a great deal of concern about Web site content, with indications that users may be quite motivated in their choice of specific sites to visit by site content, as opposed to the recreational act of browsing (Drèze & Zufryden, 1997; McDonald, 1997; Stafford & Stafford, 1998). In short, it may be that what a site offers content-wise may be the attraction which serves to bring consumers to the site, so that commercial transactions might take place.

Potential Factors Motivating Web Users

According to Stafford and Stafford (1998), Web site use might be characterized initially by process gratifications in recognition of the "Web surfing" phenomenon which has the potential to expose new users to site content. However, while initial and accidental exposure could often be due to some random browsing effect, content gratifications seem more likely to represent the reason for continued site access, a perspective in line with McGuire's (1974) "holding power" arguments.

Aimless surfing is an apt Internet characterization of the process gratification, but bookmarking a site might be more representative of motivations arising from content gratifications. When a user finds a site compelling enough to mark the return passage for a later visit, this is likely indicative of strong content interest. Researchers have expressed concern about the ability to hold the attention of Web site users (Barker & Groenne, 1997), and it appears that site designers should be working on ways to increase a user's involvement with Web sites—to actively use them and mark them for additional later use, rather than working out ways to enhance the browsing experience.

Researchers have already compared the Web to television in terms of potential effects and uses (Eighmey, 1997b; McDonald, 1997), which is ironic, since what is known about uses and gratifications theory comes from studies of television in its infancy (Stafford & Stafford, 1996). In some cases, the television metaphor is directly applicable, as in the case of Eighmey (1997a; 1997b), who investigated corporate Web sites to determine user motivations with scales developed in earlier U&G studies of television use. Certainly, television research has provided a broad understanding of general commercial media user motivations (Rubin, 1981), and the broad paradigm of uses and gratifications arising from these previous media studies can be adapted very nicely in modern application (e.g., Eighmey, 1997b; Newhagen & Rafaeli, 1996; Peterson et al., 1997). Yet, relying on methods based only on commercial television research may limit the understanding of Web-based motivations. In short, there has been little empirical work to specifically adapt the U&G perspective to commercial Web use. To that end, the objectives of this study are:

1) to develop a U&G approach specifically for examining the use of the World Wide Web.
2) to identify key factors representing consumer motivations for utilizing specific Web sites.
3) to link these factors to key indicators related to the computer and the Web.

METHOD

As demonstrated in previous television studies, the general approach to building a U&G profile is to determine key motivations for using (i.e., gratifications sought from) a particular medium. The current research accomplished this through a two-stage research design. The first stage identified a list of descriptors that were representative of Web use and gratification. The second stage involved the reduction of these descriptors into key underlying motivations. Following the suggestion of Bantz (1982) and Levy and Windahl (1984), factor analysis was used to identify dimensions of motivation.

STAGE 1

The first part of the study sought to develop a list of descriptive adjectives corresponding to the specific motivations of Web users. In order to accomplish this, cooperation was obtained from HotWired, a major Internet-themed Web site. HotWired agreed to place an open-ended questionnaire on their site, and this questionnaire was available for one week to all individuals signing on to the HotWired site.

The questionnaire included four open-ended questions that were designed to elicit a thorough list of uses and gratifications associated with the site. As proposed by Szalay and Deese (1978) and Friedmann and Fox (1989), word association techniques help in understanding the cognitive schemata of subjects. To obtain the most thorough list possible, four questions were asked to capture all potential valuable uses and gratifications. These four questions were: 1) What is the first thing that comes to mind when you think about what you enjoy most when accessing the Web? 2) What other words describe what you enjoy about interacting with the Web? 3) Using single, easy-to-understand terms, what do you use the Web for? and 4) What on-line activities are most important to you?

Results

A total of 98 individuals completed the questionnaire during the week. To encourage ready participation, personal information was not solicited, so demographic characteristics cannot be reported; however, relatively recent information on Web users suggests that the average Web site visitor has a college degree (67%), is reasonably affluent ($69,000 average income), and is married with children (Gupta, 1997).

A total of 179 individual descriptive terms were provided by the respondents. Of these 179 items, 45 were mentioned a total of 4 times or more. These items and their total number of mentions are shown in Table 1. The other 81 items were mentioned three times or less. To maintain a manageable number of items in the subsequent analysis, the 45 items mentioned four times or more were used in the questionnaire for Stage Two of the research.

STAGE 2

The Questionnaire

A questionnaire was developed that included the 45 items identified in the first stage of the research. For each of the 45 items, respondents were instructed to indicate their perceived level of importance for each item with regard to their motivations in accessing the Web. A scale of one to seven, with seven being the most important, was used.

To better understand the different motivations related to use of the technological interface with the Internet (i.e., personal computers), three additional measures were included in the questionnaire. The first was a five-item "affinity for the computer" measure adapted from Rubin's (1981; 1984) affinity for television scale. The second measure was a single item that assessed frequency of Web use, and the last measure was a single item that captured frequency of computer use.

The Sample

Digital Marketing Service (DMS), an America Online partner, agreed to participate in this research project. DMS administers AOL's on-line marketing research, and is actively engaged in the determination of motivations for commercial Internet use. The questionnaire was placed in the Opinion Place section of the America Online member services screen. Individuals were randomly selected from a pool of customer volunteers who were compensated for their participation with free on-line time for use in their AOL accounts. The questionnaire was active for this data collection over a one-week time period.

A total of 343 usable on-line questionnaires was collected. The subjects ranged in age from 18 to over 55 and included a mix of 165 men and 178 women. Fifty-seven respondents were in the 18-24 age category, 72 were 25-34, 68 were 35-44, 70 were 45-54, and 76 were 55 or older. Because it is not known how many people were offered and refused the opportunity to participate and receive the free service, a response rate ratio cannot be calculated.

ANALYSIS AND RESULTS

The analysis was a two-part process. Initially, data on the 45 individual gratifications were subjected to principal

Table 1: Initial motivations items identified in stage 1

Item	Overall Frequency of Response
Information	114
Email	49
Research	45
News	41
Software	31
Chatting	24
Entertainment	24
Communication	23
Fun	20
Access	17
Work	15
People	13
Web Sites	12
Speed	12
Updates	12
Freedom	11
Interaction	11
Games	11
Knowledge	11
Surfing	11
New	10
Technology	9
News Groups	9
Resources	9
Education	8
Interesting	8
Easy	8
Stocks	7
Answers	7
Browsing	6
Variety	6
Learning	6
Weather	6
Progressive	5
Friends	5
Shopping	5
Search Engines	5
Relaxing	4
Sports	4
Ideas	4
Money	4
Searching	4
Current	4
Homework	4
Government	4

components analysis. As a second step, factor scores for the identified underlying dimensions of Web use were then calculated and used as the dependent variables in a multiple regression analysis. In order to provide an opportunity to better understand which type of computer user and/or Web user related to specific types of media motivations, the affinity for the computer, use frequency and Web use frequency measures were specified as independent variables.

Principal Components Analysis

The principal components analysis was conducted with varimax rotation, and specified the retention of factors with eigenvalues greater than one. This resulted in

Table 2: Exploratory factor analysis results and factor loadings

Factor	**Search Factor**	**Cognitive Factor**	**New & Unique Factor**	**Social Factor**	**Entertainment Factor**
Eigenvalue	10.96	3.0	2.28	2.0	1.7
Variance explained	24.36%	7.32%	5.06%	4.43%	3.80%
Variable					
Resources	.575				
Search Engines	.686				
Searching	.685				
Software	.557				
Surfing	.590				
Technology	.661				
Updates	.529				
Web sites	.551				
Education		.671			
Information		.683			
Learning		.734			
Research		.597			
Ideas			.574		
Interesting			.703		
New			.552		
Progressive			.518		
Relaxing			.613		
Chatting				.776	
Friends				.686	
Interaction				.718	
Newsgroups				.500	
People				.711	
Entertainment					.711
Fun					.718
Games					.784

a total of 11 initial factors. A scree plot and further scrutiny of the eigenvalues indicated a natural break after the fifth factor; these five factors together accounted for about 45% of the total variance. Table 2 presents these results and reports all variable loadings above 0.5.

Factor One:

Factor one is characterized as a Search Factor. This theme was chosen based on key loadings for the variables of search engines, searching software and Web sites. Other variables loading on this factor include technology, updates and resources. Together, this suggests that the motivation underlying this dimension relates to using the Internet medium and its sites to search for the latest in informational updates and resources. The combination of key variables representative of both searching (a key Internet *process*) and informational resources (a notable *content* of the medium) implies that this initial factor represents a synergistic combination of both process and content gratifications (e.g., Stafford and Stafford 1998; Cutler and Danowski 1980). In short, it appears that users are *process* motivated to search for specific *content*.

Factor Two:

Factor two represents a theme of thinking and knowledge, and we characterize it as the Cognitive Factor. Variables loading on this factor include education, information, learning and research. This mix of variables appears to represent a primary motivation of Web-based learning and information seeking, which is highly content-specific.

Factor Three:

The third factor is termed "New and Unique," because all but one of the items loading on it seem to signify the new and unique things that are available on the Web. The variables that comprise this factor include ideas, interesting, new, progressive and relaxing. While this last item, relaxing, does not appear to be as thematic as the others, it is possible that finding new and unique things on the Internet is relaxing to some people. In general, this appears to be a content-based factor.

Factor Four:

Factor four is clearly the Social Factor, with variables such as chatting, friends, interaction, news groups, and people all loading strongly here. It appears that some people are motivated to use the Web simply for social purposes and thus receive such related *social* gratifications. This factor appears to represent a new sort of motivation: one that is neither content nor process dominant.

Factor Five:

The final factor appears to be an Entertainment Factor. Three related items (entertainment, fun and games) all load nicely here, indicating that people might obtain gratifications from the Web simply by taking advantage of the fun, games and other entertainment offered on the Web. Interestingly, this appears to be the case of a process-motivated gratification that depends on site content.

Regression Analysis

As noted, the regression analysis was conducted with affinity with the computer, frequency of Web use, and frequency of computer use as predictor variables, and the five factors (represented by the factor scores of their signifying items) as dependent variables. Results of this analysis are presented in Table 3.

As shown, the multivariate tests for both affinity with the computer and frequency of Web use were significant. For affinity with the computer, the F statistic was 4.01 (p <.05) and for frequency of Web use, the F statistic was 11.91 (p < .001). For frequency of computer use, the F-test was not significant (F =1.81, p > .10).

The univariate tests provide further understanding and details. There was a significant positive relationship between affinity with the computer and the social factor (F = 9.66, p < .05) as well as between affinity with the computer and the entertainment factor (F = 3.63, p < .05), indicating that individuals with a higher affinity for the computer tend to use the Web for, and seek gratifications related to, socialization and entertainment, as opposed to searching and cognitive gratifications.

Although the frequency of computer use is significantly and positively related to the search factor (F = 6.28, p < .05), suggesting that those who use the computer more frequently tend to use the Web for searching purposes, the multivariate statistic for frequency of computer use was not significant; thus, this univariate finding must be considered cautiously and as a chance finding.

Table 3: Regression results parameter estimates (F-tests)

	Dependent Variable					
	Multivariate F-Statistic	Search Factor	Cognitive Factor	New & Unique Factor	Social Factor	Entertainment Factor
Independent Variable						
Affinity with the Computer	4.01[a]	.013 1.46	.008 .46	.018 2.60	.036 9.66[a]	.02 3.63[a]
Frequency of Web Use	11.91[c]	.200 32.43[c]	.008 .05	.09 6.70[a]	-.003 .01	.132 12.70[c]
Frequency of Computer Use	1.81	.145 6.28[a]	-.04 .52	-.08 1.93	.04 .64	-.02 .12

[a] = p < .05
[b] = p < .01
[c] = p < .001

Additionally, frequency of Web use was significantly related to three of the dependent variables: the Search Factor ($F = 32.43$, $p < .001$), the New and Unique Factor ($F = 6.70$, $p < .05$) and the Entertainment Factor ($F = 12.70$, $p < .001$). Based on this, it appears that those individuals who frequently use the World Wide Web tend to derive gratifications from searching, finding new and unique things, and entertainment as opposed to social and informational purposes.

DISCUSSION

This chapter applied the uses and gratifications paradigm to develop an understanding of general consumer motivations for accessing commercial areas of the World Wide Web. The investigation identified five key underlying dimensions of Web use motivation: Searching, Cognition, New and Unique, Socialization, and Entertainment. Interestingly, the three dimensions of motivation represented by the searching, new/unique and entertainment factors appear to represent various mixtures of the two general media gratifications of process and content.

Moreover, the analysis indicated that certain uses and gratifications were attributed to more frequent users of the Web, while other uses and gratifications applied to those with high affinity for computers. Generally, it seems that frequent Web users are heavily motivated by process-mediated content concerns; these users are either concerned with using processes to reach specific content or enjoy the process of actually using site content in an entertainment sense. In addition, the social aspects of the Web seem to be less important to those who spend more time searching for new and interesting content on the Web. Conversely, individuals high in affinity for the computer preferred to use the Web for social and entertainment purposes. Searching, information and new and unique things seem to be less important to those who really cherish and need their computer. It is possible that those individuals who have a higher affinity for the computer may actually be more interested in using their *computers* to interface with their peers (or, perhaps, find it more *convenient* to do so), as compared to direct interpersonal social interactions and entertainment activities. Hence, for these individuals, the Web may be a primary source of socialization and fun.

There are interesting implications to this particular result, since it appears to be a case of socialization made possible *through* a commercial mass medium. The only other communication medium that even partially affords this possibility is the telephone. However, it is readily apparent that the telephone is nothing like the Internet for social purposes. For one thing, the Web provides a *rich* audiovisual environment of multimedia presentations and information transmissions, including processes that enhance mediated interpersonal interaction, such as two-way video, interactive gaming, instant messaging, and voice transmission. For another thing, telephone socialization generally takes the form of direct, identified, interpersonal contact; whereas, the Internet facilitates numerous interpersonal interaction formats that can range from direct/identified, direct/anonymous (chat rooms, for example) and indirect and/or time-shifted formats (such as e-mail and bulletin boards).

A Third General Area of Media Gratification

A rich tradition of previous U&G research has brought a generalization that gratifications generally fall into two specific areas: process-related or content-related (e.g., Cutler & Danowski, 1980). Based on the current study, we are suggesting the existence of a new, Internet-specific media gratification: socialization.

There are powerful implications of this third general gratification: The Internet is at once an interpersonal *and* a mass exposure medium, and this new medium can provide simultaneous commercial *and* noncommercial opportunities for parties to any interaction. Personal ads in newspapers are presented as "interpersonal" messages in a commercial format, but it is *not* an interactive venue. The telephone is highly interactive, and conference calls are available for group interaction, but there are generally no commercial applications during private phone calls.

However, Web-based interpersonal interactions carry the potential exposure to all manner of site-based advertising and promotional messages during interpersonal encounters between one or more individuals on-line. Marketers may find commercial Web opportunities analogous to the "personal ads" of print media, by offering sites that facilitate interpersonal interaction; a handy example is America Online's "push" for user participation in instant messaging technologies during sign-on processes. The Internet is the first true interactive commercial medium, and it appears that the general gratifications frequently identified in studies of non-interactive media must now be supplemented with the third general media use gratification of socialization.

LIMITATIONS, FUTURE RESEARCH AND CONCLUSIONS

While this study began the process of identifying key underlying uses and gratifications of the World Wide Web, there are limitations. First, self-selection in on-line research is a potential problem, but this is an issue that generally applies to on-line studies where volunteers must be recruited for participation. Moreover, in Stage Two of our study, those who volunteered to participate were further qualified based on previous participation in on-line studies and/or demographic characteristics. Our questionnaire was included with a standard Digital Marketing Service AOL user satisfaction survey which had respondent targets and qualifications designed to more fully represent the makeup of the AOL user base. Thus, our data collection process can in no way be construed as random, although it was widespread and reached diverse groups of Internet users.

Another problem inherent in on-line research is the inability to calculate traditional response rates, as compared to survey research through the mail. It is not impossible to assess the exact number of individuals who have access to a Web site and thus, who represents a sampling frame for response rate calculations. However, our commercial on-line research partners have generally been less concerned with response rates than response quality; they have no trouble recruiting participants for their studies. The primary issue is obtaining samples that are consistent demographically with their key audiences.

Another limitation is that the data from both stages of the study each accessed respondents from a single Web site (HotWired in Stage 1 and AOL in Stage 2). Although the results do not appear to be biased, future research on uses and gratifications for the World Wide Web should attempt to reach users through a wider range of sites.

Nevertheless, the initial list of 179 potential uses and gratifications presented here, along with the five underlying dimensions provide a basis from which to move forward in future research on uses and gratifications for the Web. For example, future research can use the current study's results for classic U&G measure development (e.g., Bantz, 1982; Levy & Windahl, 1984) or to segment Web and computer uses based on their individual motivations.

Moreover, this research began the process of attributing certain motivations to those with a higher affinity with the computer and those who use the Web more frequently. Results suggest that those who use the Web more frequently seek gratifications related to content, but that the process of accessing content is also very important; in heavy Web use, these gratifications may be synergistically combined to motivate use. In addition, those who have high affinity for computers tend to be highly motivated by social gratifications on the Web. Consequently, a key conclusion of this study is that Webmasters and others who manage organizational Web sites need to understand their customers in terms of their Web usage and feelings toward the computer. Such concepts appear to be highly important in determining what an individual hopes to gain by visiting a particular spot located on the World Wide Web.

REFERENCES

Applegate, L.M., McFarlan, F.W., & McKenney, J.L. (1999). *Corporate Information Systems Management.* Boston: Irwin McGraw-Hill.

Ball-Rokeach, S.J., & Reardon, K. (1988). Monologue, dialogue and telelogue: Comparing an emerging form of communication with traditional forms. In R. Hawkins, S. Wieman, & S. Pingree (Eds.), *Advancing Communication Science: Merging Mass and Interpersonal Processes.* Newberry Park, CA: Sage.

Bantz, C.R. (1982). Exploring uses and gratifications: A comparison of reported uses of television and reported uses of favorite program types. *Communication Research,* 9(July), 352-379.

Barker, C., & Groenne, P. (1997). *Advertising on the web.* http://www.samkurser.dk/advertising/research.html.

Clark, D.D. (1999). High speed data races home. *Scientific American,* 281(4), 94-99.

Cutler, N.E., & Danowski, J.A. (1980). Process gratification in aging cohorts. *Journalism Quarterly,* 57(Summer), 269-77.

Drèze, X., & Zufryden, F. (1997). Testing web site design and promotional content. *Journal of Advertising Research,* 37(2), 77-91.

Eighmey, J. (1997a). On the web: It's what you say and how you say it. http://eighmey.jlmc.iastate.edu/.

Eighmey, J. (1997b). Profiling user responses to commercial web sites. *Journal of Advertising Research,* 37(May/June), 59-66.

Fox, B. (1995). Retailing on the Internet: Seeking truth beyond the hype. *Chain Store Age*, 71 (September), 33-46, 68, 72.

Friedmann, R., & Fox, R. (1989). On the internal organization of consumers' cognitive schemata. *Psychological Reports,* (65), 115-126.

Gupta, S. (1997). Consumer survey of WWW users. http://www-personal.umich.edu/~sgupta/hermes/survey3/summary.html.

Hoffman, D.L., & Novak, T.P. (1996). Marketing in hypermedia computer-mediated environments: Conceptual foundations. *Journal of Marketing,* 60(July), 50-68.

Katz, E. (1959). Mass communication research and the study of popular culture: An editorial note on a possible future for this journal. *Studies in Public Communication,* (2), 1-6.

Katz, E., Blumler, J.G., & Gurevitch, M. (1974). Uses of mass communication by the individual. In W. Davison, & F. Yu (Eds.), *Mass Communication Research: Major Issues and Future Directions*, New York: Praeger.

Kambil, A. (1995). Electronic commerce: Implications of the Internet for business practice and strategy. *Business Economics,* 30 (October), 27-33.

Klapper, J.T. (1963). Mass communication research: An old road resurveyed. *Public Opinion Quarterly,* 27, 515-527.

Levy, M.R., & Windahl, S. (1984). Audience activity and gratifications: A conceptual clarification and exploration. *Communication Research*, 11 (January), 51-78.

Lin, N. (1977). Communication effects: Review and commentary. In B. Ruben (Ed.), Communication Yearbook 1, New Brunswick, NJ: Transaction Books.

McDonald, S.C. (1997). The once and future web: Scenarios for advertisers. *Journal of Advertising Research,* 37(2), 21-28.

McGuire, W.J. (1974). Psychological motives and communication gratification. In J. Blumler, & E. Kaatz (Eds.), *The Uses of Mass Communications: Current Perspectives on Gratifications Research*, Beverly Hills: SAGE Publications, Inc.

Newhagen, J., & Rafaeli, S. (1996). Why communication researchers should study the Internet: A dialogue. *Journal of Communication*, 46(1), 4-13.

Peterson, R.A., Balasubramanian, S., & Bronnenberg, B.J. (1997). Exploring the implications of the Internet for consumer marketing. *Journal of the Academy of Marketing Science,* 25(4), 329-346.

Philport, J.C., & Arbittier, J. (1997). Advertising: Brand communication styles in established media and the Internet. *Journal of Advertising Research*, 37(2), 68-78.

Rafaeli, S. (1988). Interactivity: From new media to communication. In R. Hawkins, J. Wieman, & S. Pingree (Eds.), *Advancing Communication Science: Merging Mass and Interpersonal Processes.* Newberry Park, CA: Sage.

Rogers, E.M. (1986). *Communication Technology: The New Media in Society.* New York: Free Press.

Rubin, A.M. (1981). An examination of television viewing motivations. *Communication Research*, 8(April), 141-165.

Rubin, A.M. (1984). Ritualization and instrumental television viewing. *Journal of Communication,* 34(Summer), 67-78.

Rubinstein, E. (1995). The retail superhighway: Take a ride on the net. *Discount Store News*, 34(August), 79-81.

Sheth, J.N. (1992). Marketing's Sacred Pigs. Presentation to the Marketing Ideas Consortium, Athens, GA.

Stafford, M.R., & Stafford, T.F. (1996). Mechanical commercial avoidance: A uses and gratifications perspective. *Journal of Current Issues and Research in Advertising*, 18(Fall), 27-38.

Stafford, T.F., & Stafford, M.R. (1998). Uses and gratifications of the World Wide Web: A preliminary study. In D. Muehling (Ed.), *The Proceedings of the 1998 American Academy of Advertising Conference,* Pullman, WA: Washington State University.

Szalay, L.B., & Deese, J. (1978). *Subjective Meaning and Culture: An Assessment through Word Association.* Hillsdale, NJ: Lawrence Erlbaum Associates.

Thomsen, M.D. (1997). *Advertising on the Web.* http://www.samkurser.dk/advertising/thomsen.html.

Chapter 8

Turning Browsers Into Buyers: User Interface Design Issues for Electronic Commerce

Rex Eugene Pereira
Drake University, USA

The chapter investigates the interaction effects between the search strategy of software agents and the consumer's product class knowledge in the context of consumers seeking to purchase cars on the Internet. The research design used was a 2 x 4, between groups, completely randomized, two-factor, factorial design. The independent variables which were manipulated were product class knowledge (HIGH KNOWLEDGE, LOW KNOWLEDGE) and agent search strategy (elimination by aspects (EBA STRATEGY), weighted average method (WAD STRATEGY), profile building (PROFILE STRATEGY), simple hypertext (HYPERTEXT STRATEGY)). The dependent variables which were measured were satisfaction with the decision process (SATISFACTION), confidence in the decision (CONFIDENCE), trust in the agent's recommendations (TRUST), propensity to purchase (PURCHASE), perceived cost savings (SAVINGS), and cognitive decision effort (EFFORT). Significant differences were found in the affective reactions of the subjects toward the agent/application depending on the level of product class knowledge possessed by the subjects. Subjects with high product class knowledge had more positive affective reactions towards agents/applications which used the WAD and EBA strategies as compared to the PROFILE strategy. Subjects with low product class knowledge had more positive affective reactions to agents/applications which used the PROFILE strategy as compared to the EBA and WAD strategies. When the systems were modified to increase the amount of information provided and to increase the degree of control provided to the subjects, their affective reactions to the agents/applications were found to be different from the original study. Subjects responded more positively to the previously "less preferred" strategy, thus weakening the interaction effect.

INTRODUCTION

Marketing managers in the consumer goods industry face a new frontier of electronic information and commerce. Understanding buyer behavior in this new marketing channel is crucial. Marketing managers would like to present consumers with information on which to base their decisions. The information presented has to be such that it allows consumers to make decisions and select products that best match their tastes and needs (Bettman, Johnson & Payne, 1991). Otherwise consumers' incentive to seek out information will be minimal (Alba, Lynch, Weitz, Janiszewski, Lutz, Sawyer, & Wood, 1997). Presenting such information is not simple. On the one hand, a vast amount of information could be relevant, even very relevant to some consumers. On the other hand, presenting superfluous information might impede consumers' ability to make good decisions (Bettman, Johnson & Payne, 1991). If consumers were predictable and all alike, presenting information would be simple – marketing managers could provide only the information that is deemed most relevant by all the consumers. However, because of the heterogeneity between consumers, and within consumers at different points in time, almost none of the potentially available information is universally perceived as relevant. Rapid advancements in Internet technology have offered a solution to this dilemma in the form of computerized decision aids, which use software smart agents to provide an intelligent interface to the consumer.

The phenomenon of consumers purchasing products on the Internet is relatively new. In this business model, consumers select items to purchase from electronic shopping malls by making queries to databases using software tools such as software smart agents. This has raised a host of interesting research issues which need to be investigated. Research that should shed light on such issues is already underway (e.g. Degeratu, Rangaswamy, and Wu's (1999) study of electronic commerce for grocery items, Lynch and Ariely's (1999) study of electronic commerce for wines, and Shankar and Rangaswamy's (1999) study of electronic commerce in the travel industry). The influence of electronic decision aids on satisfaction with the decision process, confidence in the decision, and the propensity to purchase has not been examined previously and is of crucial importance.

The objective of this research is to understand why consumers react the way they do to different forms of agent technology and to identify mechanisms which will enable us to optimize the cognitive fit between an individual's knowledge and expertise and the decision strategy used by the software agent. To achieve this objective, four different decision environments were created which varied the process used for filtering the information. A simulated Web site is used which supports various agent strategies. The strategies used by the agent for information filtering are discussed below:

1. The Weighted Average (WAD) strategy uses all the information about the subject's preferences and computes a weighted preference matching score for each alternative based on the degree to which the attribute values of that alternative match the attribute values entered by the subject as his preferred values and the preference weights allocated to each of the attributes by the subject. The alternatives are then sorted by the computed preference matching scores and this sorted list is presented to the subject in descending order of the preference matching score. The subject can browse this list and narrow his choice set by first selecting the subset of alternatives which he would like to consider further in his decision process and then systematically eliminating alternatives from the choice set until he arrives at his final choice. The design of the application using the WAD strategy is similar to that of the Personal Logic web site (www.personalogic.com).

2. The Elimination By Aspects (EBA) strategy (Payne, Bettman, & Johnson 1993) obtains cutoff values from the decision maker on a set of product attributes. Alternatives that do not meet these specified criteria are eliminated from the choice set and the remaining alternatives make up the reduced choice set.

3. The "Profile Building" (PROFILE) strategy matches the user with "similar others" based on his demographic profile (age, household income, gender, educational level). The agent deduces the user's preferences by matching him with a group of similar individuals based on his demographic profile and expressed preferences and predicts that their preferences in the product category under consideration will also be similar to the user's. The agent will query the user for ratings on cars previously owned. Based on the demographic profile of the user and the ratings of previously owned cars, the agent will group the user with other individuals who responded similarly and recommend the current car models that those individuals have rated positively, inferring the user's similar preferences. Choices made by these similar others in the product category under consideration are used to form the recommended reduced choice set for the decision maker. The data to set up the different profiles was provided by IntelliChoice Inc., Campbell, California. Six different profile categories were created which included "Commuter", "College Freshman", "Executive", "Soccer Mom", "Sport Driver", and "Weekend Warrior". For example, when a user logs onto the Amazon.com web site, he is presented with a list of recommended books based on the books which he has purchased previously. Similarly, when a user logs onto the Personal Logic web site, he can select a profile which he feels best matches his own and then view the alternatives which the agent recommends. The design of the application using the PROFILE strategy is similar to that of the Firefly web site (www.firefly.net).

4. The "Simple Hypertext" (HYPERTEXT) strategy does not provide any information filtering support to the user. The user is presented with a set of

hypertext links to all the alternatives and is allowed to narrow the choice set at his own pace by sequentially eliminating alternatives from the initial choice set.

THEORETICAL DEVELOPMENT OF HYPOTHESES

Many factors, including demographics and prior product class experience have been studied in an attempt to account for individual differences in consumers' responses to a given set of information (Capon & Burke, 1980; Jacoby, Chestnut, & Fischer, 1978; Moore & Lehmann, 1980). Drawing on the information processing paradigm, this paper examines the effect of prior knowledge on information search behavior. A crucial element in the information processing model of human behavior is information stored in memory – i.e., prior knowledge. Much empirical evidence supports the view that prior knowledge affects information processing activities (Chase & Simon 1973a, 1973b; Chi, Glaser, & Rees, 1981; Chiesi, Spilich, & Voss, 1979; Larkin, McDermott, Simon & Simon, 1980). A number of studies have found a negative relationship between amount of product experience and amount of external search (Anderson, Engledow & Becker, 1979; Katona & Mueller, 1955; Moore & Lehmann, 1980; Newman & Staelin, 1971, 1972; Swan, 1969). An explanation for these results holds that experienced consumers perform more efficient information searches because they know which attributes are most useful for discriminating between brands and can more quickly determine which alternatives are inferior. Knowledgeable consumers substitute internal search for external search, thus reducing their amount of external search for information. Furthermore, knowledgeable consumers search more efficiently. Evidence that knowledgeable consumers recognize product alternatives as belonging to categories and subcategories is found in Sujan (1985). Efficiency in information search may occur in attribute selection as well as in alternative selection. Specifically, highly knowledgeable consumers may search only those attributes that are useful for discriminating among alternatives. Knowledgeable consumers possess three types of knowledge that contribute to search efficiency by allowing a quicker elimination of unsuitable alternatives: criteria for evaluating attributes, perceived covariance of attributes, and usage situation knowledge. Knowledge of criteria for evaluating attributes permits the individual to decide whether an alternative is acceptable by allowing him/her to compare it to reference points stored in memory. Knowledge of attribute covariation allows inferences to be made about some attributes without external search. Usage situation knowledge leads to earlier – and possibly more accurate – categorization of alternatives, based on their appropriateness for the intended usage situation. And finally, in situations where known brands rather than hypothetical or unknown brands are used, knowledge of the attribute values of available brands is used as a substitute for more effortless external search.

In providing agent services to consumers, intelligent agent tools depend on the accuracy of preference prediction to provide benefits to the consumer (Gershoff &

West, 1998). The majority of the literature examining intelligent agent-assisted electronic commerce assumes that consumers possess and are able to convey established preferences in the product category. As Gershoff and West (1998) point out, their research on intelligent agents assumes "well-defined" and "stable" preferences. Pazgal and Vulkan (1998) claim that search agents provide users with several useful advantages including increased productivity if the user can specify precisely what he or she is looking for. As noted by Bettman, Luce and Payne (1998), an important property of the constructive viewpoint is that preferences will often be extremely context-dependent. As such, an agent's goal in a choice situation characterized by constructive preferences is not just to inform, provide alternatives and uncover existing preferences, but to help the consumer build preferences with the ultimate goal of aiding in choice.

We define an expert as someone who has acquired domain specific knowledge through experience and training. This knowledge results in observable differences in cognitive processes (Chi, Glaser, & Farr, 1988) but may or may not lead to better performance in judgment and decision making. This definition is consistent with most research reported in the behavioral decision-making literature. To formulate a judgment, a decision maker must select, evaluate, and combine information that is available either internally or externally. Empirical findings indicate that knowledgeable decision makers are more selective in the information they acquire (Johnson, 1988; Shanteau, 1992a), are better able to acquire information in a less-structured environment (Brucks, 1985), are more flexible in the manner in which they search for information (Johnson, 1980), and agree more than novices regarding what information is important (Shanteau, 1988). A finding that has widespread support is that experts are more confident in their decisions than are novices (Mahajan, 1992).

How problems are cognitively represented affects the strategy by which problems are solved. Experts and novices have been found to exhibit differences in their problem-solving strategies. Experts categorize problems on the basis of solution procedures or underlying concepts; whereas, novices tend to categorize problems on the basis of surface features (Chi, Feltovich, & Glaser, 1981; Larkin, McDermott, Simon, & Simon, 1980). Because of this difference, experts use more efficient top-down or knowledge-based strategies, starting with known quantities to deduce unknowns (Chi, Feltovich, & Glaser, 1981; Johnson, 1980). Should a solution path fail, the decision maker can trace back a few steps and then proceed again, a valuable process in determining what actions are appropriate. The bottom-up or means-end decision strategy used by novices is not so practical. Decision makers start with the goal and determine what conditions are necessary to achieve the goal. Because novices focus their attention on goals instead of essential features of the task, learning is inhibited; they devote insufficient attention to acquiring valid schemas. The net effect is that experts are credited with having better-developed procedural knowledge (Chi & Glaser, 1980). If experts' procedural knowledge is appropriate for the task, they can encode and interpret information more quickly than can novices (Chase & Simon, 1973a; Chi, Feltovich, & Glaser, 1981; Johnson,

1988): They evoke a knowledge framework that is based on prior experience that expedites problem solving (Alba & Hasher, 1983).

A view that addresses the effects of task characteristics on expert judgments is that simple, well-structured domains do not give experts the opportunity to display their unique skills (Brucks, 1985; Johnson, 1980). Instead, general knowledge is sufficient to solve the problem. Johnson (1980) reviews a collection of real-world studies that compared experts' judgments with novices' and concludes that there are benefits to expertise if the combination rules are complex (environments that lend themselves to nonlinear cue use) and the task requires the decision maker to evaluate inputs (what he calls "complex cue representation").

Brucks (1985) argues that traditional laboratory tasks that organize the problem space by arranging decision alternatives and attributes in a matrix are inappropriate to use when studying expertise effects on judgment or choice processes. In the real-world, all the attributes and alternatives may not be readily available when the decision maker first confronts the problem. Providing a matrix in the laboratory therefore could eliminate the special advantages that experts have in structuring problems. Empirical findings from Brucks' research support her argument. Domain expertise benefited consumers when the intended usage situation was complex, that is, when many attributes could be potentially relevant. In contrast, there were no significant expertise effects when the intended usage situation was simple. These findings support Punj and Stewart's (1983) supposition that task characteristics, as opposed to individual differences, are "the most important determinants of behavior when the task is well-defined and unambiguous" (p. 182); by implication, individual differences therefore could take precedence as task ambiguity increases.

Smith (1988) proposes that problems can be characterized as structured, structurable, or unstructured for a particular problem solver at a given point in time. A problem is structured if the solver can readily identify a viable solution strategy. This might be the result of prior experience solving the problem or of a problem being stated in such a way that identifying a solution strategy is transparent. The application in which the search agent uses the PROFILE strategy would be characterized as a structured problem since the solution strategy is apparent to even the novice user. A problem is structurable if additional information would produce a solution strategy or if the solver can reformulate the problem into manageable subproblems, perhaps with the aid of a structuring methodology. Although this class of problems is called structurable, only those with access to the right information or knowledge can structure it reliably. The applications in which the search agent uses the EBA strategy or the WAD strategy would be termed as structurable problems because an expert with high product class knowledge would be able to add structure to the problem and formulate a solution strategy; whereas, a novice with low product class knowledge would not be able to add structure to the problem because of a lack of product class knowledge. For structurable problems, a complex but knowable solution strategy exists. A problem is inherently unstructured if a reliable solution strategy cannot be located by any means. The HYPERTEXT strategy would be termed as unstructured because even experts cannot utilize their product class knowledge to formulate a solution strategy to this problem. Problems that are unstructured are not necessarily unsolvable. Smith (1988, p. 1499) asserts that when faced with an unstructured problem, "one is forced to employ less reliable methods and hope for the best."

When tasks are inherently unstructured (for example, for the HYPERTEXT strategy), even experts cannot apply known solution strategies. Instead, they must use heuristics, and their resulting judgments are subject to all the biases associated with human judgment processes (Shanteau & Stewart, 1992). As Shanteau (1992b) observes, expert performance under these conditions is often times poor. Conversely, in domains that can be characterized as well structured (for example, for the PROFILE strategy), general problem-solving knowledge could be sufficient to solve the problem. Novices therefore could be expected to induce reasonable problem-solving strategies on the spot, so their performance might rival that of experts, which is consistent with Brucks' (1985) argument. It is with tasks in the middle category, the set of ill-structured but structurable problems (for example, the EBA and WAD strategies), that experts would be expected to significantly outperform novices. Problems of this nature are information rich and require large amounts of internal knowledge (Voss & Post 1988). Using existing knowledge, experts can reformulate, decompose, and/or impose constraints onto the problem, all of which reduce the size of the problem space and hence its ambiguity (Newell & Simon, 1972; Reitman, 1965; Voss & Post, 1988). The problem is now internally represented as one or more structured problems. Therefore, within the category of structurable problems, the more structure that is provided in the problem's initial condition the better novices will do, decreasing the performance differential between experts and novices. As problems become more ill-structured, the performance differential between experts and novices also should decrease, because of experts' decreasing ability to structure the decision problem. The relationship

Table 1: Summary of conceptual framework

	Inherent Problem Structure		
	Initially well-structured	Initially ill-structured, but structurable	Inherently unstructured
Experts	Experts solve the problem on the basis of their internal knowledge and external information.	Experts apply their knowledge to form an internally well-structured problem, which then can be solved more easily.	Experts reason by analogy or use simplifying heuristics.
Novices	Novices figure out how to solve the problem on the basis of general knowledge & external information.	Novices cannot reliably structure the problem; they evoke simplifying and often inappropriate heuristics.	Novices cannot reliably structure the problem; they evoke simplifying and often inappropriate heuristics.

Table 2: Problem characteristics that affect structure

	Ease of selecting inputs
	Ease of evaluating inputs
Inputs	Noise inherent in inputs
	Number and complexity of inputs
	Organization of inputs
	Number of allowable transformations
Transformation	Ease with which the problem can be decomposed
Rules	Specificity of transformations
Goals	Clarity of goals
	Number of acceptable goal states

among expertise, initial problem structure, and decision performance is capsulized in Table 1.

To be useful, this conceptualization requires us to be able to identify factors affecting a problem's structure. Early researchers in this area propose that a problem's initial structure is a function of how clearly specified are the goals, inputs, and/or allowable transformation rules—procedures used to integrate data inputs to reach a decision (Reitman, 1965; Simon, 1973, 1978; Taylor, 1974). Taking this notion further, Smith (1988) provides a list of problem attributes that contribute to a problem's level of structure. Using this and other literature, a partial set of problem characteristics is provided in Table 2. For a problem to be (at least initially) ill-structured, at least one of these characteristics must be ambiguous.

To formulate a judgment about a prespecified criterion, a decision maker first must decide which inputs to use (Klayman, 1988). Empirical findings on information search point to dual benefits of expertise. On the one hand, expertise facilitates information processing, potentially increasing amount of search; but on the other hand, expertise allows for more efficient searching, potentially decreasing search (Brucks, 1985; Johnson & Russo, 1984). Whether the facilitating effect or the efficiency effect dominates in a specific context depends partly on the demands of the task. If the decision maker has access to large amounts of external information, much of which is irrelevant or redundant, it is likely that experts will be more selective in their use of available information than will novices, because they can activate domain specific schemas that direct attention to relevant information. In contrast, novices are less able to discern the diagnosticity of the available data and/or the relationships among them.

Previous studies have found that experts find attributive statements such as those provided by WAD and EBA strategies informative; whereas, novices consider benefit statements such as those provided by the PROFILE strategy informative (Conover, 1982; Walker, Celsi, & Olson, 1987). Walker, Celsi, and Olson (1987) noted that experts tended to use technical attributes (e.g., nutritional information) in distinguishing among food items; whereas, novices performed this task on the basis of benefits (e.g., good for you).

When attribute information is presented, as in the EBA and WAD strategies, experts have the knowledge to infer the benefits implied by attribute information and are likely to be motivated to make such inferences as a basis for judgments because they perceive attribute information to be highly informative. As Alba and Hutchinson (1987, p. 426) note, a technical attribute focus is likely to be effective because experts are "able to infer all of the related benefits and find the technical description to be more convincing ....". By contrast, it seems unlikely that experts would process a benefits only message, such as that provided by the PROFILE strategy, in detail or be persuaded by such an appeal. The absence of attribute information prevents experts from using their knowledge to evaluate the claimed benefits. Without this information, experts may reject the communication as uninformative.

Novices are expected to respond differently than experts to the attribute-oriented (EBA and WAD) and benefit-oriented (PROFILE) appeals. Alba and Hutchinson (1987, p. 426) note that "physical features may be meaningless to novices, so advertisements directed at them are structured around easily comprehended benefits." This implies that attribute-oriented information (EBA and WAD) would not be informative and therefore not processed in detail by novices. By contrast, communications that focus on benefits (PROFILE) could be understood and perceived as informative by novices.

In the EBA strategy, as the decision process requires consideration of each product attribute and expression of cutoff values for some of the attributes, it seems reasonable to expect that it will be easier for individuals with high product class knowledge and thus will be preferred by them. Research by Payne, Bettman, and Johnson (1993) finds that experts prefer to use noncompensatory strategies like elimination by aspects and tend to process relevant information more efficiently than novices (Fiske, 1993). Brucks (1985) finds that experienced consumers know which attributes are useful for distinguishing between options and may search only on those.

While knowledgeable consumers are well equipped to process attribute information, individuals with low product class knowledge will likely find such a task more difficult. Attribute-oriented messages are found to be less informative to novices (Maheswaran & Sternthal, 1990; Alba & Hutchinson, 1987) as they do not process attribute information as efficiently as experts. Given the added effort for individuals with low product class knowledge to process attribute information, it is expected that they will show negative affective reactions to the agent/application when the agent is using the EBA strategy.

Hypothesis 1a: Subjects who have high product class knowledge will have more positive affective reactions to applications in which the search engines use the elimination by aspect filtering strategy than subjects who have low product class knowledge.

As the weighted average (WAD) strategy requires consideration of each product attribute and expression of preference with regard to each, it seems reasonable to expect that it will be easier for individuals with high product class knowledge and thus will be preferred by them.

Hypothesis 1b: Subjects who have high product class knowledge will have more positive affective reactions to applications in which the search engines use the weighted average filtering strategy than subjects who have low product class knowledge.

Given their inability to process attribute information as efficiently as individuals with higher levels of product knowledge, consumers with low product class knowledge have been found to seek more summary information (Brucks, 1985). Because of the lower level of effort required, individuals with low product class knowledge are predicted to prefer the PROFILE strategy as compared to the EBA or WAD strategies. Conversely, individuals with high product class knowledge may base their search only on product attributes (Brucks, 1985). The absence of attribute information in the PROFILE strategy prevents experts from using their knowledge to evaluate alternatives. Without this opportunity experts may reject the communication as uninformative (Maheswaran & Sternthal, 1990) and will have negative affective reactions towards agents/applications which use the PROFILE strategy.

Thus, it is predicted that individuals with high product class knowledge will show less favorable response to agents using the PROFILE strategy than individuals with low product class knowledge. The logic behind this is that experts are not permitted to use their attribute knowledge; rather, their preferences are inferred by matching them with "similar others". An underlying factor in this negative response may also have to do with the actual source of the recommendation – unidentified similar others versus an internal agent algorithm driven by the user's own preferences. Herr, Kardes, & Kim (1991) cite literature that shows that consumers trust their own opinions more than they trust the opinions of others (Hoch & Deighton, 1989). These authors contend that while other individuals are thought to exhibit knowledge or reporting biases (Wood & Eagly, 1981), making information provided by other sources ambiguous, self-generated information is less likely to be contaminated by knowledge or reporting biases.

Hypothesis 1c: Subjects who have low product class knowledge will have more positive affective reactions to applications in which the search engines use the profile building filtering strategy than subjects who have high product class knowledge.

Since subjects with high product class knowledge have a greater ability to discriminate among alternatives and to eliminate undesirable alternatives from the choice set, it is expected that they will experience more positive affective reactions to the HYPERTEXT strategy than subjects who have low product class knowledge. However, because of the lack of agent support in filtering the information, it is expected that subjects in both the groups will experience significantly negative affective reactions to the HYPERTEXT strategy as compared to the EBA, WAD, and PROFILE strategies.

DESCRIPTION OF VARIABLES

The scale items used to measure each of the constructs is presented in the Appendix.

Independent Variables Being Manipulated

Agent Search Strategy (STRATEGY)

This refers to the search and decision strategy employed by the agent in making recommendations to the user. The system was designed to have four treatment conditions, viz., Weighted Average Strategy (WAD), Elimination By Aspects Strategy (EBA), Profile Building Strategy (PROFILE), and Simple Hypertext Strategy (HYPERTEXT).

Product Class Knowledge (KNOWLEDGE)

Product class knowledge refers to the knowledge about the product and the familiarity with the product which the subject has.

Dependent Variables

Trust in the Agent's Recommendations (TRUST)

Trust in the agent's recommendations refers to the degree to which the subject feels that the software agent has recommended alternatives to him which most closely match his preferences.

Propensity to Purchase (PURCHASE)

This represents the subject's perception that he would purchase the selected alternative following the experiment if he were going to make a purchase in that particular product class.

Satisfaction With the Decision Process (SATISFACTION)

This represents the subject's subjective state of satisfaction with all aspects of the computerized decision process immediately after the decision has been made.

Confidence in the Decision (CONFIDENCE)

This refers to the confidence expressed by the subject that he has selected the best alternative from the set of feasible alternatives.

Perceived Cost Savings (SAVINGS)

This reflects the degree to which the subject feels that the use of the system has helped him to realize significant cost savings in his purchase decision.

Cognitive Decision Effort (EFFORT)

Cognitive decision effort refers to the psychological costs of processing information. This represents the ease with which the subject can perform the task of obtaining and processing the relevant information in order to enable him to arrive at his decision.

RESEARCH METHODOLOGY
FOR EXPERIMENT # 1

Industry Selection

The product category "cars" was selected to maximize the likelihood of a wide variation in product class knowledge for the subject group used in the experiment. There are more than 400 car models currently available in the USA and there exists a large number of attributes which customers typically use in their selection of cars.

Experimental Design

The research design used was a 2 x 4, between groups, completely randomized, two-factor, factorial design. The independent variables which were manipulated were product class knowledge (HIGH KNOWLEDGE, LOW KNOWLEDGE) and agent search strategy (EBA STRATEGY, WAD STRATEGY, PROFILE STRATEGY, HYPERTEXT STRATEGY). Subjects in each group (HIGH KNOWLEDGE and LOW KNOWLEDGE) were randomly assigned to one of the four treatment conditions (EBA, WAD, PROFILE, HYPERTEXT). The experiment was administered to 160 MBA students. Independent samples testing was used. Twenty subjects were assigned to each cell.

The 2x4 design resulted in 8 cells as is illustrated in Figure 1.

Figure 1. 2x4, between-groups, two-factor, factorial design

		Agent Filtering Strategy Employed			
		Elimination By Aspect Strategy (EBA)	Weighted Average Strategy (WAD)	Profile Building Strategy (PROFILE)	Simple Hypertext Strategy (HYPERTEXT)
Subject Groups	High Product Class Knowledge				
	Low Product Class Knowledge				

Factors Controlled in the Experiment

In order to test the hypothesized effects, the following factors were controlled in the experiment:

1. *Information Presentation Format and Graphics*: This was achieved through the use of a Web site on a local server which was designed specifically for the purpose of this research.

2. *Information Content of the Web Sites*: For each alternative which the subject examined, the set of attributes for which information was provided was the same. The attributes used included model year, body type, price, size (in terms of number of passengers, number of doors, cargo capacity), technical features (in terms of engine type, transmission type, drive train type, brake type, number of cylinders, fuel efficiency, acceleration, braking distance, towing capacity), safety record and features (in terms of antilock brakes, air bags, child safety locks, traction control), maintenance costs, car manufacturer, and country of manufacture. In addition, a photograph of the car model under examination was also placed on the Web site.

3. *Download Time of the Web Pages*: The download time of the Web pages was constant for all the alternatives.

4. *Number of Alternatives in the Feasible Set*: The initial choice set which was presented to the subjects was the same, regardless of the treatment condition.

5. *Choice Task*: All the respondents were given the same choice task, a setting where they were asked to select a car to purchase from among the cars in the database.

6. *Market Segment*: The sample is based on a convenience sample of MBA students. This represents a fairly homogeneous market segment for the decision-making task.

These controls limit the generalizability of the research, but are necessary to test the effects of interest.

Choice Environment

A laboratory experiment served as the vehicle for testing the hypotheses. Eight workstations in a behavioral decision laboratory provided a controlled environment where subjects participated in the experiment.

Choice Procedures

Subjects were first administered a pre-experiment questionnaire, which was intended to determine initial knowledge in the product category. This included measures of familiarity with the product category and knowledge about the product category. The pre-experiment questionnaire was also used to collect demographic information from the subjects (e.g., their age, household income, education level, gender, etc.). The level of product class knowledge was then manipulated by providing each of the subjects who were identified following the initial questionnaire as belonging to the group "high product class knowledge" with training on product attributes and features. This consisted of a series of screens of terminology used to describe and assess attributes of the product with the opportunity to click on any of the terms and receive additional information. Subjects in the "low product class knowledge" group received no training on the product category. All subjects were then required to list from memory the attributes that they would use in their purchase decision for this product. This provided a more objective measure of product class knowledge. In accordance with West, Brown, and Hoch (1996), consumers who have a consumption vocabulary are better able to develop and express preferences in a product category. The subjects in each of the two groups, "high" and "low" product class knowledge, were then allocated at random to one of the four treatment conditions. After completion of the choice task, subjects were asked to rate the choice task on the following dependent variables: cognitive effort, confidence in their decision, satisfaction with the decision process, propensity to purchase, perceived cost savings, and trust in the product alternatives recommended by the agent.

Manipulation Check

The initial subjective measure of product class knowledge showed some difference in product class knowledge between subjects in the "high product class knowledge" and "low product class knowledge" groups. The initial measure of product class knowledge was done by using the multi-item seven-point Likert scale measure. Means for product class knowledge (high knowledge = 4.12; low knowledge = 2.77; p = .155) were not significantly different. Following the training task, a question was presented to test subjects' objective knowledge about the product category. The responses to the question on choice factors (List the attributes you would consider in your purchase decision for cars?) were analyzed. The number of distinct, correct answers to the question was tallied to come up with an objective knowledge score. An independent scorer familiar with the product category and blind to the hypotheses being tested also graded the subjects' responses. Inter-rater reliability was .93. The scores on this objective measure of product class knowledge differed significantly between the "high product class knowledge" and the "low product class knowledge" groups in the direction predicted, with subjects in the "high product class knowledge" group being more knowledgeable about the terminology and choice factors than those in the "low product class knowledge" group (F [1,158] = 12.99; p = .001; mean high knowledge = 6.82; mean low knowledge = 3.15; scores ranged from 0 to 11 for list of car attributes considered).

RESULTS FOR EXPERIMENT # 1

Following extensive pretests and the procedures required for instrument purification, the measures used in the main experiment were found to have values for Cronbach a ranging from .73 to .94. The results of the reliability tests are presented in Table 3. From this analysis, it can be concluded that the measures used had high reliability. Factor analysis of the data indicated that the scale items loaded onto the constructs they were a priori expected to load on. There were no cross-loadings. Furthermore, the number of factors which emerged was identical to those expected a priori. Thus, there is statistical evidence to support the claim that the scales have adequate unidimensionality, convergent and discriminant validity at the monomethod level of analysis. Hence it can be concluded that the measures used had high validity. The results of the factor analysis are presented in Table 5. The measures used for the dependent variables SATISFACTION, CONFIDENCE, TRUST, PURCHASE, SAVINGS and EFFORT were represented as the mean-centered scores of the seven-point Likert scale items which were used to measure these constructs. Correlation analysis shows that product class knowledge is significantly correlated with several dependent variables, including satisfaction with the decision process (r=.23, p=.037), how much they trusted that the agent represented them well in selecting alternatives (r=.27, p=.085) and how effortful they found the task (r=-.21, p=.039). The results of the correlation analysis are presented in Table 4.

Table 3: Reliability of measures used

Acronym	**Measure**	α
SATISFACTION	Satisfaction with the Decision Process	.86
CONFIDENCE	Confidence in the Decision / Choice	.73
TRUST	Trust in the Agent's Recommendations	.84
PURCHASE	Propensity to Purchase	.79
SAVINGS	Perceived Cost Savings	.94
EFFORT	Cognitive Decision Effort	.92
KNOWLEDGE	Product Class Knowledge	.91

Table 4: Correlations between the constructs

	Effort	Satisf-action	Confi-dence	Savings	Trust	Purch-ase	Know-ledge
Effort	1.00						
Satisfaction	-.1546	1.00					
Confidence	.0947	.0443	1.00				
Saving	-.2027	.1973	.1498	1.00			
Trust	.0423	.0619	.2497**	.2538**	1.00		
Purchase	.0316	.0618	.2192	.2519**	.1683	1.00	
Knowledge	-.2142**	.2341**	.2893***	.1052	.2716***	.1865	1.00

*** Significant LE .01 (2-tailed)** Significant LE .05 (2-tailed)

Table 5: Summary of the factor analysis of the variables

Scale #	Effort	Satisfa-ction	Confi-dence	Savings	Trust	Purch-ase	Know-ledge
E.1	.57						
E.2	.76						
E.3	.69						
E.4	.72						
E.5	.58						
E.6	.81						
S.1		.89					
S.2		.56					
S.3		.91					
S.4		.96					
S.5		.72					
S.6		.67					
C.1			.52				
C.2			.69				
C.3			.78				
C.4			.57				
C.5			.81				
C.6			.64				
Save.1				.91			
Save.2				.95			
Save.3				.64			
Save.4				.81			
Save.5				.79			
Save.6				.90			
T.1					.59		
T.2					.62		
T.3					.72		
T.4					.74		
T.5					.61		
T.6					.89		
T.7					.91		
T.8					.72		
T.9					.79		
P.1						.57	
P.2						.59	
P.3						.56	
P.4						.61	
P.5						.78	
P.6						.81	
P.7						.72	
P.8						.69	
K.1							.82
K.2							.73
K.3							.57
K.4							.72
K.5							.68
K.6							.75

To rule out any potentially confounding effects, the sample means for computer familiarity were statistically compared across cells. Results of these tests indicated that each cell contained subjects who, on average, had the same level of computer familiarity. In addition, subjects were distributed approximately equally across cells by gender. Hence, effects identified in the experimental data can be assigned with greater certainty to the experimental variables under investigation.

Table 6 presents the cell means obtained for each of the dependent variables. The detailed discussion of the statistical tests conducted and the results obtained for each of the dependent variables is presented below.

Satisfaction With the Decision Process (SATISFACTION)

A two-factor 2 x 4 ANOVA was performed to test the interaction effects of the independent variables "product class knowledge" (KNOWLEDGE) and "agent search strategy" (STRATEGY) on the dependent variable "satisfaction with the decision process" (SATISFACTION). The factors used were KNOWLEDGE and STRATEGY. This analysis yielded a significant overall interaction effect $F(3, 152) = 8.23, p < .001$. The presence of interaction effects between KNOWLEDGE and

Table 6: Cell means for each emotion as a function of agent search strategy and product class knowledge for experiment #1

| | High Product Class Knowledge | | | | | | | |
| | Eba | | Wad | | Profile | | Hypertext | |
	Mean	S.d.	Mean	S.d.	Mean	S.d.	Mean	S.d.
Satisfaction	5.11	1.27	5.32	1.35	2.91	.76	2.82	.71
Confidence	5.39	1.38	5.63	1.43	2.52	.61	2.78	.73
Trust	5.26	1.29	5.17	1.34	2.19	.48		
Purchase	4.18	1.28	4.25	1.35	2.53	.52	2.42	.75
Savings	5.63	1.44	5.79	1.41	2.05	.48	2.53	.62
Effort	2.71	.61	2.96	.75	4.82	1.13	5.51	1.34

| | Low Product Class Knowledge | | | | | | | |
| | Eba | | Wad | | Profile | | Hypertext | |
	Mean	S.d.	Mean	S.d.	Mean	S.d.	Mean	S.d.
Satisfaction	3.01	.75	2.91	.72	5.25	1.29	2.49	.63
Confidence	3.43	.88	3.47	.84	4.49	1.18	3.12	.87
Trust	2.92	.74	2.68	.68	4.24	1.05		
Purchase	1.96	.63	1.92	.65	4.92	1.21	1.96	.54
Savings	3.27	.82	3.02	.77	4.41	1.12	2.23	.56
Effort	4.65	1.12	4.75	1.21	2.79	.72	5.81	1.51

STRATEGY for the dependent variable SATISFACTION is clearly demonstrated in Figure 2.

This was followed by an investigation of the simple effects of the independent variable KNOWLEDGE on the dependent variable SATISFACTION. For the EBA STRATEGY, subjects with HIGH KNOWLEDGE experienced higher SATIS-FACTION than subjects with LOW KNOWLEDGE, $F(1, 152) = 11.54$, $p < .001$. For the WAD STRATEGY, subjects with HIGH KNOWLEDGE experienced higher SATISFACTION than subjects with LOW KNOWLEDGE, $F(1, 152) = 12.62$, $p < .001$. For the PROFILE STRATEGY, subjects with LOW KNOWL-EDGE experienced higher SATISFACTION than subjects with HIGH KNOWL-EDGE, $F(1, 152) = 7.29$, $p < .01$. For the HYPERTEXT STRATEGY, no significant difference in SATISFACTION was detected between subjects with HIGH KNOWL-EDGE and subjects with LOW KNOWLEDGE, $F(1, 152) = 1.95$, $p > .10$. Examination of the cell means shows clearly that for the EBA STRATEGY and the WAD STRATEGY, SATISFACTION was higher for the HIGH KNOWLEDGE group as compared to the LOW KNOWLEDGE group. For the PROFILE STRAT-EGY, SATISFACTION was higher for the LOW KNOWLEDGE group as com-pared to the HIGH KNOWLEDGE group. An investigation of the simple effects of the independent variable STRATEGY on the dependent variable SATISFACTION yielded significant results for both levels of KNOWLEDGE. For the HIGH KNOWL-EDGE group, $F(3, 152) = 6.19$, $p < .001$. For the LOW KNOWLEDGE group, $F(3, 152) = 5.87$, $p < .001$.

Figure 2. KNOWLEDGE x STRATEGY interaction for SATISFACTION

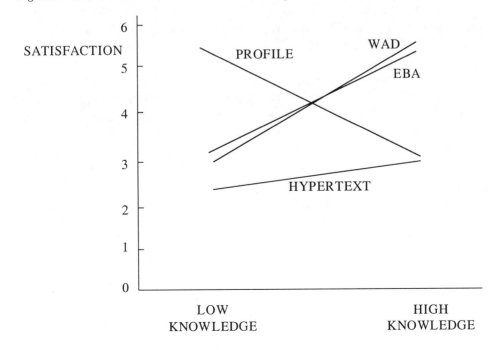

This was followed by a series of planned contrasts to investigate the effect of the independent variable STRATEGY on the dependent variable SATISFACTION. The weighting for the planned contrasts was consistent with the hypotheses being tested (Rosenthal & Rosnow, 1985). A planned contrast comparing the combined data from the cells (HIGH KNOWLEDGE, EBA STRATEGY) and (HIGH KNOWLEDGE, WAD STRATEGY) with the combined data from the cells (HIGH KNOWLEDGE, PROFILE STRATEGY) and (HIGH KNOWLEDGE, HYPERTEXT STRATEGY) indicated that subjects with HIGH KNOWLEDGE experienced significantly higher SATISFACTION when using the EBA STRATEGY or the WAD STRATEGY as compared to those who used the PROFILE STRATEGY or the HYPERTEXT STRATEGY, $F(1, 152) = 10.92$, $p < .001$. A one way ANOVA which was conducted on the two cells (HIGH KNOWLEDGE, EBA STRATEGY) and (HIGH KNOWLEDGE, WAD STRATEGY) which were combined for the purpose of the planned contrast did not yield a significant difference, $F(1, 38) = .83$, $p > .10$. A one way ANOVA which was conducted on the two cells (HIGH KNOWLEDGE, PROFILE STRATEGY) and (HIGH KNOWLEDGE, HYPERTEXT STRATEGY), which were combined for the purpose of the planned contrast, did not yield a significant difference, $F(1, 38) = 1.29$, $p > .10$. A planned contrast comparing the data from the cell (LOW KNOWLEDGE, PROFILE STRATEGY) with the combined data from the cells (LOW KNOWLEDGE, EBA STRATEGY), (LOW KNOWLEDGE, WAD STRATEGY), and (LOW KNOWLEDGE, HYPERTEXT STRATEGY) indicated that subjects with LOW KNOWLEDGE experienced significantly higher SATISFACTION when using PROFILE STRATEGY as compared to those who used the EBA STRATEGY, the WAD STRATEGY, or the HYPERTEXT STRATEGY, $F(1, 152) = 12.37$, $p < .001$. A one way ANOVA which was conducted on the three cells (LOW KNOWLEDGE, EBA STRATEGY), (LOW KNOWLEDGE, WAD STRATEGY), and (LOW KNOWLEDGE, HYPERTEXT STRATEGY), which were combined for the purpose of the planned contrast, did not yield a significant difference, $F(2, 57) = 1.67$, $p > .10$. Examination of the cell means shows clearly that the HIGH KNOWLEDGE group experienced higher SATISFACTION when using the EBA STRATEGY or the WAD STRATEGY and the LOW KNOWLEDGE group experienced higher SATISFACTION when using the PROFILE STRATEGY.

This was followed by a complex interaction contrast to investigate the interaction effects of the independent variables KNOWLEDGE and STRATEGY on the dependent variable SATISFACTION. The weighting for the complex interaction contrast was consistent with the hypothesis being tested (Rosenthal & Rosnow, 1985). A complex interaction contrast to detect the interaction effects of KNOWLEDGE (HIGH, LOW) and STRATEGY (combined EBA + WAD, PROFILE) yielded a significant result $F(1, 152) = 14.28$, $p < .001$. From the above-mentioned series of statistical analyses, it was concluded that there exists a strong interaction effect between the independent variables KNOWLEDGE and STRATEGY on the dependent variable SATISFACTION. Subjects with HIGH KNOWLEDGE experience significantly higher SATISFACTION when using the EBA STRATEGY or the WAD STRATEGY. Subjects with LOW KNOWLEDGE experience significantly higher SATISFACTION when using the PROFILE STRATEGY.

Confidence in the Decision (CONFIDENCE)

A two-factor 2 x 4 ANOVA was performed to test the interaction effects of the independent variables "product class knowledge" (KNOWLEDGE) and "agent search strategy" (STRATEGY) on the dependent variable "confidence in the decision" (CONFIDENCE). The factors used were KNOWLEDGE and STRATEGY. This analysis yielded a significant overall interaction effect $F(3, 152) = 6.58$, $p < .001.$. The presence of interaction effects between KNOWLEDGE and STRATEGY for the dependent variable CONFIDENCE is clearly demonstrated in Figure 3.

This was followed by an investigation of the simple effects of the independent variable KNOWLEDGE on the dependent variable CONFIDENCE. For the EBA STRATEGY, subjects with HIGH KNOWLEDGE experienced higher CONFIDENCE than subjects with LOW KNOWLEDGE, $F(1, 152) = 12.17$, $p < .001$. For the WAD STRATEGY, subjects with HIGH KNOWLEDGE experienced higher CONFIDENCE than subjects with LOW KNOWLEDGE, $F(1, 152) = 12.29$, $p < .001$. For the PROFILE STRATEGY, subjects with LOW KNOWLEDGE experienced higher CONFIDENCE than subjects with HIGH KNOWLEDGE, $F(1, 152) = 8.91$, $p < .01$. For the HYPERTEXT STRATEGY, no significant difference in CONFIDENCE was detected between subjects with HIGH KNOWLEDGE and

Figure 3. KNOWLEDGE x STRATEGY interaction for CONFIDENCE

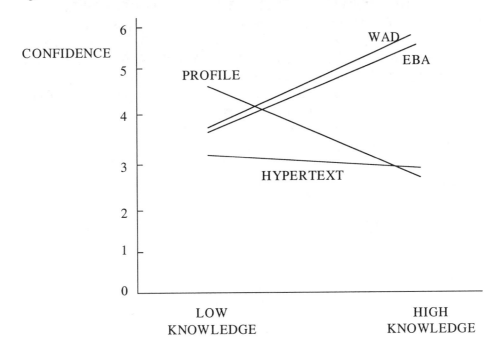

subjects with LOW KNOWLEDGE, $F(1, 152) = .92$, $p > .10$. Examination of the cell means shows clearly that for the EBA STRATEGY and the WAD STRATEGY, CONFIDENCE was higher for the HIGH KNOWLEDGE group as compared to the LOW KNOWLEDGE group. For the PROFILE STRATEGY, CONFIDENCE was higher for the LOW KNOWLEDGE group as compared to the HIGH KNOWLEDGE group. An investigation of the simple effects of the independent variable STRATEGY on the dependent variable CONFIDENCE yielded significant results for both levels of KNOWLEDGE. For the HIGH KNOWLEDGE group, $F(3, 152) = 8.53$, $p < .001$. For the LOW KNOWLEDGE group, $F(3, 152) = 2.91$, $p < .05$.

This was followed by a series of planned contrasts to investigate the effect of the independent variable STRATEGY on the dependent variable CONFIDENCE. The weighting for the planned contrasts was consistent with the hypotheses being tested (Rosenthal & Rosnow, 1985). A planned contrast comparing the combined data from the cells (HIGH KNOWLEDGE, EBA STRATEGY) and (HIGH KNOWLEDGE, WAD STRATEGY) with the combined data from the cells (HIGH KNOWLEDGE, PROFILE STRATEGY) and (HIGH KNOWLEDGE, HYPERTEXT STRATEGY) indicated that subjects with HIGH KNOWLEDGE experienced significantly higher CONFIDENCE when using the EBA STRATEGY or the WAD STRATEGY as compared to those who used the PROFILE STRATEGY or the HYPERTEXT STRATEGY, $F(1, 152) = 13.11$, $p < .001$. A one way ANOVA which was conducted on the two cells (HIGH KNOWLEDGE, EBA STRATEGY) and (HIGH KNOWLEDGE, WAD STRATEGY), which were combined for the purpose of the planned contrast, did not yield a significant difference, $F(1, 38) = 1.12$, $p > .10$. A one-way ANOVA which was conducted on the two cells (HIGH KNOWLEDGE, PROFILE STRATEGY) and (HIGH KNOWLEDGE, HYPERTEXT STRATEGY), which were combined for the purpose of the planned contrast, did not yield a significant difference, $F(1, 38) = .81$, $p > .10$. A planned contrast comparing the data from the cell (LOW KNOWLEDGE, PROFILE STRATEGY) with the combined data from the cells (LOW KNOWLEDGE, EBA STRATEGY), (LOW KNOWLEDGE, WAD STRATEGY), and (LOW KNOWLEDGE, HYPERTEXT STRATEGY) indicated that subjects with LOW KNOWLEDGE experienced significantly higher CONFIDENCE when using PROFILE STRATEGY as compared to those who used the EBA STRATEGY, the WAD STRATEGY, or the HYPERTEXT STRATEGY, $F(1, 152) = 4.17$, $p < .05$. A one way ANOVA which was conducted on the three cells (LOW KNOWLEDGE, EBA STRATEGY), (LOW KNOWLEDGE, WAD STRATEGY), and (LOW KNOWLEDGE, HYPERTEXT STRATEGY), which were combined for the purpose of the planned contrast, did not yield a significant difference, $F(2, 57) = 2.19$, $p > .10$. Examination of the cell means shows clearly that the HIGH KNOWLEDGE group experienced higher CONFIDENCE when using the EBA STRATEGY or the WAD STRATEGY and the LOW KNOWLEDGE group experienced higher CONFIDENCE when using the PROFILE STRATEGY.

This was followed by a complex interaction contrast to investigate the interaction effects of the independent variables KNOWLEDGE and STRATEGY on the dependent variable CONFIDENCE. The weighting for the complex interaction contrast was consistent with the hypothesis being tested (Rosenthal & Rosnow, 1985). A complex interaction contrast to detect the interaction effects of KNOWL-EDGE (HIGH, LOW) and STRATEGY (combined EBA + WAD, PROFILE) yielded a significant result $F(1, 152) = 7.81$, $p < .01$. From the above-mentioned series of statistical analyses, it was concluded that there exists a strong interaction effect between the independent variables KNOWLEDGE and STRATEGY on the dependent variable CONFIDENCE. Subjects with HIGH KNOWLEDGE experience significantly higher CONFIDENCE when using the EBA STRATEGY or the WAD STRATEGY. Subjects with LOW KNOWLEDGE experience significantly higher CONFIDENCE when using the PROFILE STRATEGY.

Trust in the Agent's Recommendations (TRUST)

A two-factor 2 x 3 ANOVA was performed to test the interaction effects of the independent variables "product class knowledge" (KNOWLEDGE) and "agent search strategy" (STRATEGY) on the dependent variable "trust in the agent's recommendations" (TRUST). The factors used were KNOWLEDGE and STRAT-EGY. This analysis yielded a significant overall interaction effect $F(2, 114) = 9.17$, $p < .001$. The presence of interaction effects between KNOWLEDGE and STRAT-EGY for the dependent variable TRUST is clearly demonstrated in Figure 4.

This was followed by an investigation of the simple effects of the independent variable KNOWLEDGE on the dependent variable TRUST. For the EBA STRAT-EGY, subjects with HIGH KNOWLEDGE experienced higher TRUST than subjects with LOW KNOWLEDGE, $F(1, 114) = 13.85$, $p < .001$. For the WAD STRATEGY, subjects with HIGH KNOWLEDGE experienced higher TRUST than subjects with LOW KNOWLEDGE, $F(1, 114) = 14.63$, $p < .001$. For the PROFILE STRATEGY, subjects with LOW KNOWLEDGE experienced higher TRUST than subjects with HIGH KNOWLEDGE, $F(1, 114) = 12.19$, $p < .001$. Examination of the cell means shows clearly that for the EBA STRATEGY and the WAD STRATEGY, TRUST was higher for the HIGH KNOWLEDGE group as compared to the LOW KNOWLEDGE group. For the PROFILE STRATEGY, TRUST was higher for the LOW KNOWLEDGE group as compared to the HIGH KNOWLEDGE group. An investigation of the simple effects of the independent variable STRATEGY on the dependent variable TRUST yielded significant results for both levels of KNOWLEDGE. For the HIGH KNOWLEDGE group, $F(2, 114) = 8.92$, $p < .001$. For the LOW KNOWLEDGE group, $F(2, 114) = 7.96$, $p < .001$.

This was followed by a series of planned contrasts to investigate the effect of the independent variable STRATEGY on the dependent variable TRUST. The weighting for the planned contrasts was consistent with the hypotheses being tested (Rosenthal & Rosnow, 1985). A planned contrast comparing the combined data from the cells (HIGH KNOWLEDGE, EBA STRATEGY) and (HIGH KNOWLEDGE, WAD STRATEGY) with the data from the cell (HIGH KNOWLEDGE, PROFILE STRATEGY) indicated that subjects with HIGH KNOWLEDGE experienced significantly higher TRUST when using the EBA STRATEGY or the WAD STRATEGY as compared to those who used the PROFILE STRATEGY, $F(1, 114) = 13.19$, $p < .001$. A one way ANOVA which was conducted on the two cells (HIGH KNOWLEDGE, EBA STRATEGY) and (HIGH KNOWLEDGE, WAD STRATEGY), which were combined for the purpose of the planned contrast, did not yield a significant difference, $F(1, 38) = 1.27$, $p > .10$. A planned contrast comparing the data from the cell (LOW KNOWLEDGE, PROFILE STRATEGY) with the combined data from the cells (LOW KNOWLEDGE, EBA STRATEGY), and (LOW KNOWLEDGE, WAD STRATEGY) indicated that subjects with LOW KNOWLEDGE experienced significantly higher TRUST when using PROFILE STRATEGY as compared to those who used the EBA STRATEGY or the WAD STRATEGY, $F(1, 114) = 11.92$, $p < .001$. A one way ANOVA which was conducted on the two cells (LOW KNOWLEDGE, EBA STRATEGY) and (LOW KNOWLEDGE, WAD STRATEGY) which were combined for the purpose of the planned contrast, did not yield a significant difference, $F(1, 38) = .93$, $p > .10$. Examination of the cell means shows clearly that the HIGH KNOWLEDGE group experienced higher TRUST when using the EBA STRATEGY or the WAD STRATEGY and the LOW KNOWLEDGE group experienced higher TRUST when using the PROFILE STRATEGY.

This was followed by a complex interaction contrast to investigate the interaction effects of the independent variables KNOWLEDGE and STRATEGY on the

Figure 4. KNOWLEDGE x STRATEGY interaction for TRUST

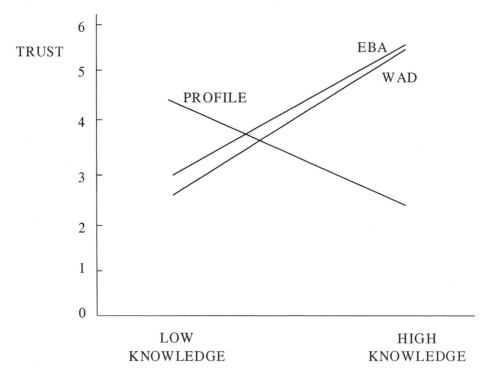

dependent variable TRUST. The weighting for the complex interaction contrast was consistent with the hypothesis being tested (Rosenthal & Rosnow, 1985). A complex interaction contrast to detect the interaction effects of KNOWLEDGE (HIGH, LOW) and STRATEGY (combined EBA + WAD, PROFILE) yielded a significant result $F(1, 114) = 12.19$, $p < .001$. From the above-mentioned series of statistical analyses, it was concluded that there exists a strong interaction effect between the independent variables KNOWLEDGE and STRATEGY on the dependent variable TRUST. Subjects with HIGH KNOWLEDGE experience significantly higher TRUST when using the EBA STRATEGY or the WAD STRATEGY. Subjects with LOW KNOWLEDGE experience significantly higher TRUST when using the PROFILE STRATEGY.

Propensity to Purchase (PURCHASE)

A two-factor 2 x 4 ANOVA was performed to test the interaction effects of the independent variables "product class knowledge" (KNOWLEDGE) and "agent search strategy" (STRATEGY) on the dependent variable "propensity to purchase" (PURCHASE). The factors used were KNOWLEDGE and STRATEGY. This analysis yielded a significant overall interaction effect $F(3, 152) = 6.92$, $p < .001$. The presence of interaction effects between KNOWLEDGE and STRATEGY for the dependent variable PURCHASE is clearly demonstrated in Figure 5.

This was followed by an investigation of the simple effects of the independent variable KNOWLEDGE on the dependent variable PURCHASE. For the EBA STRATEGY, subjects with HIGH KNOWLEDGE experienced higher PURCHASE than subjects with LOW KNOWLEDGE, $F(1, 152) = 8.72$, $p < .01$. For the WAD STRATEGY, subjects with HIGH KNOWLEDGE experienced higher PURCHASE than subjects with LOW KNOWLEDGE, $F(1, 152) = 7.91$, $p < .01$. For the PROFILE STRATEGY, subjects with LOW KNOWLEDGE experienced higher PURCHASE than subjects with HIGH KNOWLEDGE, $F(1, 152) = 10.97$, $p < .001$. For the HYPERTEXT STRATEGY, no significant difference in PURCHASE was detected between subjects with HIGH KNOWLEDGE and subjects with LOW KNOWLEDGE, $F(1, 152) = 2.33$, $p > .10$. Examination of the cell means shows clearly that for the EBA STRATEGY and the WAD STRATEGY, PURCHASE was higher for the HIGH KNOWLEDGE group as compared to the LOW KNOWLEDGE group. For the PROFILE STRATEGY, PURCHASE was higher for the LOW KNOWLEDGE group as compared to the HIGH KNOWLEDGE group. An investigation of the simple effects of the independent variable STRATEGY on the dependent variable PURCHASE yielded significant results for both levels of KNOWLEDGE. For the HIGH KNOWLEDGE group, $F(3, 152) = 5.41$, $p < .01$. For the LOW KNOWLEDGE group, $F(3, 152) = 4.94$, $p < .01$.

This was followed by a series of planned contrasts to investigate the effect of the independent variable STRATEGY on the dependent variable PURCHASE. The weighting for the planned contrasts was consistent with the hypotheses being tested (Rosenthal & Rosnow, 1985). A planned contrast comparing the combined data from the cells (HIGH KNOWLEDGE, EBA STRATEGY) and (HIGH KNOWL-

EDGE, WAD STRATEGY) with the combined data from the cells (HIGH KNOWL-
EDGE, PROFILE STRATEGY) and (HIGH KNOWLEDGE, HYPERTEXT
STRATEGY) indicated that subjects with HIGH KNOWLEDGE experienced
significantly higher PURCHASE when using the EBA STRATEGY or the WAD
STRATEGY as compared to those who used the PROFILE STRATEGY or the
HYPERTEXT STRATEGY, $F(1, 152) = 10.51$, $p < .01$. A one way ANOVA which
was conducted on the two cells (HIGH KNOWLEDGE, EBA STRATEGY) and
(HIGH KNOWLEDGE, WAD STRATEGY), which were combined for the pur-
pose of the planned contrast, did not yield a significant difference, $F(1, 38) = 1.77$,
$p > .10$. A one way ANOVA which was conducted on the two cells (HIGH
KNOWLEDGE, PROFILE STRATEGY) and (HIGH KNOWLEDGE,
HYPERTEXT STRATEGY) which were combined for the purpose of the planned
contrast did not yield a significant difference, $F(1, 38) = 2.42$, $p > .10$. A planned
contrast comparing the data from the cell (LOW KNOWLEDGE, PROFILE
STRATEGY) with the combined data from the cells (LOW KNOWLEDGE, EBA
STRATEGY), (LOW KNOWLEDGE, WAD STRATEGY), and (LOW KNOWL-
EDGE, HYPERTEXT STRATEGY) indicated that subjects with LOW KNOWL-
EDGE experienced significantly higher PURCHASE when using PROFILE STRAT-
EGY as compared to those who used the EBA STRATEGY, the WAD STRAT-
EGY, or the HYPERTEXT STRATEGY, $F(1, 152) = 12.91$, $p < .001$. A one way
ANOVA which was conducted on the three cells (LOW KNOWLEDGE, EBA

Figure 5. KNOWLEDGE x STRATEGY interaction for PURCHASE

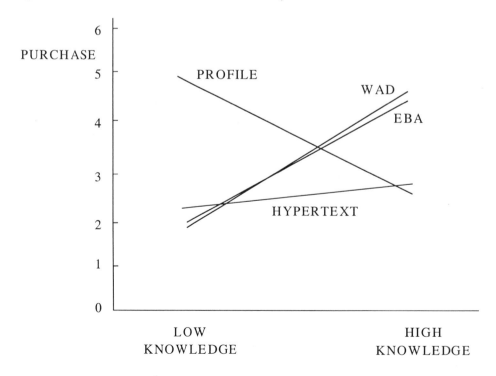

STRATEGY), (LOW KNOWLEDGE, WAD STRATEGY), and (LOW KNOWL-EDGE, HYPERTEXT STRATEGY) which were combined for the purpose of the planned contrast did not yield a significant difference, F(2, 57) = .17, p > .10. Examination of the cell means shows clearly that the HIGH KNOWLEDGE group experienced higher PURCHASE when using the EBA STRATEGY or the WAD STRATEGY and the LOW KNOWLEDGE group experienced higher PURCHASE when using the PROFILE STRATEGY.

This was followed by a complex interaction contrast to investigate the interaction effects of the independent variables KNOWLEDGE and STRATEGY on the dependent variable PURCHASE. The weighting for the complex interaction contrast was consistent with the hypothesis being tested (Rosenthal & Rosnow, 1985). A complex interaction contrast to detect the interaction effects of KNOWLEDGE (HIGH, LOW) and STRATEGY (combined EBA + WAD, PROFILE) yielded a significant result F(1, 152) = 11.17, p < .001. From the above-mentioned series of statistical analyses, it was concluded that there exists a strong interaction effect between the independent variables KNOWLEDGE and STRATEGY on the dependent variable PURCHASE. Subjects with HIGH KNOWLEDGE experience significantly higher PURCHASE when using the EBA STRATEGY or the WAD STRATEGY. Subjects with LOW KNOWLEDGE experience significantly higher PURCHASE when using the PROFILE STRATEGY.

Perceived Cost Savings (SAVINGS)

A two-factor 2 x 4 ANOVA was performed to test the interaction effects of the independent variables "product class knowledge" (KNOWLEDGE) and "agent search strategy" (STRATEGY) on the dependent variable "perceived cost savings" (SAVINGS). The factors used were KNOWLEDGE and STRATEGY. This analysis yielded a significant overall interaction effect F(3, 152) = 6.19, p < .001. The presence of interaction effects between KNOWLEDGE and STRATEGY for the dependent variable SAVINGS is clearly demonstrated in Figure 6.

This was followed by an investigation of the simple effects of the independent variable KNOWLEDGE on the dependent variable SAVINGS. For the EBA STRATEGY, subjects with HIGH KNOWLEDGE experienced higher SAVINGS than subjects with LOW KNOWLEDGE, F(1, 152) = 10.17, p < .01. For the WAD STRATEGY, subjects with HIGH KNOWLEDGE experienced higher SAVINGS than subjects with LOW KNOWLEDGE, F(1, 152) = 9.69, p < .01. For the PROFILE STRATEGY, subjects with LOW KNOWLEDGE experienced higher SAVINGS than subjects with HIGH KNOWLEDGE, F(1, 152) = 10.91, p < .001. For the HYPERTEXT STRATEGY, no significant difference in SAVINGS was detected between subjects with HIGH KNOWLEDGE and subjects with LOW KNOWLEDGE, F(1, 152) = 1.12, p > .10. Examination of the cell means shows clearly that for the EBA STRATEGY and the WAD STRATEGY, SAVINGS was higher for the HIGH KNOWLEDGE group as compared to the LOW KNOWL-EDGE group. For the PROFILE STRATEGY, SAVINGS was higher for the LOW

KNOWLEDGE group as compared to the HIGH KNOWLEDGE group. An investigation of the simple effects of the independent variable STRATEGY on the dependent variable SAVINGS yielded significant results for both levels of KNOWL-EDGE. For the HIGH KNOWLEDGE group, $F(3, 152) = 7.91$, $p < .001$. For the LOW KNOWLEDGE group, $F(3, 152) = 6.11$, $p < .001$.

This was followed by a series of planned contrasts to investigate the effect of the independent variable STRATEGY on the dependent variable SAVINGS. The weighting for the planned contrasts was consistent with the hypotheses being tested (Rosenthal & Rosnow, 1985). A planned contrast comparing the combined data from the cells (HIGH KNOWLEDGE, EBA STRATEGY) and (HIGH KNOWL-EDGE, WAD STRATEGY) with the combined data from the cells (HIGH KNOWL-EDGE, PROFILE STRATEGY) and (HIGH KNOWLEDGE, HYPERTEXT STRATEGY) indicated that subjects with HIGH KNOWLEDGE experienced significantly higher SAVINGS when using the EBA STRATEGY or the WAD STRATEGY as compared to those who used the PROFILE STRATEGY or the HYPERTEXT STRATEGY, $F(1, 152) = 14.42$, $p < .001$. A one way ANOVA which was conducted on the two cells (HIGH KNOWLEDGE, EBA STRATEGY) and (HIGH KNOWLEDGE, WAD STRATEGY) which were combined for the purpose of the planned contrast did not yield a significant difference, $F(1, 38) = .47$, $p > .10$. A one way ANOVA which was conducted on the two cells (HIGH KNOWLEDGE, PROFILE STRATEGY) and (HIGH KNOWLEDGE, HYPERTEXT STRAT-

Figure 6. KNOWLEDGE x STRATEGY interaction for SAVINGS

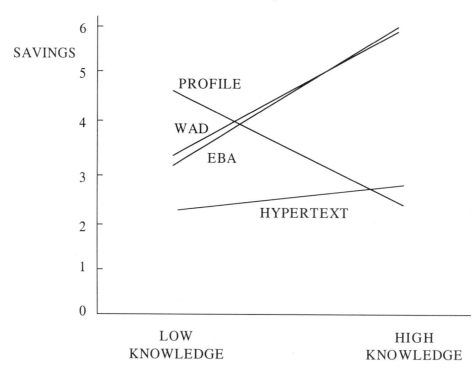

EGY), which were combined for the purpose of the planned contrast, did not yield a significant difference, $F(1, 38) = 1.33, p > .10$. A planned contrast comparing the data from the cell (LOW KNOWLEDGE, PROFILE STRATEGY) with the combined data from the cells (LOW KNOWLEDGE, EBA STRATEGY), (LOW KNOWLEDGE, WAD STRATEGY), and (LOW KNOWLEDGE, HYPERTEXT STRATEGY) indicated that subjects with LOW KNOWLEDGE experienced significantly higher SAVINGS when using PROFILE STRATEGY as compared to those who used the EBA STRATEGY, the WAD STRATEGY, or the HYPERTEXT STRATEGY, $F(1, 152) = 4.72, p < .05$. A one way ANOVA which was conducted on the three cells (LOW KNOWLEDGE, EBA STRATEGY), (LOW KNOWLEDGE, WAD STRATEGY), and (LOW KNOWLEDGE, HYPERTEXT STRATEGY), which were combined for the purpose of the planned contrast, did not yield a significant difference, $F(2, 57) = 2.39, p > .10$. Examination of the cell means shows clearly that the HIGH KNOWLEDGE group experienced higher SAVINGS when using the EBA STRATEGY or the WAD STRATEGY and the LOW KNOWLEDGE group experienced higher SAVINGS when using the PROFILE STRATEGY.

This was followed by a complex interaction contrast to investigate the interaction effects of the independent variables KNOWLEDGE and STRATEGY on the dependent variable SAVINGS. The weighting for the complex interaction contrast was consistent with the hypothesis being tested (Rosenthal & Rosnow, 1985). A complex interaction contrast to detect the interaction effects of KNOWLEDGE (HIGH, LOW) and STRATEGY (combined EBA + WAD, PROFILE) yielded a significant result $F(1, 152) = 11.92, p < .001$. From the above-mentioned series of statistical analyses, it was concluded that there exists a strong interaction effect between the independent variables KNOWLEDGE and STRATEGY on the dependent variable SAVINGS. Subjects with HIGH KNOWLEDGE experience significantly higher SAVINGS when using the EBA STRATEGY or the WAD STRATEGY. Subjects with LOW KNOWLEDGE experience significantly higher SAVINGS when using the PROFILE STRATEGY.

Cognitive Decision Effort (EFFORT)

A two-factor 2 x 4 ANOVA was performed to test the interaction effects of the independent variables "product class knowledge" (KNOWLEDGE) and "agent search strategy" (STRATEGY) on the dependent variable "cognitive decision effort" (EFFORT). The factors used were KNOWLEDGE and STRATEGY. This analysis yielded a significant overall interaction effect $F(3, 152) = 5.71, p < .001$. The presence of interaction effects between KNOWLEDGE and STRATEGY for the dependent variable EFFORT is clearly demonstrated in Figure 7.

This was followed by an investigation of the simple effects of the independent variable KNOWLEDGE on the dependent variable EFFORT. For the EBA STRATEGY, subjects with HIGH KNOWLEDGE experienced lower EFFORT than subjects with LOW KNOWLEDGE, $F(1, 152) = 10.17, p < .01$. For the WAD STRATEGY, subjects with HIGH KNOWLEDGE experienced lower EFFORT than subjects with LOW KNOWLEDGE, $F(1, 152) = 9.77$, $p < .01$. For the PROFILE STRATEGY, subjects with LOW KNOWLEDGE experienced lower EFFORT than subjects with HIGH KNOWLEDGE, $F(1, 152) = 6.91$, $p < .01$. For the HYPERTEXT STRATEGY, no significant difference in EFFORT was detected between subjects with HIGH KNOWLEDGE and subjects with LOW KNOWL-EDGE, $F(1, 152) = .45$, $p > .10$. Examination of the cell means shows clearly that for the EBA STRATEGY and the WAD STRATEGY, EFFORT was lower for the HIGH KNOWLEDGE group as compared to the LOW KNOWLEDGE group. For the PROFILE STRATEGY, EFFORT was lower for the LOW KNOWLEDGE group as compared to the HIGH KNOWLEDGE group. An investigation of the simple effects of the independent variable STRATEGY on the dependent variable EFFORT yielded significant results for both levels of KNOWLEDGE. For the HIGH KNOWLEDGE group, $F(3, 152) = 5.17$, $p < .01$. For the LOW KNOWL-EDGE group, $F(3, 152) = 5.31$, $p < .01$.

This was followed by a series of planned contrasts to investigate the effect of the independent variable STRATEGY on the dependent variable EFFORT. The weighting for the planned contrasts was consistent with the hypotheses being tested (Rosenthal & Rosnow, 1985). A planned contrast comparing the combined data from the cells (HIGH KNOWLEDGE, EBA STRATEGY) and (HIGH KNOWL-EDGE, WAD STRATEGY) with the combined data from the cells (HIGH KNOWL-

Figure 7. KNOWLEDGE x STRATEGY interaction for EFFORT

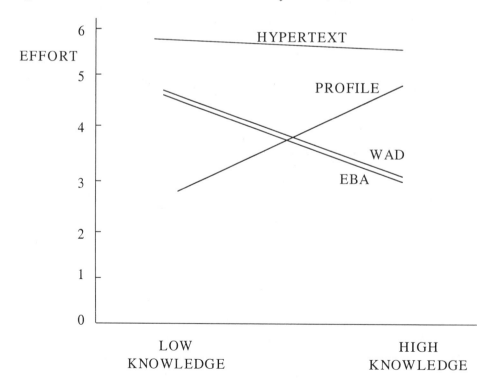

EDGE, PROFILE STRATEGY) and (HIGH KNOWLEDGE, HYPERTEXT STRATEGY) indicated that subjects with HIGH KNOWLEDGE experienced significantly lower EFFORT when using the EBA STRATEGY or the WAD STRATEGY as compared to those who used the PROFILE STRATEGY or the HYPERTEXT STRATEGY, $F(1, 152) = 12.91, p < .001$. A one way ANOVA which was conducted on the two cells (HIGH KNOWLEDGE, EBA STRATEGY) and (HIGH KNOWLEDGE, WAD STRATEGY), which were combined for the purpose of the planned contrast, did not yield a significant difference, $F(1, 38) = .67$, $p > .10$. A one way ANOVA which was conducted on the two cells (HIGH KNOWLEDGE, PROFILE STRATEGY) and (HIGH KNOWLEDGE, HYPERTEXT STRATEGY) which were combined for the purpose of the planned contrast did not yield a significant difference, $F(1, 38) = 2.29, p > .10$. A planned contrast comparing the data from the cell (LOW KNOWLEDGE, PROFILE STRATEGY) with the combined data from the cells (LOW KNOWLEDGE, EBA STRATEGY), (LOW KNOWLEDGE, WAD STRATEGY), and (LOW KNOWL-EDGE, HYPERTEXT STRATEGY) indicated that subjects with LOW KNOWL-EDGE experienced significantly lower EFFORT when using PROFILE STRAT-EGY as compared to those who used the EBA STRATEGY, the WAD STRAT-EGY, or the HYPERTEXT STRATEGY, $F(1, 152) = 16.12, p < .001$. A one way ANOVA which was conducted on the three cells (LOW KNOWLEDGE, EBA STRATEGY), (LOW KNOWLEDGE, WAD STRATEGY), and (LOW KNOWL-EDGE, HYPERTEXT STRATEGY), which were combined for the purpose of the planned contrast, did not yield a significant difference, $F(2, 57) = 1.92, p > .10$. Examination of the cell means shows clearly that the HIGH KNOWLEDGE group experienced lower EFFORT when using the EBA STRATEGY or the WAD STRATEGY and the LOW KNOWLEDGE group experienced lower EFFORT when using the PROFILE STRATEGY.

This was followed by a complex interaction contrast to investigate the interaction effects of the independent variables KNOWLEDGE and STRATEGY on the dependent variable EFFORT. The weighting for the complex interaction contrast was consistent with the hypothesis being tested (Rosenthal & Rosnow, 1985). A complex interaction contrast to detect the interaction effects of KNOWLEDGE (HIGH, LOW) and STRATEGY (combined EBA + WAD, PROFILE) yielded a significant result $F(1, 152) = 10.17, p < .01$. From the above-mentioned series of statistical analyses, it was concluded that there exists a strong interaction effect between the independent variables KNOWLEDGE and STRATEGY on the dependent variable EFFORT. Subjects with HIGH KNOWLEDGE experience significantly lower EFFORT when using the EBA STRATEGY or the WAD STRATEGY. Subjects with LOW KNOWLEDGE experience significantly lower EFFORT when using the PROFILE STRATEGY.

RATIONALE FOR EXPERIMENT # 2

Given these differing responses to agent search strategies based upon the level of product class knowledge of the user, the next step was to examine more closely the specific characteristics of each strategy that contribute to this interaction, alterations to which could eliminate the interaction effect.

THEORETICAL DEVELOPMENT OF HYPOTHESES FOR EXPERIMENT # 2

Luce (1998) hypothesizes that decision environments that are characterized by higher tradeoff difficulty and/or higher conflict will be associated with increased negative emotion as well as increased tendencies for decision makers to choose avoidant options. The ability to choose an avoidant option (skip making the decision) is found to reduce this negative emotion (Luce, 1998). Hence, the ability to avoid specifying preference values for certain attributes or to provide a neutral response ("don't know" or "don't care") may reduce individuals' negative response toward the agent search strategy. Additionally, if individuals are permitted to provide a measure of their confidence in their preference specifications, they may feel more confident that the recommendation given by the agent reflects a weighting of the attributes in terms of their confidence level. It is expected that by modifying the application in the following two ways, the negative affective reactions of subjects with low product class knowledge towards agents/applications which use the EBA and WAD strategies will be eliminated or significantly reduced.

1) Increasing the amount of information provided. When the subjects are expressing their preference values for the attributes and when they are browsing the attribute information for the alternatives, instead of just being presented with the attribute names on the screen, they are presented with hypertext links for each attribute. If they click the hypertext link for any attribute, they are presented with a screen of information which provides detailed information about that attribute.

2) Increasing the degree of control the subjects have in expressing their preferences and making their decisions. This increase in the degree of control is achieved through three mechanisms:

   (i)   The subjects are given the option to skip attributes when expressing preference or cut-off values for the attributes.

   (ii) The subjects are given the option of specifying confidence levels in their preference specifications for each attribute.

   (iii) The subjects are given the option of returning to the preference specification stage from any stage in the decision process and changing the preference values specified. Thus after subjects have obtained some information about attributes, they are able to utilize that information in specifying their preferences.

Hypothesis 2: Changes to the functionality of the application such as (1) increasing the amount of information provided in the description of each attribute and (2) increasing the degree of control the subject has in expressing his preferences and making his decision, will reduce the negative affective reactions of subjects with low product class knowledge towards the agents/ applications which employ the EBA and WAD strategies.

RESEARCH METHODOLOGY FOR EXPERIMENT # 2

One hundred twenty MBA students participated in the study. The subjects used in Experiment # 2 were different from the subjects used in Experiment # 1. This was done to eliminate bias due to history effects and learning effects. Measures of subjective knowledge for the product category were taken. Subjects identified as belonging to the group "high product class knowledge" received further training in the product class. Subjects identified as belonging to the group "low product class knowledge" did not receive further training. This was done to manipulate product class knowledge. Subjects in each of the groups, "high" and "low" product class knowledge, were then randomly assigned to one of three treatment conditions – MODIFIED EBA, MODIFIED WAD, or PROFILE. This yielded a sample size of 20 subjects for each of the cells in the 2 x 3 research design. The HYPERTEXT strategy was omitted from experiment # 2 since it did not yield any significant results in experiment # 1. Following the experiment, measures of affective response to each agent search strategy such as satisfaction with the decision process, confidence in the decision, propensity to purchase, perceived cost savings, cognitive decision effort, and trust in the agent's recommendations were taken.

RESULTS FOR EXPERIMENT # 2

Table 7 presents the cell means obtained for each of the dependent variables in Experiment # 2 when the modified applications were used as the treatment conditions. The 2 x 3, two-factor ANOVAs which were conducted did not yield any significant overall interaction effects between the independent variables KNOWL-EDGE and STRATEGY for any of the dependent variables SATISFACTION, CONFIDENCE, TRUST, PURCHASE, SAVINGS, or EFFORT. The planned contrasts which were conducted yielded only one significant result, that subjects in the HIGH KNOWLEDGE group expressed significantly higher positive affective preferences for the MODIFIED EBA STRATEGY and the MODIFIED WAD STRATEGY as compared to the PROFILE STRATEGY. Subjects in the LOW KNOWLEDGE group did not express significantly higher positive affective preferences for the PROFILE STRATEGY as compared to the MODIFIED EBA STRATEGY or the MODIFIED WAD STRATEGY. Thus the interaction effects of KNOWLEDGE and STRATEGY were significantly reduced by modifying the EBA and WAD treatment conditions to increase the degree of control provided to the user and to increase the amount of information provided to the user. Examination of the cell means shows clearly that the LOW KNOWLEDGE group responded much more positively to the modified EBA and WAD strategies than they did in Experiment # 1.

Table 7: Cell Means for Each Emotion as a Function of Agent Search Strategy and Product Class Knowledge for Experiment # 2

| | High Product Class Knowledge | | | | | |
| | Modified Eba | | Modified Wad | | Profile | |
	Mean	S.d.	Mean	S.d.	Mean	S.d.
Satisfaction	5.27	1.35	5.41	1.40	2.83	.74
Confidence	5.48	1.41	5.59	1.41	2.57	.62
Trust	5.26	1.31	5.29	1.37	2.27	.51
Purchase	4.31	1.37	4.27	1.36	2.46	.49
Savings	5.68	1.46	5.76	1.39	1.94	.44
Effort	2.57	.55	2.94	.74	4.79	1.12

| | Low Product Class Knowledge | | | | | |
| | Modified Eba | | Modified Wad | | Profile | |
	Mean	S.d.	Mean	S.d.	Mean	S.d.
Satisfaction	4.29	1.12	4.57	1.21	5.32	1.32
Confidence	4.71	1.25	4.78	1.25	4.58	1.13
Trust	4.21	1.06	4.26	.98	4.29	1.07
Purchase	3.17	.79	3.19	.75	4.79	1.14
Savings	4.29	1.08	4.25	1.12	4.37	1.11
Effort	3.21	.81	3.32	.83	2.89	.75

CONCLUSIONS

The experimental results presented here demonstrate that the cognitive fit of agent search strategy and subjects' product class knowledge has a significant impact on consumers' ability to integrate information, to understand inputs to their judgments, and to be confident about their judgments. This research has implications for a number of settings within the realm of marketing and consumer behavior, especially in the electronic commerce environment. Understanding the reasons behind individuals' varying reactions to agent strategies based on the level of their product class knowledge allows web retailers to modify their web sites and include functionality in their agents/applications to make the agent's search strategy more appealing to both those with high as well as low product class knowledge. Specific recommendations to managers would include making at least two agent search strategies (WAD or EBA, and PROFILE) available to users and allowing the users to use the one they prefer. Alternatively, managers could include the functionalities demonstrated in Experiment # 2 which reduce negative reactions by individuals with differing states of product class knowledge.

This research has demonstrated that optimizing the cognitive fit between agent search strategy and consumers' product class knowledge significantly increases consumer satisfaction with the decision process. However, it has been noted that although some decision aids may improve decision making, abuse is possible (Todd & Benbasat, 1994). In particular, Widing and Talarzyk (1993) have shown that the decision aid most likely to be a part of an electronic commerce environment (i.e., a cutoff rule that allows the formation of a consideration set containing only those alternatives that pass consumer-specified attribute cutoffs) can lead to suboptimal decisions in efficient choice sets. A separate stream of research has shown that a second likely characteristic of an electronic commerce environment, i.e., a visually rich presentation, can distort the decision process by diverting attention away from information that is most important for the task at hand (Jarvenpaa, 1989, 1990).

Managerial Implications

This research has significant managerial implications in terms of providing guidelines for the design of web sites in order to optimize the interface between the consumer and the system.

Design of User Interfaces for Electronic Commerce

This research should help designers of web sites to make accurate generalizations about the effects of computerized decision aids on strategy selection so that they can then design their web sites to provide the optimal interface for a given task environment.

Impact on Consumer Satisfaction and Confidence

Given the large number and variety of decision aids currently emerging on the Internet, it is imperative that we investigate how these decision aid formats impact consumer satisfaction and confidence in the decision. This is necessary to avoid consumer perceptions of nonutility, and ultimately nonuse of the computerized decision aids.

Marketing Strategy of Online Vendors

Many merchants who have set up electronic shopping malls on the Internet fear that the reduced cognitive search effort associated with this environment will lead to increased price competition and lower profit margins. This is consistent with arguments proposed by Bakos (1997), Lynch and Ariely (1999), and Alba, Lynch, Weitz, Janiszewski, Lutz, Sawyer, and Wood (1997). This may lead to merchants adopting a strategy of providing a suboptimal Web site so as to make it difficult for consumers to use this medium to obtain price comparisons, quality comparisons and comparisons across web sites. This research has demonstrated that optimizing the cognitive fit of agent search strategy with consumers' product class knowledge results in an increased perception of cost savings among consumers and increased satisfaction with the decision process. This will lead to the consumers using this channel more extensively to search for prepurchase information and making their purchases through this channel. Merchants who adopt the strategy of not providing the optimal interface to consumers on their web sites will risk losing a substantial portion of the business which will be transacted via this channel.

Limitations of the Research

As with any experimental investigation, there are a number of limitations present in this research. This research was restricted to the selection of cars on the Internet. Clearly, a variety of choice situations as well as products must be investigated before generalizable comments can be made to guide the development of computerized decision aids. Another limitation of this research is the composition of the group which participated in the study. The sample is homogeneous, and presumably has greater than average cognitive capabilities. A more diverse sample would have offered greater opportunity for generalization of the findings.

Directions for Future Research

This research has examined the influence of computerized decision aids on decision making and their impact on different aspects of performance and satisfaction with the decision process. Much more work needs to be done on examining the influence of these computerized decision aids on consumer preferences. Some of the potential research areas are discussed below.

The Use of Query-Based Decision Aids in Different Information Environments

Ample evidence exists that information is not simply acquired in reaction to predefined preferences, but that it also helps decision makers define their own values and preferences as they engage in the process of acquiring information (Tversky, Sattath & Slovic, 1988; Payne, Bettman & Johnson, 1993). In other words, the information itself changes the way preferences are constructed, and therefore one cannot define the decision space in advance. There exist potential liabilities for computerized decision aids in dynamic environments in which innovation can change the correlation structure of alternatives in the environment. As long as the information environment is stable and does not change much, the structure of preferences can be expected to have some stability. Hence in such environments computerized decision aids can be beneficial. However, in situations in which information changes over time, consumers served by computerized decision aids alone would be unlikely to notice the changing correlational structure of the environment. In these environments, additional mechanisms would need to be built into the system to continuously update the knowledge base. Expert systems could play a vital role in these decision environments.

Planning Upgrade Paths

Under some circumstances, it might be better to have a simple user interface that does not require much effort to learn and use. The advantages of such interfaces are primarily at the initial stages of usage, when knowledge is low. Over time, as knowledge accumulates, the advantages of more powerful and flexible interfaces become more apparent. The challenge for marketing managers is to provide consumers with information systems that change over time such that they fulfill the consumers' short term needs without sacrificing the consumers' long term interests.

REFERENCES

Alba, J.W., & Hasher, L. (1983). Is memory schematic?, *Psychological Bulletin*, 93 (March), 203-231.

Alba, J.W., & Hutchinson, J.W. (1987). Dimensions of consumer expertise, *Journal of Consumer Research*, 13(4), 411-454.

Alba, J.W., Lynch, J., Weitz, B., Janiszewski, C., Lutz, R., Sawyer, A. & Wood, S. (1997). Interactive home shopping: Incentives for consumers, retailers, & manufacturers to participate in electronic marketplaces, *Journal of Marketing*, 61(3), 38-53.

Anderson, R.D., Engledow, J.L., & Becker, H. (1979). Evaluating the relationships among attitude toward business, product satisfaction, experience, and search effort, *Journal of Marketing Research*, 16 (August), 394-400.

Bakos, Y. J. (1997). Reducing buyer search costs: Implications for electronic marketplaces, *Management Science*, 43(12), 1676-1692.

Bettman, J.R., Luce, M.F., & Payne, J.W. (1998). Constructive consumer choice processes, *Journal of Consumer Research*, forthcoming.

Bettman, J.R., Johnson, E.J. & Payne, J.W. (1991). Consumer decision making, in T.S. Robertson and H.H. Kassarjian (eds.), *Handbook of Consumer Behavior*, 50-84, Englewood Cliffs, NJ: Prentice-Hall.

Brucks, M. (1985). The effects of product class knowledge on information search behavior, *Journal of Consumer Research*, 12 (June), 1-16.

Capon, N., & Burke, M. (1980), Individual, product class, and task-related factors in consumer information processing, *Journal of Consumer Research*, 7 (December), 314-326.

Chase, W.G., & Simon, H. (1973a). Perception in chess, *Cognitive Psychology*, 4 (January), 55-81.

Chase, W.G., & Simon, H. (1973b). The mind's eye in chess, in *Visual Information Processing*, ed. Chase, W. G., New York: Academic Press.

Chi, M.T.H., Feltovich, P.J., & Glaser, R. (1981). Categorization and representation of physics problems by experts and novices, *Cognitive Science*, 5 (April/June), 121-152.

Chi, M.T.H., & Glaser, R. (1980). The measurement of expertise, in *Educational Testing and Evaluation*, E.L. Baker & E.S.Quellmalz, eds. Newbury Park, CA: Sage Publications.

Chi, M.T.H., Glaser, R., & Rees, E. (1981). Expertise in problem solving, in *Advances in the Psychology of Human Intelligence*, ed. Sternberg, Hillsdale, New Jersey: Lawrence Erlbaum.

Chiesi, H.L., Spilich, G.J., & Voss, J.T. (1979). "Acquisition of domain-related information in relation to high and low domain knowledge," *Journal of Verbal Learning and Verbal Behavior*, 18(June), 257-273.

Conover, Jerry N. (1982). Familiarity and the structure of product knowledge, in *Advances in Consumer Research*, vol. 9, ed. Andrew A. Mitchell, Ann Arbor, MI: Association for Consumer Research, 494-498.

Degeratu, A., Rangaswamy, A., & Wu, J. (1999). Consumer choice behavior in online and regular stores: The effects of brand name, price, & other search attributes, unpublished working paper.

Earle, E. (1999). GM launches sales site on Web, *USA Today*, Section B, Page 1B, March 11, 1999.

Fiske, S. (1993), Social cognition and social perception, in *Annual Review of Psychology*, 44, 155-194.

Gershoff, A. & West, P. (1998). Using a community of knowledge to build intelligent agents, *Marketing Letters*, 9(1), 79-91.

Gupta, S. (1995). HERMES: A research project on the commercial uses of the world wide web, www.umich.edu/~sgupta/hermes/.

Herr, P., Kardes, F., & Kim, J. (1991). Effects of word-of-mouth and product-attribute information on persuasion: An accessibility-diagnosticity perspective, *Journal of Consumer Research*, 17 (March), 454-462.

Hoch, S.J. & Deighton, J. (1989). Managing what consumers learn from experience, *Journal of Marketing*, 53 (April), 1-20.

Hoffman, D.L. & Novak, T.P. (1996a). Marketing in hypermedia computer-mediated environments: Conceptual foundations, *Journal of Marketing*, 60 (Winter), 50-68.

Hoffman, D.L. & Novak, T.P. (1996b). The future of interactive marketing, *Harvard Business Review* (6), 151-162.

Hoffman, D.L., Novak, T.P., & Chatterjee, P. (1995). Commercial scenarios for the web: opportunities and challenges, *Journal of Computer-Mediated Communication*, jcmc.huji.i1/vol1/issue3/vol1no3.html.

Jacoby, J., Chestnut, R.W., & Fischer, W.A. (1978). A behavioral approach in non-durable purchasing, *Journal of Marketing Research*, 15 (November), 532-544.

Jarvenpaa, S.L. (1989). The effect of task and graphical format congruence on information processing strategies and decision-making performance, *Management Science*, 35, 285-303.

Jarvenpaa, S.L. (1990). Graphical displays in decision making – The visual salience effect, *Journal of Behavioral Decision Making*, 3, 247-262.

Johnson, E.J. (1980). Expertise in Admissions Judgment, unpublished dissertation, Department of Psychology, Carnegie-Mellon University.

Johnson, E.J. (1988). Expertise and decision under uncertainty: Performance and process, in *The Nature of Expertise*, M.T.H. Ch, R. Chi, & M.J. Farr, eds. London: Lawrence Erlbaum and Associates.

Johnson, E.J., & Russo, E. (1984). Product familiarity and learning new information, *Journal of Consumer Research*, 11 (June), 542-550.

Katona, G. & Mueller, E. (1955). A study of purchase decisions, in *Consumer Behavior: The Dynamics of Consumer Reaction*, ed. Clark, L.H., New York: New York University Press, 30-87.

Klayman, J. (1988). On the how and why (not) of learning from outcomes, in *Human Judgment: The SJT View*, B. Brehmer & C.R.B. Joyce, eds. New York: Elsevier Science Publishing Company.

Larkin, J.H., McDermott, J., Simon, D.P., & Simon, H.A. (1980). Expert and novice performance in solving physics problems, *Science*, 208, 1335-1342.

Luce, M.F. (1998). Choosing to avoid: Coping with negatively emotion-laden consumer decisions, *Journal of Consumer Research*, 24(4), 409-433.

Lynch, J.G.Jr. & Ariely, D. (1999). Interactive home shopping: Effects of search cost for price and quantity information on consumer price sensitivity, satisfaction with merchandise, & retention, *Journal of Consumer Psychology*, forthcoming.

Mahajan, J. (1992). The overconfidence effect in marketing management predictions, *Journal of Marketing Research*, 29 (August), 329-342.

Maherwaran, D. & Sternthal, B. (1990). The effects of knowledge, motivation, and type of message on ad processing and product judgments, *Journal of Consumer Research*, 17 (June), 66-73.

Moore, W.L. & Lehmann, D.R. (1980). Individual differences in search behavior for a nondurable, *Journal of Consumer Research*, 7 (December), 296-307.

Newell, A., & Simon, H.A. (1972). *Human Problem Solving*. Englewood Cliffs, NJ: Prentice-Hall.

Newman, J.W. & Staelin, R. (1971). Multivariate analysis of differences in buyer decision time, *Journal of Marketing Research*, 8 (May), 192-198.

Newman, J.W. & Staelin, R. (1972). Prepurchase information seeking for new cars and major household appliances, *Journal of Marketing Research*, 9 (August), 249-151.

Payne, J.W., Bettman, J.R., & Johnson, E.J. (1993). *The Adaptive Decision Maker*, Cambridge University Press, Cambridge, England.

Pazgal, A. & Vulkan, N. (1998). Have your agent call mine: Software agents, the internet, and marketing, working paper, Washington University.

Punj, G. N., & Stewart, D.W. (1983). An interaction framework of consumer decision making, *Journal of Consumer Research*, 10 (September), 181-196.

Reitman, W.R. (1965). *Cognition and Thought: An Information Processing Approach*. New York: John Wiley & Sons.

Rosenthal, R., & Rosnow, R.L. (1985). *Contrast analysis: Focused comparisons in the analysis of variance*, Cambridge, England: Cambridge University Press.

Saad, G. & Russo, J.E. (1996). Stopping criteria in sequential choice, *Organizational Behavior and Human Decision Processes*, 67(3), 258-270.

Shankar, V. & Rangaswamy, A. (1999). The impact of Internet marketing on price sensitivity and price competition, unpublished working paper.

Shanteau, J. (1988). Psychological characteristics and strategies of expert decision makers, *Acta Psychologica*, 68, 203-215.

Shanteau, J. (1992a). How much information does an expert use? Is it relevant?, *Acta Psychologica*, 81, 75-86.

Shanteau, J. (1992b). Competence in experts: The role of task characteristics, *Organizational Behavior and Human Decision Processes*, 53, 252-266.

Shanteau, J., & Stewart, T.R. (1992). Why study expert decision making? Some historical perspectives and comments, *Organizational Behavior and Human Decision Processes*, 53, 95-106.

Simon, H.A. (1973). The structure of ill-structured problems, *Artificial Intelligence*, 4, 181-201.

Simon, H.A. (1978). Information Processing Theory of Human Problem Solving, in *Handbook of Learning and Cognitive Processes*, vol. 5, W.K. Estes, ed. Hillsdale, NJ: Lawrence Erlbaum Associates, 271-296.

Smith, G. F. (1988). Towards a heuristic theory of problem structuring, *Management Science*, 34 (12), 1489-1506.

Sujan, M. (1985). Consumer knowledge effects on evaluation strategies mediating consumer judgments, *Journal of Consumer Research*, 12 (June), 31-46.

Swan, J.E. (1969). Experimental analysis of predecision information seeking, *Journal of Marketing Research*, 6 (May), 192-197.

Taylor, R.N. (1974). Nature of problem ill-structuredness: Implications for problem formulation and solution, *Decision Sciences*, 5, 632-643.

Todd, P. & Benbasat, I. (1994). The influence of decision aids on choice strategies: an experimental analysis of the role of cognitive effort, *Organization Behavior and Human Decision Processes*, 60, 36-74.

Tversky, A., Sattath, S., & Slovic, P. (1988). Contingent weighting in judgment and choice, *Psychological Review*, 95, 371-384.

Voss, J.F., & Post, T.A. (1988). On the solving of ill-structured problems, in *The Nature of Expertise*, M.T.H. Chi, R. Glaser, & M.J. Farr, eds. London: Lawrence Erlbaum Associates.

Walker, B., Celsi, R., & Olson, J. (1987). Exploring the structural characteristics of consumers' knowledge, in *Advances in Consumer Research*, vol. 14. Eds. Wallendorf, M, & Anderson, P., Provo, UT: Association for Consumer Research, 17-21.

Wernerfelt, B. (1994). On the function of sales assistance, *Marketing Science*, 13(1), 68-82.

West, P.M., Brown, C.L., & Hoch, S.J. (1996). Consumption vocabulary and preference formation, *Journal of Consumer Research*, 23 (September), 120-135.

Widing, R.E.II & Talarzyk, W.W. (1993). Electronic information systems for consumers: An evaluation of computer-assisted formats in multiple decision environments, *Journal of Marketing Research*, 30, 125-141.

Wilkie, W. (1990). *Consumer Behavior*, 2nd. Edition, John Wiley & Sons, Inc.

Wood, W. & Eagly, A. (1981). Stages in the analysis of persuasive messages: The role of causal attributions and message comprehension, *Journal of Personality and Social Psychology*, 40 (February), 246-259.

APPENDIX: SCALE ITEMS USED TO MEASURE THE CONSTRUCTS

The following scale items were used to measure the constructs. The respondents were told to mark each of the responses on a seven-point Likert scale ranging from "Strongly Disagree" to "Strongly Agree".

Independent Variables Being Manipulated

Product Class Knowledge (KNOWLEDGE)

K.1   I am an expert in cars
K.2   I am very experienced in purchasing cars
K.3   I am very knowledgeable about cars
K.4   I understand the features of cars well enough to evaluate the alternative car models
K.5   I am not at all familiar with cars (r)
K.6   I have a great interest in cars

Dependent Variables

Trust in the Agent's Recommendations (TRUST)

T.1   I believe that the alternatives which the agent recommended to me were consistent with the preferences I expressed
T.2   The agent can be trusted to recommend alternatives which closely match the preferences I expressed
T.3   I am convinced that the agent recommended alternatives which most closely matched my preferences
T.4   The alternatives recommended by the agent were not credible (r)
T.5   The agent recommended alternatives which were consistent with my preferences
T.6   The agent has probably used my preference specifications in recommending alternatives to me
T.7   It is questionable whether the agent used my preference specifications in recommending alternatives to me (r)
T.8   The agent can be relied on to use my preference specifications when it recommends alternatives to me
T.9   The agent can be depended on to recommend alternatives which closely match my preferences

Propensity to Purchase (PURCHASE)

P.1 I would like to purchase this car
P.2 If I purchased a car right now I would purchase this car model
P.3 I would purchase this car if I had the money available
P.4 I feel a strong urge to purchase this car
P.5 I am willing to pay the price quoted for this car
P.6 It is very likely that I will purchase this car
P.7 I would definitely like to purchase this car
P.8 It is important that I purchase this car

Satisfaction with the Decision Process (SATISFACTION)

S.1 This system is one of the best ways to select a car
S.2 If I could do it over again, I'd rather not use this system to select a car (r)
S.3 I am not happy that I used this system to select a car (r)
S.4 This system was very useful in helping me to select the best car model to suit my requirements
S.5 If I had to select a car in future, and a system such as this was available, I would be very likely to use it
S.6 If my friend was searching for information in order to purchase a car, and I knew that a system such as this was available, I would be very likely to recommend this system to him

Confidence in the Decision (CONFIDENCE)

C.1 I am confident that I selected the best car model to suit my needs
C.2 I am confident that I selected the car model which best matches my preferences
C.3 I am not confident that I selected the best car model (r)
C.4 There are probably other car models I should have examined more closely (r)
C.5 I would select this same car model if I had to make the decision again
C.6 This is clearly the best car model available for my budget

Perceived Cost Savings (SAVINGS)

SAVE.1 By using this system to select a car, I was able to obtain the best value for my money
SAVE.2 The use of this system has enabled me to save a lot of money in purchasing a car
SAVE.3 If I had not used this system I would have obtained a better deal for my money (r)
SAVE.4 This car is a real bargain
SAVE.5 This system enabled me to compare the prices of different car models very efficiently
SAVE.6 I could have obtained a better deal from a car dealer (r)

Cognitive Decision Effort (EFFORT)

E.1   The task of selecting a car model using this system was very frustrating

E.2   I easily found the information I was looking for (r)

E.3   The task of selecting a car model using this system took too much time

E.4   The task of selecting a car model using this system was easy (r)

E.5   Selecting a car model using this system required too much effort

E.6   The task of selecting a car model using this system was too complex

Chapter 9

4I: A New Premise for Marketing Online

Amit Pazgal and Sandeep Sikka
Washington University, USA

New technologies require new paradigms and a fresh perspective in analyzing and comprehending their implications. Computer networks, the Internet and the World Wide Web (WWW) in particular have already revolutionized many business practices. The satisfactory application of traditional marketing models to the analysis of online marketing practices is difficult at best. Thus, this chapter offers a new and an intuitive conceptual framework for analyzing, interpreting and managing the marketing process in a connected world. Specifically, we propose a model consisting of four crucial aspects: Intensity, Integration, Interaction, and Identification (4I). Each of these four aspects should be carefully analyzed according to prespecified guidelines to ensure the success of any online business. The chapter describes characteristics that will be intrinsic to marketing in the future connected world. We investigate the reasons underlying these characteristics. We suggest a detailed procedure for managing these future attributes using the 4I model. In the process of doing so, we also compare and contrast our model to traditional marketing models and demonstrate its superiority.

INTRODUCTION

The emergence of the Internet throughout the 1990s as a force in daily life is one of the most important events to date in the history of information technology. The introduction of the World Wide Web (WWW) has been one of the main reasons for this revolution. It took the Internet less than seven years to be adopted by 30 percent of Americans, compared to 13 years for PCs, 17 for televisions, and 38 for telephones (Stewart, 1998).

The emergence of the Internet and the World Wide Web has fundamentally changed the rules of business in several industries. It has presented new opportunities and challenges, and forced leading companies in these industries to rethink and reorganize themselves. Business to consumers electronic commerce, which can be loosely characterized as the process of customers carrying out business transactions over the Internet (Peterson, 1997), has been a big driver of this growth. (According to Forrester research 28.7 million Americans will generate $38.8 billion in on-line retail spending in the year 2000.) Companies like Amazon.com, PlanetRx.com, and Etoys.com sell their products and services exclusively using the WWW. These companies have forced their well-established competitors like Barnes & Nobles, Walgreen, and Toys 'R' Us to incorporate the WWW in some form as a part of their business strategy. Several intermediaries like travel agents, car dealers, insurance agents, stockbrokers, and ticketing companies have seen a big fraction of their sales threatened by the emergence of firms like Priceline.com, Autoweb.com, E-Trade.com and Tickets.com over the WWW.

As a consequence of this growing activity over the Internet, marketing using the WWW has emerged as a significantly important way for a company to connect with both its existing and potential customers. As early as 1967, Doody and Davidson introduced the business world to their own form of online retailing. "City-Wide" was their synonym for a system that would allow for 'retail transaction to be made by electronic telecommunications and push-button devices installed in private homes and hooked on-line to data processing networks'. Whereas they identified certain basic sources of competitive advantage – such as low price, easy accessibility, and timesaving – the ability to proactively engage in novel marketing strategies is now being identified as one of the significant advantages of conducting business via the Internet. Firms have been making considerable investments in pursuing marketing strategies like interactive advertising, incentive marketing, building virtual communities, developing customer ownership, and forming alliances with portals. Several companies have also been experimenting with developing databases of customer profiles, helping their customers conduct product research, offering complementary services and pricing using auctions, all via the WWW.

The present day Internet and the WWW will gradually evolve into a universal information infrastructure characterized by convergence of audio, video and data communication. We term an environment characterized by such omnipresent connectivity and convergence as the *connected medium*. The connected nature of the medium not only enhances the potential of marketing activities described above but also makes possible marketing strategies unimaginable in the non-virtual world. This in turn has the potential to radically alter the way business is conducted in many industries.

In this chapter we propose an analytical model (4I) to help firms interpret, strategize and manage marketing processes in the *connected* medium. Traditional marketing models such as the 4P model (Kotler, 1997) have been of somewhat limited applicability, due to the fact that the marketing activities in the real world are fundamentally different from issues underlying o*nline* marketing activities. A *connected* medium like the Internet has some remarkable differences from various other media, such as print, that have emerged so far. For example, the WWW shifts the balance of power in favor of buyers by increasing choice, allowing interaction, integrating the value chain, enabling direct contact, and breaking down geographical barriers. In this chapter we characterize such a futuristic marketing process by extrapolating the influence of the attributes of the connected medium. We believe that these characteristics will remain invariant even as the Internet evolves[1]. The 4I model, unlike traditional marketing models, focuses on precisely these characteristics that are of consequence to an *online* marketing process.

Previous work in Internet marketing has varied across a diverse spectrum. Peterson (1997) and Peterson, Balasubramanian, and Bronnenberg (1997), two very thought-provoking articles, examine issues like channel intermediary functions, price competition, classification schemes for understanding the impact of marketing activities on various products and services, and consumer decision sequences, in the context of marketing to consumers using the Internet. However the authors doubt the usefulness of peering into the future because of the rapid pace of change inherent in the Internet. While we fully agree that the Internet is changing rapidly, we believe that it is possible to spot certain fundamental trends that will remain invariant as this changing landscape unfolds. We identify these trends, analyze them, and propose a model to manage them. In the process we address a question raised in Peterson et al. (1997) – "What are some of the major implications of the Internet for consumer marketing?"

Hoffman and Novak (1997) outline the need for a new marketing paradigm as electronic commerce transforms conventional marketing activities. The model we present is an attempt to develop one such paradigm. In another article, Hoffman and Novak (1996) construct a structural model of consumer behavior using the concept of a *flow construct*. We indirectly use their model by incorporating its conclusions while describing the attributes of the connected medium. They also define the concept of a hypermedia CME. Our usage of the term, *connected medium*, resembles that of a hypermedia CME. In Capton and Glazer (1987), Glazer (1991), Blattberg, Glazer and Little (1994), the authors analyze the implications of information on marketing. Information is central to the Internet and continues to be so in the connected medium. Thus, we believe the work of these authors is of importance in understanding marketing over the Internet. Our analysis of marketing processes in the connected medium captures the issues they highlight. Blattberg and Deighton (1991) explore the opportunities of interactive marketing. Interaction, like information, is also central to the Internet and to marketing processes pursued using the Internet. Alba et al. (1997) analyze the incentives for consumers, retailers, and manufacturers to participate in an electronic marketplace like Interactive Home Shopping. Similarly Burke (1997) examines issues and incentives of online retailing. As the Internet evolves into a universal connected medium, we believe these incentives will become even stronger. Thus, it will become even significantly important for firms to pursue and carefully manage marketing activities through the connected medium.

The rest of our chapter is organized as follows. The next section describes characteristics intrinsic to marketing in the connected world. Some of these aspects are already in place while the rest are expected to materialize in the foreseeable future. Then we outline the rationale for these characteristics. While doing so we emphasize those attributes of the connected medium that we expect to remain invariant as it evolves. The 4I model is described in detail and we illustrate its use and contrast it to traditional marketing models. Finally, we present our conclusions and plans for future work.

A PEEK INTO THE FUTURE

Current technology trends point to a futuristic world in which humans and microprocessor-based appliances will be continuously interconnected via fast, reliable, inexpensive, and standardized means of communication. This improved connectivity will transform the way the world works, sells, buys, receives information and entertains. Recent alliances between the communication and computing industries continue to create (at an escalating pace) new electronic platforms that enhance the potential value of businesses. The future world is shaping up to be a dichotomous one, consisting of a *virtual* world that both cuts across and coexists with tangible structures in the *physical* world. *Cyberspace,* made possible by the Internet, is just one early manifestation of such a connected medium (Stewart, 1998). In the near future the physical limitations of the Internet—such as congestion and reliability and security - will be alleviated, transforming it into a sophisticated superset of virtual networks linked by a set of open standards. It is these changes that make our model crucial to the analysis of online marketing.

The following section describes in detail some of the most essential properties of marketing processes within a connected environment. We illustrate the early manifestations of each property in today's electronic commerce and conjecture its inevitable unfolding[2] as marketplaces become increasingly virtual.

Interaction—Interaction and communication will be at the core of every aspect of a marketing process in a totally connected environment. We define interaction to be any many-to-many communication process in which the current exchange of information heavily influences that to come (Hoffman and Novak, 1996). There are many important aspects to this interaction, and we will elaborate on them in detail.

Amazon.com's "collaborative" story project with Pulitzer Prize-winning author John Updike, where customers were encouraged to contribute ideas, and paragraphs for the story, which was concluded by John Updike himself, is one example of interaction (Amazon.com Press Releases). Firms, such as The Motley Fool, let customers interact with other customers on their Web sites and provide tools to assemble an end product suitable to their needs. Firms are also using interaction to define their brands. The Ragu brand of Italian food has made the discount-coupon process interactive. At its web site, visitors register, forming a community, in exchange for coupons. This in turn lets Ragu build a brand for all things Italian (Schwartz, 1998). Interactive advertising is becoming increasingly popular on the Web (Jupiter Communications 1999). Marketers have also been using the WWW as an interactive branding and communication tool (Briggs, 1997; LeFurgy, 1997).

Narrative Communication's *Enliven Software* helps advertisers create interactive banners that expand when site visitors interact with them and shrink back when left alone. These banners also allow users to make purchases and queries directly through them. Online music companies have been toying with the idea of having customers select and suggest songs for composing an album. Proactive, sustained service dialogue via e-mail centers, chat centers or bulletin boards which are open 24 hours, 7 days a week, is being used heavily by firms to build long-lasting relationships with customers. Such dialogue initiates customer queries. While processing these queries companies can supply information regarding new products, new promotions and also report the status of customer specific orders or problems.

Customization—The marketing process will be highly personalized and one-to-one in nature. Technology will enable mass customization, i.e., mass production of custom goods (see Elfson and Robinson, 1998, for one such example). It will target individual customers and strive to satisfy their specific needs. Moreover, customers will come to expect and value such individual treatment.

Bank of America's "Build your own bank" program illustrates this concept by allowing customers to build and use their own ideal, custom-made financial service (Stewart 1998). Companies like Levi's and Lands' End gather personal information about their customers, such as favorite designer, waist size, colors and patterns preferred by each customer, and the time of the year preferred for shopping. On-line catalogues can easily facilitate the concept of one-to-one mass customization. Programs can identify the shopper and suggest various pieces of clothing tailored to the individual needs. The company's Web site can be automatically redesigned to show only garments that are of interest to the individual. The known individual preferences and purchasing patterns allow for customization of colors, sizes, materials, and even designers.

Furthermore, niche markets too small to currently be profitable will become identifiable and viable. Consolidators (Elfson and Robinson, 1998), a new breed of intermediaries, will help materialize these markets. As a result consumers will have a wider range of alternatives and combinations to choose from. Amazon.com reported that a number of items in its Top 100 list for books and CDs were produced by obscure artists (Amazon.com Press Releases). These items were unavailable in traditional stores, which can't justify the necessary shelf space to carry these titles. This kind of effect will push out the overall demand curve and expand the total market.

Customer Power – In the virtual world acquiring and especially retaining customers will become crucial to the success of any on-line business. Firms will need to invest considerable effort and resources in managing customer relationships in order to maintain lifelong customers. The core value to a firm's business would be the various affinities of its customer base that will determine its actions.

As an example consider the expansion of several on-line businesses into related areas due to the influence of their customer base. For example, E-Trade (an online broker firm) and CNN Finance have opened a shopping center for their visitors; Amazon.com extended its line of products to include presents, music CDs, videos, and gifts. *Customer portfolio management* (Blattberd, Glazer and Deighton, 1991) i.e., measuring, ensuring, and retaining the quality of a customer base, will become every firm's primary goal. The latest development of portals with their dedication to managing the complete needs of their customers and their emphasis on repeat visitors rather than merely acquiring new ones illustrates this. For a complete analysis of portals see Moran, Pazgal and Reike (1998). For example Yahoo!, the leading Internet portal, has launched many specialty services like Yahoo! Calendar, Yahoo! Movies, Yahoo! Pager, Yahoo! Real Estate, Yahoo! Travel, and Yahoo! Shopping for its visitors.

The power balance will shift towards the customers who as a consequence will become more confident and sophisticated. The basis of this power shift is twofold. First, customers will frequently group via virtual communities, in order to leverage their numbers (Armstrong and Hagel, 1996). By uniting, customers can achieve greater buying power and better bargaining positions. Virtual car communities are forcing dealers to standardize their prices and eliminate haggling. The *Motley Fool* is an example of a site advocating financial information exchange and advice sharing. Second, consumers can easily and with little cost search for information about product attributes, prices, and possible substitutes. The increasing use of shopping agents to search for airline tickets from travel agencies on the Web is a prime example of the new information consumers easily obtain. In the future these agents may negotiate deals and make the actual purchases on behalf of their users.

The future marketplace will be *"pull-based,"* i.e., demand for new products will be fueled by consumer needs rather than manufacturer suggestions. Customers, when provided tangible returns, will be more open about revealing their preferences and desires. Thus they will become active participants in the marketing process. However they are likely to demand more both concrete compensation (Hagel and Rayport, 1997) and effective control over (Cheskin Research, 1999; Hoffman, Novak, and Peralta, 1998) the information they supply. This prediction is not necessarily harmful to firms' bottom line as it implies that they will be able to predict demand more easily, thus lowering response times and required inventory.

Sensitivity – Customers will have more and more choices, thus, when faced with low switching costs they will become very sensitive to the various variables of the marketing mix. As Amazon.com's CEO Jeff Bezos remarks, "Competition is just a click away" (Kotha, 1998). Technology will enable efficient and automated comparison-shopping. In some product categories (especially homogeneous products such as books or music CDs) consumers will likely be extremely price sensitive, opting to buy only at the lowest price. The marketing management process will need to combat this sensitivity phenomenon by creating product or service differentiation, branding and finding ways to increase customers' loyalty (Shankar, 1998).

Service Oriented – in a connected world much of the added value to customers will come from the services provided along with the core offering. These services will add intangible value, which in turn will be a viable strategy for firms to deal with competition. This intangible value will allow vendors to create product differentiation and escape fierce price competition. In the connected medium, such differentiation can be achieved through the provision of information-based or other novel services and by the *association* of a particular customer with the firm's other customers. Thus, firms will increasingly shift towards offering more services on the product-centered to service-centered continuum (Blatberg, Glazer, and Little, 1994).

FedEx provides better information by allowing real-time tracking of packages while Ebay offers a ranking system that grades the satisfaction of previous customers with different auctioneers. Amazon.com offers such value-adding intangibles as books reviewed by peers or recommendations based on others readers' preferences. Dell has created virtual communities within company intranets to allow potential customers in the company to discuss their choices and the merits and faults of various configurations. These services are helping both companies sustain their market dominance and build customer loyalty despite not offering the lowest price.

Vertical Integration – For certain kinds of information-based products, such as software or digital music, the networked medium can be used to serve all stages of the marketing process. It can simultaneously serve as a communication, transaction, and distribution channel, thus creating highly vertically integrated channels. This in turn will necessitate an equally integrated marketing management process. For example, Dell has managed to integrate almost its entire business process via the Internet. It now strives to pursue equally integrated marketing strategies that are more inline with its "direct model" business processes (Magretta 1998).

Speed—Customers using the connected medium will tend to be hyper-impulsive because this medium permits a much closer conjunction of need, transaction and payment compared to any other existing medium. These channels also provide for better perceptual experiences. This along with automation will result in the customers making rapid progress along the buying process as they spend less time in each of the required steps. Various examples for this newly acquired speed are transaction banners that allow customers to order just by clicking, Amazon.com's "1-Click Ordering" program, and automated trip planning.

The resulting speed will also encourage a high degree of change. The dynamic nature of these channels will necessitate highly flexible and adaptive strategies that optimally respond to shifting conditions. The practice of *change management* (Blattberg, Glazer, and Deighton, 1994), i.e., identifying likely changes and implementing policies to handle them will evolve to be an indispensable part of the marketing management process.

Barrierless—The marketing process will transcend barriers imposed by the physical world. Geographical, political, social and even linguistic barriers will diminish with time (Quelch and Klein, 1996). For example Amazon.com used its U.S.-based Web site to sell books in more than 125 different countries. It's *"Advantage 4 Music"* program makes it possible for unsigned artists and independent label CDs to reach millions of music fans worldwide. Auction sites like Ebay are allowing small vendors to sell their products to millions of consumers worldwide.

Small local stores such as Peppers.com in Dewey Beach, Delaware find themselves faced with the opportunities of a global and diverse marketplace. Such a marketplace eliminates the restrictions of size and distance. Not only are geographical barriers smashed, but also traditional 9-5 stores are non existent in the connected world. Sites are open 24 hours a day every day without exception. Some stock trading sites report constant high volume of orders by traders interested in different global markets.

Automation - The buying process will be highly interactive and as such will require high involvement levels from both customers and the firm. High mental effort levels can not be justified across all product categories and over all stages of the purchasing process. Thus, a substantial portion of customer and firm activities will get automated. Software programs will automatically accomplish processes like information gathering, comparison shopping, and transaction completion. In other words technology will be actively sought and will eventually automate many stages of the marketing process.

Intelligent software agents catalog the Web in order to help users locate needed information. They employ robots or subagents that transverse the WWW on behalf of the user and perform simple comparisons of a pre-specified pattern, like a price or a key word. Currently they search the Web for a completely specified product and then record and tabulate the sites where the product can be bought and for what price. In the future these agents will even be able to negotiate deals and make actual purchases without requesting explicit authorization at each stage. For a detailed analysis see Pazgal (1999) or Caglayan and Harrison (1997).

Efficient - The marketing process in a connected environment will be highly efficient. Not only will the cost of doing business be reduced, firms will also be able to asses their cost, predict demand, and evaluate process duration with much higher precision. Such streamlining will allow quicker implementations of innovations at various stages of production, distribution, and service.

As transaction costs and overhead expenses drop, firms will be able to customize their product to better fit the customer needs. For example Booz Allen and Hamilton calculate the direct variable costs of banking at the following per transaction levels: Teller: $1.07, Telephone: $0.52, ATM: $0.27, PC Banking: $0.015, Internet: $0.01. More accurate information about customer preferences together with detailed and timely customer feedback will result in firms being able to better predict customer demand and needs. The immediate result is lower inventories, reduced reaction time, and more just-in-time activities. As an example consider Dell Computers' online distribution channel that allows the firm to build computers to order and ship them within a few days. Marketing and advertising campaigns will be better targeted and achieve their goals at lower costs.

The market will move towards mass customization where decisions based on average values of marketing variables will be replaced by ones based on individual consumer preferences. The size of market segments could potentially be reduced to one single consumer. Targeted advertising that is practiced today by portals allows consumers to only see banners that are directly related to their interests or prespecified search parameters. Many online stores recommend books or music CDs based on the customers' previous shopping trips or the experiences of similar clients. Such developments will increase the utility and efficiency of marketing processes.

The characteristics described above will gradually unfold as the Internet evolves. In the following section we describe reasons explaining these characteristics. These reasons have their genesis in the attributes of the underlying connected medium. We believe that even as the connected medium evolves, these attributes will continue to persist.

FROM THE PRESENT INTO THE FUTURE

Although the characteristics described above are not pervasive in the present marketing processes, early trends can be seen on the WWW. For example *interaction* is limited. At best the commonly used interaction is asynchronous and between individual customers and the firm. Customers barely get to interact with each other in real time. Even the widely touted *Customization* is still limited to certain product categories such as computers and services like banner advertising. However, efficient tools and facilities to enable customization are being rapidly developed by various companies such a Broadvision and Double Click.

We believe that the Internet is an early precursor of the *connected* world. Personal computers are the focal points of connectivity today. Besides being cumbersome to use, they are relatively immobile and fixed in a particular point in space. Thus, networks between these personal computers are not what connectivity may ultimately end up being all about. The WWW is nothing more than a reasonable interface to this kind of *static* connectivity.

The ultimate milestone in this futuristic world of ubiquitous connectivity would perhaps be a wired human body. While this is still in the realm of science fiction, technical advances like mobile wireless technology, home networks, satellite connectivity, speech recognition, and networked information appliances are quickly gaining acceptance. Thus an entirely new medium for marketers to reach consumers will be born. With the advent of more advanced technology, the WWW will be extended or replaced by more elegant representations of this connectivity. We are not completely sure of the eventual form of this medium. Nevertheless we think it should exhibit at least the following characteristics:

Information - Information will become a staple commodity in this world. Vast amounts of it will be produced, collected, searched, organized, interpreted, refreshed, structured, disseminated, and rated inexpensively in real time.

Global - The medium would permeate society at all levels. It shall enable people to connect and do so across geographically wide areas.

Time - The *connectivity* offered by this medium would be available all the time. People will be able to connect whenever they wish.

Interaction - The medium shall promote many-to-many communication between users of the medium and the medium itself. This communication will also be quick, reliable and inexpensive. It will be a mix of audio, video and data communication.

Reach - The medium will make it possible to address along the entire spectrum of communication from individual to broadcast.

User Control - The medium will offer a lot of control and self-selection to the user.

Anonymous -The medium will redefine the notion of privacy and identity. It will enable users to effectively organize information about them. Users will trade this information for tangible returns (Hagel and Rayport, 1997). It will also foster an identity for a user distinct from her physical identity because of a lack of physical cues like body language and cultural nuances.

Efficient - The medium will be highly efficient in terms of resource utilization and very low marginal costs. It will also permit a high degree of accountability and accuracy in its use.

Swiftness - The medium shall offer great speed to interactions. Results of actions will manifest themselves at the speed of light.

Engaging - The users of this medium will demonstrate high involvement, concentration and consequently a loss of sense of time (Hoffman and Novak 1996).

Search - The medium will encourage and facilitate users to actively seek, search and hunt for everything from pleasure to information.

Note that the WWW exhibits all the above characteristics, although in primitive and chaotic forms. However, the trends are clearly observable. Table 1 illustrates the influence of these characteristics on those highlighted. A 'P' denotes a positive influence whereas a 'N' entry denotes a negative influence. An 'I' denotes an indirect influence that could either be positive or negative, and a blank denotes no direct meaningful influence.

MANAGING THE FUTURE: THE 4I MODEL

So far we have described and analyzed a futuristic online marketing process. In this section we present a framework (4I) that firms may adopt to better manage their marketing activity. Using the 4I model firms can analyze, strategize and implement marketing processes in the connected medium.

Our model in its present form is applicable only to those marketing processes that take place entirely in the online world. Such processes in all their constituent stages will use only the connected medium. However we believe that this assumption can be relaxed, and the model can be appropriately modified to accommodate departures from this assumption such as the physical delivery of the purchased good. In particular we think the model can be adapted by firms to synchronize both their online and offline marketing processes.

Table 1: Influences of the medium's characteristics on those of a marketing process

Marketing Process Characteristics	Connected Medium Characteristics										
	Information	Global	Time	Interaction	Reach	User Control	Anonymous	Efficient	Swiftness	Engaging	Search
Interaction	P	I	I	P	P	I	I	P	P	P	I
Customization	P	I	I	P	P	P	I	P			
Customer Power	I	P	P	P	P	P	P	I		I	
Service Oriented	P			P	I	P	N	P	I		P
Vertical Integration	I	N	N	I	P	N		P	P		I
Speed	P	P	P	P	P	P		P	P	P	P
Sensitivity	P	P	P	P		P	P		P	P	P
Barrier-less		P	P		P			P			
Automation	P	I	I	P		P		P	P	P	P
Efficient	P	P	P	P	P	P	P	P	P		

Our model is a mix of four aspects: Integration, interaction, identification, and intensity. These four aspects can be used to fully manage the characteristics presented earlier. We depict the abstract issues underlying each of these aspects. Resolving each issue involves making a choice. The variety of choices available while making these decisions will depend on the representative form of the connected medium. Since we can do no more than speculate on these forms, we describe the range of choices available in the current form of this connected medium, i.e., the World Wide Web.

Integration

Integration covers three related processes. The first is the process of integrating consumers. The second is the process of the firm integrating with other firms while the third is the process of integrating with the medium.

Consumer Integration is the process of organizing consumers into groups, or what we choose to call as *aggregates*[3]. Aggregates help in directing the marketing process in a manner appropriate for that aggregate by incorporating characteristics representative of that aggregate. Consumer integration requires a firm to first decide on its customer base i.e., its target audience. It then needs to decide on various aspects like the number and granularity of aggregates, overlap amongst aggregates, the attributes used for constructing these aggregates, the methodology for constructing these aggregates, and last but not the least formulate strategies for profitably using these aggregates.

Numerous choices are available while deciding on each of these aspects. An online firm could decide if its customer base should be limited only to people that visit its own Web site or include browsers at related competitors' Web sites. It could form small or big aggregates. For example a community portal could build micro-communities spread across the connected medium along with larger communities at its own Web site. It could allow for aggregates to overlap i.e., manage the same customer via different aggregates. It could also adjust for the strength of a customer's presence in various aggregates. It could use geographic, demographic, psychographic, and behavioral attributes to construct these aggregates. However in the connected medium novel attributes like content, context, virtual location[4], navigation behavior[5], and technology can also be used. These are made possible because of the measurement and accountability techniques offered by the underlying medium. It could use various methodologies like market research, collaborative filtering, and customer participation to create these aggregates. It could encourage customers to form aggregates on their own or actively structure these aggregates. It could use these aggregates for various purposes like defining its offerings, setting prices, defining points of contact, and formulating strategies to differentiate from competitors. For example a community portal could use the aggregates it develops to organize niche portals based on these aggregates.

Firm integration is the process by which a firm positions itself in the competitive landscape. Since a firm will have a virtual presence in the connected world, it may choose to be present at numerous places, in the same form, at the same time, with many other firms. The collective presence could help it to command higher visibility, a bigger target audience, and develop stable trust-building value-added relationships with customers. Firm integration will require a firm to actively manage this collective presence. This presence could take varying forms. For example a firm could integrate with other firms based on whether it desires to share revenues from actual sales or whether it wants to improve its visibility by increasing its target audience. It will also be subject to frequent negotiation and rapid change. A firm while integrating itself with other firms will need to figure out various issues like its affinities with other firms, the presence of competitors, the strength of its own presence, and formulate strategies to effectively exploit this integration.

On the World Wide Web, a firm could choose to be present at many places. It could locate itself at Internet service providers, portals, community sites, information centers, or build its own Web site. It could present itself as a transaction agent, as an integrator, as a mediator, or as a sponsor. It could choose to be present only at specific times of the day or even use its presence to consolidate existing markets, explore new markets, or manage risk.

Medium Integration is the process of integrating various underlying features of the medium such as available information, access points, and the different interaction facilities. Online ticket booking agencies and comparison shopping sites for music and books are obvious examples. A firm could aggregate various services provided by the medium to build new services. For example an online firm that aggregates free e-mail services over the Web and helps customers make a choice between them builds a new service out of services already available in the medium. As it integrates and syndicates available services, it could choose to provide only a few core services by itself. For example, an online broker such as Etrade may aggregate stock quotes, news and charts provided on the web with its internal trading mechanism to offer a complete solution to the customer. Since interconnected links are intrinsic to this connected medium, a firm could aggregate these links. A firm, such as egroups.com, which develops e-mail discussion lists by helping people organize e-mail addresses is an example. Portals, like Yahoo!, which organize links to ease navigation, are also examples. A firm could also use medium integration to offer services to its customers that help it differentiate itself from competitors.

Interaction

Interaction stands for a many-to-many communication process spread across time. As mentioned before, this would be a key defining point for firms because the connected world enables fast, reliable, and inexpensive communication. While formulating strategies for interaction a firm will need to decide on the enablers, the parties involved, the nature, the initiation aspects, and the use of this interaction.

The medium could offer various enablers for interaction. Presently the WWW offers enablers ranging from e-mail lists and chat sites to Web pages. Since each enabler has its own strengths and weaknesses the firm will need to evaluate them, and form a strategy for using these enablers. Such a strategy could involve deciding on issues like sequencing the use of these enablers, judging their relative importance, and the frequency of their use. A firm presently marketing on the Web can start with interactive banners, which motivate customers to join broad opt-in e-mail discussion lists. As a next step it can encourage customers interacting over these broad lists to form more focused niche buddy lists. Finally, it could motivate them to register online accounts and publish Web pages at its Web site.

The communicating parties can be endogenously determined out of the set of possible partners. This set includes the selling firm, other firms (including competitors), an individual customer, groups of customers, intermediaries, suppliers or even the medium itself. A firm could enable interaction between its various customers to build communities or between itself and its customers in order to promote new products, get feedback, and improve its responsiveness to customers. It could take the lead in fostering interaction between itself and its competitors in order to promote the basic underlying product or service category by enhancing awareness and providing information about the product or service. A manufacturer with a well-established brand could initiate interaction between retailers and its customers in order to get attractive deals from retailers. (Thus the distribution of power in the channel might roll back to the manufacturers.) It could also enable interaction between the various communities it builds in order to make them grow. The firm could enable a number of interactions in various forms between any of these parties.

The interaction could be asynchronous, with each party responding at its own convenience or real-time in nature. E-mail lists and bulletin boards could do the former while like chat sites could achieve the latter. For example, in order to encourage and reinforce repeat discussions, a firm could build only a small archive and limited summaries of past interactions. The interaction could be well structured, where every stage is carefully choreographed or left in a free form with few limitations. The firm could play various roles like that of a moderator, contributor, facilitator, and propagator in the interaction. Interactions could be initiated by either party or by the medium.

Interaction could be used to mold all aspects of the marketing process. A firm could use interaction to define various aspects of its offering. It could interact with its target audience to identify bundles of products and services, which it can profitably market. It could interact with its customers to develop pricing strategies that allow it to capture consumer surplus. It could enable interaction between its customers and other firms that complement its core offering. For example a firm selling software online could have its customers interact with hardware manufactures who optimize their platforms for its software products.

A firm could use interaction to consolidate and extend its target audience. It can consolidate by enabling interaction in various forms between customers and building virtual communities. It can extend its target audience by enabling, and motivating interaction between the various communities it builds. For example a firm selling music online can build two communities: one for listeners who love rock music, another for listeners who love classical music. Then by organizing programs (like affiliate programs) and special promotional offers it can have these two communities interact, in the process increasing its customer base from sales of both rock and classical music. It could also build communities based on loyalty, and have the most fiercely loyal community interact with communities built by its competitors in order to grab market share.

Interaction can be used to evaluate the results of marketing strategies and tailor them in real time to a changing environment. It could be used to differentiate a firm from its competitor by building its brand and allowing customers to interact with its competitors' offerings. A firm could have its customers build their own stores on its basic Web site, in the process interactively building its brand. For example a firm marketing clothes online could have its customers build stores to sell products like music and cosmetics, which in turn will slowly build its brand. A firm could also allow its customers to interact with its competitors' products in the process generating feedback, improving its own offering, and thus differentiating itself from its competitors. For example a firm marketing software products online could allow its customers to experiment with its competitors' products in the process refining the design of its own product for future versions and thus automatically differentiating itself from its competitors.

Identification

A firm needs to identify and define three different attributes: customers, environment, and itself. As a part of the identification process, the firm will need to rigorously define the meaning of *identity*, the granularity and extent of identification, the methodologies it uses for identifying, the frequency of the process, and the intended uses of the identification profiles it develops.

Customer identity could have various interpretations. It could involve developing profiles on attributes derived from cultural, social, demographic, psychological, behavioral, and technological characteristics. However in the connected medium we believe that the attributes of central importance would be those derived from customer preferences, affinities, needs, attitudes, awareness, behavior and relationships. Identities may be developed for individual customers and aggregates of customers. For example a firm selling music online could build profiles for individual listeners based on their musical tastes and then build other profiles for on all listeners having similar tastes. Identities may also differ based on the context they are developed in. For example a firm selling both music CDs and music software could build different profiles for the same customer based on whether it was planning to market CDs or software to the customer. A music profile could be built on cultural and social attributes; whereas, a software profile could be build on technological attributes.

A firm may use various methods to build these profiles. Using reasoning systems (like data mining tools), tracking systems and predictive techniques could automate the process. Customers could build these profiles on their own in exchange for tangible incentives like price discounts or premium services. A firm could provide tools to assist customers in building these profiles by helping them organize information about them. These tools can allow customers to upload the information they organize into the firm's databases. As an example, a firm marketing groceries online could build online accounts for its customers that help them organize information about their past purchases and future needs. A firm could also use the customer identity profiles it develops in various ways. First and foremost it could use these profiles to develop strong relationships with its customers and in the process slowly get to *own* the customer. It could also use these profiles to acquire more customers and improve the accuracy of its marketing process. It could use these profiles to catalyze community formation by providing appropriate content and structure at its Web site.

A firm's environment due to its virtual presence could potentially span the entire connected world. To deal with the resulting complexity, a firm will need to clearly define its environment. A firm will need to reconcile its virtual environment against boundaries of physical location and time to efficiently accommodate economic, political, cultural, and more importantly technological differences. This is especially true if a firm needs to exploit the global marketplace that a connected medium can potentially offer. For example, a firm like Amazon.com needs to understand incorporate cultural and social attitudes of people towards books in order to sell books across different continents. By virtue of being online a firm also needs to identify the technological characteristics of its environment. Presently a firm needs to know the bandwidth of its customers' Internet connections in order to decide on the amount of rich media it can add and still have pages download fast enough on their computers. Due to the interconnected nature of the medium, a firm will have a large number of approach points to itself in this medium. On the WWW, a firm may have numerous links pointing to its web site, some within its knowledge and some not. To market efficiently it will need to continuously understand and identify all these approach points. Last but not the least, a firm will also need to identify competition, trends, and cost structures, which will change at an even faster pace in this connected medium.

Along with identifying its environment and its customers a firm will also need to identify itself so that it can effectively manage the speed and continuous change intrinsic in its marketing processes. Identifying itself would require it to keep track of its core competencies with respect to its customer base. A web portal, for example, could identify itself as a search, navigation, commerce, content or a community portal depending on its competencies. The identity the firm selects and develops will depend on the visitors it plans to attract to its Web site. In order to use the customer profiles it develops towards satisfying consumers' wants, it will frequently need to revisit the make-or-outsource decision. Clear self identification is crucial for making an optimal decision on the trade-off between the services and products a firm provides to its customers. By being present in the virtual world, it will also need to continuously adapt its organizational structure to this evolving connected medium. As firms have started using the Internet to provide customer services, they have been establishing e-mail centers and learning to use them instead of call centers. However as the connected medium brings about a convergence of data, audio and video, it will need to merge both e-mail, call and customer service centers and learn to operate them in a synchronized manner, in order to effectively manage its marketing processes. This in turn will make it change the ways it organizes its customer service employees. A virtual presence will also imply that its employees communicate primarily through this medium, which in turn will also influence the way it manages its marketing processes. The Motley Fool is one example of a firm that has employees who are located in geographically diverse locations and interact at work via the Internet.

Intensity

Intensity can be exercised on three independent dimensions. The first is the *push-pull* axis. A firm could take a fairly intensive stance towards it customers by pushing information and products or could encourage customers to pull the process towards them. The second dimension relates to using the connected medium as a communication, transaction, and distribution channel. As a communications channel, tuning intensity will amount to controlling the amount of information exchanged, the frequency, and the style of exchange. For example a community portal could provide efficient and elaborate tools like those for publishing home pages, organizing discussion threads and bulletin boards. A firm could also limit the scope of communication by restricting the visibility of its messages in (virtual) space and time. As a transaction channel, managing intensity will amount to controlling the speed and conduct of transactions. It would also involve simplifying complex and costly transactions. An online firm providing realtor services could simplify the arduous task of buying a house by integrating all the transactions involved. The connected medium, due to its very nature, also makes it possible to distribute via numerous links. The distribution on each of these links can differ in its scope, size, and frequency. Controlling the intensity of distribution will involve decisions on these issues. For example an online retailer can improve the ease of navigation, interface design, usability, and the look and feel of its Web site to make it simpler to shop for its customers. It could also set up a path in the medium where customers can interact with its banner advertisements, see information about the product and purchase the product, all without leaving the advertising Web site. In contrast it could also set up a path in the medium where users are required to register, become a part of the community, show a certain level of involvement before they can conduct transactions with the firm. It could set up the former paths for repeat customers, and set up the latter kind of paths for acquiring new customers.

The third dimension can be understood in terms of the various stages of the consumer buying process. Although there are several consumer buying behavior models quoted in literature, none has yet been established for use online. Thus, for the purpose of our discussion we use the standard five-stage model (see Kotler, 1997). The five stages are: problem recognition, information search, evaluation of alternatives, purchase decisions, and postpurchase behavior. Note that each of these stages can be done via the connected medium.

Understanding intensity in each stage amounts to deciding on the speed, duration and effort invested by both the firm and its customer. At each of these stages, the customer will be faced by myriad choices. A firm could handle intensity by providing tools to the customer to help her simplify and streamline each stage. Further since all these stages will occur in the same medium, customers might increasingly vacillate across all these stages. Thus a firm will also need to provide facilities to a customer to coordinate her activities across all these stages. Further the firm could enable paths of varying intensity across these five stages. Some paths could short-circuit certain stages; some could invest more resources in certain stages. The firm could influence customers, depending on their characteristics, to take either of these paths by placing them at appropriate points in the medium. It could also influence customers to switch paths depending on the progress they make.

USING THE 4I MODEL

We start this section by describing the dependencies between the four aspects of our model. We next illustrate the effectiveness of our model by describing the ways in which it can be used to manage a futuristic marketing process. We also contrast our model with traditional marketing models. Finally we apply our model by constructing a classification of various marketing strategies that have been employed by Amazon.com.

Dependencies

The four aspects—integration, interaction, identification and intensity—of our marketing model are far from independent. They influence and interact with each other. Deciding on one involves thinking about the other. The influence graph between them, with examples, is presented in Figure 1. Each of four aspects affects all the others. The graph also illustrates possible forms of these pair wise influences.

Integration can determine the end result of identification. In other words profile attributes can be chosen on the basis of the integration attributes. For example the attributes used for customer integration could be used to determine the attributes of the customer profiles. The attributes used for firm integration could be used to construct the firm profile. The attributes used for medium integration could be used to build an environment profile. Similarly integration can be used to define the

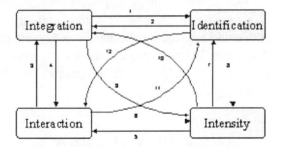

Figure 1. Dependencies between the four aspects of the 4I model

	Cause	Effect
1:	Attributes of integration	Identification method used
2:	Accuracy of identification	Accuracy of integration
3:	Interaction	An integration method
4:	Aggregates	Interacting parties
5:	Intensity	Form of interaction
6:	Interaction	Intensity
7:	Intensity	A form of identification
8:	Identification	Intensity at each stage
9:	Integration at each stage	Intensity at that stage
10:	Intensity	Nature of integration
11:	Interaction	An identification method
12:	Identification	Nature of interaction enabled

parties between which interaction might be enabled by the firm. The aggregates constructed by the firm can determine the intensity of the marketing process at each stage, especially for those processes which are constructed per aggregate.

Interaction can determine integration. The simplest relationship between the two is to use interaction as a methodology for integration, which results in *interactive* aggregates. Virtual communities are one manifestation of such aggregates. Similarly to its affect on integration, interaction can also be used as an identification methodology, where the firm enables interactions appropriate to building customer, firm, and environment profiles. Interaction can affect intensity. Different kinds of interaction can have different effects in various stages of the consumer buying process.

Identification can affect integration in many ways. The accuracy of the identification process can determine the reliability of the aggregates formed. Similarly identification can determine interaction. The results of the identification process can help a firm organize and implement interaction between parties. The identification process can help a firm develop knowledge about the various parameters of intensity. For instance it can help a firm in deciding between a push versus pull strategy.

Intensity can be used to determine the attributes of Integration. For example a firm might want to aggregate customers based on the suitability of push versus pull processes for them. It could aggregate customers based on the parameters of each stage of the buying process. Intensity can also be used to direct the identification process. For example, a firm might want to understand the effects of using the

Figure 2. An approach to using 4I

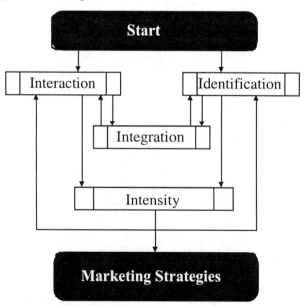

connected medium as a transaction channel on various customers, which in turn implies that it needs to build customer profiles on transaction attributes. Similarly intensity can drive interaction. A firm would want to facilitate interaction between various customers if it believes that interaction can lead to a more efficient exchange of communication.

These are just some illustrations of the ways in which the four aspects of our model can interact. Given that these interactions can be complex, we need to operationalize our model. We depict one such possible road map in Figure 2.

A firm may start by working on the identification and interaction aspects. It can use the results from these two aspects to understand the issues underlying Integration. Having developed an initial understanding, it can feedback and fine-tune the identification and interaction aspects again. At the same time it can take results from each of these three aspects and use these results to understand the issues underlying intensity. It can use the results obtained to go back and refine its analysis of identification and interaction. This is just one way of using our model; it can be used in other ways depending on the situation it is being applied to. Exploring these approaches is a subject for future study for us.

Effectiveness of the 4I Model

This subsection describes the use of the 4I model to effectively manage the characteristics of the future environment.

The first and most important characteristic is *interaction*. We believe it to be so important that we made it into an aspect by itself of our model. Figure 1, which illustrates the way these aspects interact is in effect a way of managing this characteristic. Another characteristic we list is *customization*. Integration can be used to decide on the amount of customization that needs to be provided with the core offering. For example if the integration is very granular, and there are a large number of very small aggregates, then a very high level of customization needs to be provided. Interaction can be used to optimally shift a certain amount of effort involved in customization on the customer. A firm with very well developed channels of interaction can provide the basic components to a user and expect her to assemble the customized end product. Identification can be used by a firm to decide on the kind of customization that is required and will be profitably accepted by its customers. A firm can use intensity to decide on the form of customization available to its customers.

Our model can also handle *customer power*. By choosing appropriate aggregates, customer power can be directly managed. Very large aggregates will be more powerful and harder to manage than finer aggregates. Interaction can be used to channel customer power in an effective manner. Identification can be used to identify sources of customer power beyond the firm's immediate control. It can be used to identify the pros and cons of various strategies available in managing customer power. Intensity can be manipulated depending on customer power. A situation where the customer is more powerful can be subject to a fairly intense process, thus requiring less investment and effort on part of the firm. The fourth characteristic is *service based*. Integration can once again be used to decide on the overall quality, number, and flexibility of services provided to customers. Interaction can be used to measure the effectiveness of these services. Identification can be used to precisely define the nature of these services. Intensity can be used to decide on kind of services provided. If a process is to be very less intense then the customer needs to be provided with a large number of services.

Integration and interaction can be used to reduce the effects of *sensitivity*. Both can be used by a firm to differentiate itself from its competitors, while simultaneously reducing the sensitivity of its customers. Identification can be used by a firm to identify sources of sensitivity and deepen its understanding of sensitivity. Intensity can also directly affect sensitivity. A very intense process could increase the sensitivity of a customer and make her switch to a competitor, whereas, a less intense process could decrease this sensitivity.

Integration and *speed* are two other characteristics best tackled by integration. For example choosing a very fine integration could help lessen the speed and change in various processes. Whereas choosing large aggregates may actually subject management processes organized per aggregate to change more frequently. Interaction can be used to shift the burden of managing these characteristics on the customer. Identification can be used to understand the sources, and develop information about these characteristics. Intensity has a direct correlation to these characteristics. A fairly intense process could increase the speed. Controlling intensity might help integrate the process more efficiently.

In order to manage the *barrier-less* nature of the futuristic marketing process, all four aspects can be used to effectively understand and exploit the global, diverse and timeless nature of the marketing online. Another characteristic that we highlight is *automation*. Integration can be used to decide on the way automation is provided and organized. For example certain marketing processes could be automated per aggregate but certain will need to be automated per customer in an aggregate. An example of using interaction to automate is using software tools for automated negotiation. Identification can be used to identify the actual subprocesses which require automation. Decisions on intensity control can lead to high or low levels of automation.

The last characteristic that we highlight is *efficiency*. Integration can be used to enhance efficiency by amortizing costs across aggregates. Interaction can help firms get accurate feedback and build accountability, thus increasing efficiency. Identification can be used to identify sources of inefficiency in the processes and take steps on removing them. Manipulating intensity can be used to make the process more efficient. For example by streamlining cumbersome and tedious stages in the marketing process, efficiency can be improved.

Contrasting the 4I Model
With Traditional Marketing Models

We contrast our model with the traditional 4P model of marketing (Kotler, 1997; McCarthy, 1978). We believe that our model highlights issues that are orthogonal to those highlighted by the 4P model. One can reach the same optimal marketing plan when using the traditional marketing models. However, we believe that our suggested way is more intuitive in the connected world and highlights the fundamental issues critical to understanding marketing activities in the virtual environment. This in turn makes our model easier to use for analyzing marketing processes online.

The 4P model of marketing categorizes decision-making about marketing into four categories: *product, price, place and promotion*. Product stands for the firm's tangible offer to the market, including the product quality, design, features, branding, and packaging. Price stands for the amount of money that customers need to pay for the product. Place stands for the various activities the company undertakes to make the product accessible and available to target customers. Promotion stands for the various activities the firm undertakes to communicate and promote its products to the target markets

While our model is fundamentally different in the issues it highlight, the 4P model is still hidden in our model as figure 3 shows. The horizontal lines represent the four aspects of our model. Deciding on these aspects can be interpreted as the process of *indirectly* deciding on the four P's. However each aspect of our model also helps make decisions on issues other than the four P's. Consider issues like customer relationships and knowledge management. These are not at the core of the 4P model. The way a firm manages integration, interaction, identification and

Figure 3. Contrasting 4I to 4P

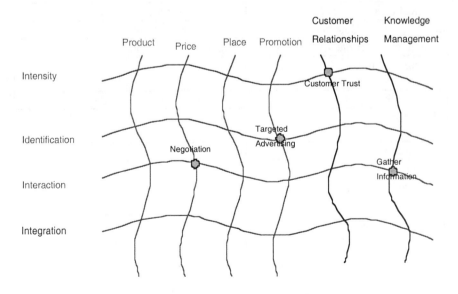

intensity will *directly* determine the way its relationships develop and the utility of the information it accumulates. For example, effectively managing the intensity in online marketing processes can help a firm build trust with its customers. A firm while interacting with its customers, can use those interactions to learn more about them, which in turn improves its customer knowledge base. Deciding on the four P's influences these issues but an explicit cause-and-effect analysis is cumbersome to do by concentrating only on the four Ps.

An Example Analysis

We now use our model to construct a classification of several marketing strategies that have been pursued by Amazon.com. The strategies we list were obtained by exhaustively browsing through the press releases filed by Amazon.com at its web site (Amazon.com Press Releases) and from a few other papers profiling Amazon.com (Kotha, 1998; Kotha and Dooley, 1998). Due to space constraints we request the reader to refer to these press releases and papers for details of these marketing activities.

Table 2: 4I applied to Amazon.com

Strategy	Model Parameter
Customer, author, peer reviews	Customer-Customer Interaction
Related titles, author interviews	Customer-Firm Interaction
Eye's service, Editor's service	Identification, Interaction
Customer databases, Cookies	Customer identification, Integration
Agreements with Portals	Firm Integration
Micro franchises (Associate Program)	Medium Integration, Intensity
Geographical location (Seattle)	Environment identification
Discounted Pricing , Customer service	Firm identification
Providing huge selection, virtual service	Medium Integration
Building communities of book readers	Customer Integration, Interaction
Interactive book project	Customer-Firm Interaction
1-Click ordering	Customer identification, intensity
Entering a fragmented industry	Environment identification
Information broker for books	Information Intensity
"Visible" and "Invisible" customers	Customer-Customer Interaction
Transaction banners at other Web sites	Transaction Intensity
Expansion into videos, CDs, Gifts	Customer identification
"Shop the Web" program	Customer identification, medium Integration
Advantage 4 Music program	Customer identification

CONCLUSIONS

In this chapter we describe characteristics intrinsic to a futuristic online marketing process. We do so by analyzing attributes of the connected medium, and extrapolating the influence of these attributes on the characteristics of a marketing process. We believe these characteristics will remain central, and even reinforced, as the connected medium continues to evolve.

Technology always advances; it is society, which tries to catch up, whether that is in the form of acceptance by people, government regulation, or commercial viability. One of the most pervasive activities that modern society engages in is market driven commerce. As technology leaps forward and markets struggle to cope, it is necessary to introduce changes in our thought processes too. We do so by proposing a comprehensive framework that is oriented towards understanding and managing the marketing implications of the new connected medium. Our model presents a significant departure from widely accepted traditional marketing models but we believe such a shift is inevitable. We also illustrate our model with an example, where the model naturally leads to strategies that have so far been regarded as complete innovations. As we improve our understanding, and society adapts, innovations *become* intuitive. It is this journey from innovation to intuition, that we hope our model makes possible by highlighting the appropriate issues.

Our model is only the first step in the right direction. It needs to be refined further. In order to improve the applicability of our model, we need to rigorously parameterize each of the four aspects of the model. Once parameterized, we need to develop guidelines for tackling these aspects in a pragmatic manner. Another aspect is the development of quantifiable measures for evaluation. We would like to exhaustively understand all the various choices available for the firm when deciding on the issues underlying each of the four aspects of our model. In particular we would like to identify choices that will remain invariant even as the connected world continues to change. The model could be extended in a straightforward manner to illustrate and analyze online marketing processes like developing customer ownership, one-to-one marketing, building portals, and organizing metamediaries.

REFERENCES

Alba, J., J. Lynch, B. Weitz, C. Janiszewski, R. Lutz, A. Sawyer, and S. Wood (1997). "Interactive Home Shopping: Consumer, Retailer, and Manufacturer Incentives to Participate in Electronic Marketplaces," *Journal of Marketing* 6: 38-53.

Amazon.Com, "Press Releases," http://www.amazon.com/exec/obidos/subst/misc/news.html.

Atkinson, R.D., and R. H. Court (1998). "The New Economy Index: Understanding America's Economic Transformation," Progressive Policy Institute, Technology, Innovation, and New Economy Project. http://www.dlcppi.org/ppi/tech/neweconomy_site/.

Armstrong A. and J. Hagel (1996). "The Real Value of On-Line Communities,"

Harvard Business Review, pp 134-141.

Blattberg R. C. and J. Deighton (1991) "Interactive Marketing: Exploiting the Age of Addressability," *Sloan Management Review*, 5-14.

Blattberg R. C., R. Glazer, and J. D. C. Little Eds. (1994). *"The Marketing Information Revolution,"* Boston: Harvard Business School Press.

Briggs R. (1997) *"A Roadmap to Marketing Online,"* Internet Advertising Bureau report.

Burke R. R. (1997) "Do You See What I See? The Future of Virtual Shopping," *Journal of the Academy of Marketing Science* 25(4) , 352-360.

Caglayan A. K. and C. G. Harrison (1997) *"AGENT Sourcebook,"* Wiley Computer Publishing.

Capton N. and R. Glazer (1987). "Marketing and Technology: A Strategic Coalignment," *Journal of Marketing* 51, 1-14.

Cheskin Research (1999). "eCommerce Trust Study," A Joint Research Project by *Cheskin Research and Studio Archetype/Sapient,* January 1999.

Doody, A. F. and W. R. Davidson (1967). "Next Revolution in Retailing," *Harvard Business Review* (45), 4-20.

Elfson G. and W. N. Robinson (1998). "Creating a Custom Mass-Production Channel on the Internet," *Communications of the ACM,* 41(3).

Ernst & Young LLP (1999), "Internet Shopping '99," The second annual Ernst & Young Internet Shopping Study, http://www.ey.com/industry/consumer/internetshopping/download.asp.

Glazer R, (1991), "Marketing in an information intensive environment: Strategic implication of knowledge as an asset," *Journal of Marketing* 55, 1-19.

Hagel J. and Rayport J. F. (1997). "The Coming Battle for Customer Information," *Harvard Business Review,* January-February.

Hoffman, D. L., T. P. Novak, and M. A. Peralta (1998), "Building Consumer Trust in Online Environments: The Case for Information Privacy," Working Paper, Project 2000, University of Vanderbilt.

Hoffman, D. L., W. D. Kalsbeek, and T. P. Novak (1996). "Internet and Web Use in the U.S.," *Communications of the ACM,* 39(12), 36-46.

Hoffman, D. L. and T. P. Novak (1996). "Marketing in Hypermedia Computer Mediated Environments: Conceptual Foundations," *Journal of Marketing,* Vol. 60, 50-68.

Hoffman, D. L. and T. P. Novak (1997). "A New Marketing Paradigm for Electronic Commerce," *The Information Society,* Special Issue on Electronic Commerce 13, 43-54.

Jupiter Communications (1999) *"1999 Online Advertising Report: Revenue Models, Market Strategies, & Projections,"* Online Advertising Group.

Kotler, P. (1997). *Marketing Management: Analysis, Planning, Implementation and Control*, 9th edition, Prentice Hall.

Kotha, S. (1998). "Competing on the Internet: How Amazon.com is rewriting the rules of competition," *Advances in Strategic Management*, Vol. 15, 239-265.

Kotha, S. and E. Dooley (1998). "Amazon.com" In Hill, C. & Jones, G. *Strategic*

Management Theory and Cases. New York: Houghton Mifflin.

LeFurgy, R. (1997). *"1997 IAB Online Advertising Effectiveness Study,"* Internet Advertising Bureau and Millard Brown Interactive.

Magretta, J. (1998). "The Power of Virtual Integration: An Interview with Dell Computer's Michael Dell," *Harvard Business Review,* March-April, 73-84.

Margherio, L., D. Henry, S. Cooke, S. Montes, and K. Hughes (1998) "The Emerging Digital Economy," Secretariat on Electronic Commerce, US Department of Commerce.

McCarthy, E. J. (1978). *Basic Marketing: A Managerial Approach*, 6th edition, Richard D. Irwin Inc.

Moran, S. P. M and A. I. Pazgal (1999). "Portal Vendor Relationships: Building Blocks of Future Online Retailing." Working paper.

Quelch, J. A. and L. R. Klein (1996). "The Internet and International Marketing," *Sloan Management Review,* 37: 60-75.

Pazgal, A. I. (1999). "Software agents: The future of marketing on the Internet," *Proceedings of the Conference on Information Systems & Technology,* Cincinnati.

Peterson, R. A. (1997). "Electronic Marketing: Visions, Definitions, and Implications," In *Electronic Marketing and the Consumer.* Ed. Robert A. Peterson. Thousand Oaks, CA: Sage, 1-16.

Peterson, R. A., S. Balasubramanian, and B. J. Bronnenberg (1997). "Exploring the Implications of the Internet for Consumer Marketing," *Journal of the Academy of Marketing Science,* 25, 329-346.

Shankar, V., Rangaswamy A., and Pusateri M. (1998). "The Impact of Internet Marketing on Price Sensitivity," Memo, Penn State University.

Schwartz, E. I. (1998). "Webonomics: Nine essential principles for growing your web business on the WWW," Broadway Books.

Stewart T. R. (1998). "The e-business tidal wave: Perspectives on business in cyberspace," Deloitte Touche Tohmatsu.

ENDNOTES

1 This invariance over time enhances the applicability of our contributions.

2 While our descriptions of each feature use the future tense, our examples are in the present.

3 The concept of *consumer aggregation is* clearly conceptually similar to that of market *segmentation* (Kotler, 1997).

4 Even though a consumer could travel almost anywhere in a connected world, in reality she will stay within a certain boundary. For instance she may visit only certain news Web sites on a regular basis, and rarely go to others. This boundary could be used to define her virtual location.

5 Concentration span and click-stream are two examples of navigation behavior.

Chapter 10

Exploring Consumers' Willingness to Contribute to Internet Web Sites

Benedict G.C. Dellaert
Tilburg University, The Netherlands

INTRODUCTION

One of the most interesting opportunities when introducing e-commerce in producer consumer networks is that the new information technology structure may be used to empower consumers to be more active participants in the economic value creation process (e.g., Hoffman and Novak, 1996; Alba et al., 1997). Consumers may for example create their own personalized version of a Web site or services, or communicate with other consumers about products they have bought. Many Internet-based firms have recognized the potential benefits of these opportunities and are encouraging consumers to make contributions to their Web sites. Some examples of Web sites encouraging various types of consumer contributions are presented in Table 1.

Allowing consumers to contribute more actively to different stages of the supply chain can create three main types of economic benefits. First, consumers can assist producers in achieving lower production costs and creating higher consumption utility for the consumer's own benefit (e.g., by lowering transaction costs or by allowing producers to make more customized products). Secondly, they can also assist producers in generating similar benefits for other consumers. Thirdly, the Internet can be a vehicle through which consumers can generate additional value for each other, directly and without business intermediation (e.g., by providing suggestions for new product designs or by sharing information about past consumption experiences).

Table 1: Examples of Internet web sites encouraging consumer contributions

Type of Web site	Internet location	Suggested consumer contributions
Auctioning	Ebay.com	"Sell your item" "Get news and chat" "Leave your feedback [about this seller]"
Books	Amazon.com	"Write an online review" "… jump into the world of electronic commerce today by joining the Amazon.com Associates Program"
Computers	Dell.com	"Point, click, configure, buy. It doesn't get any easier" "Support your Dell: Documentation, troubleshooting, files and more…"
Portal	Yahoo.com	"Join a chat" "Customize your My Yahoo Headlines to see only the news of interest to you" "Start a club"
Travel	Expedia.msn.com	"E-mail a free spring break card to a friend" "Share your travel experiences and tips in bulletin boards and chats. […] Read and share romantic travel tips!"

The success of such potential additional value creation depends of course on consumers' willingness to make such contributions to Internet Web sites. However, little is known about what drives consumers' decisions whether or not to contribute to Web sites. Therefore, the current study analyzes the impact of some potentially important drivers of such consumer contributions to value creation on the Internet. Based on household production theory (e.g., Kooreman and Wunderink 1997), hypotheses are formulated on the relationships between consumer, product and exchange process characteristics and the likelihood of the consumer choice to contribute to Internet Web sites. The validity of these hypotheses is explored drawing on data from the 10th GVU WWW survey on Internet usage (Georgia Tech Research Corporation, 1998).

THEORY

Household production theory is based on the notion that consumers will only participate in those activities that will increase the total value of their consumption experiences. In this view on consumers' contributions to Internet Web sites, the key question is whether or not consumers will benefit from making such contributions and if so, what costs are attached to making the contributions.

Three main types of variables are distinguished that may determine whether or not consumers will wish to contribute to Internet Web sites. They are consumer characteristics, product characteristics and exchange process characteristics. The

Table 2: Hypothesized impact of consumer, product and exchange process characteristics on consumer contributions in Internet-based value creation

Category	Variables	Hypothesized effects on consumer contributions
Consumer related	Consumer experience and education	Consumers' time required for contributing on the Internet decreases and the value of their contributions increases if their experience with the Internet and/or their education level is higher.
	Consumer income	Consumers' contribution costs on the Internet depend on the consumers' value of time. The higher the consumer's value of time the higher the costs of making contributions on the Internet.
	Consumer costs	The higher the costs of Internet access, the less likely it is that consumers will contribute. The costs of making contributions increase if the consumers' primary language is not English.
Product related	Product modularization	Making use of consumer contributions in Internet-based customization of production and facilitation is less expensive if products can be modularized.
	Product digitization	Integrating consumer contributions in the production process by using the Internet is less expensive if products can be digitized.
Exchange process related	Internet production costs	The higher the costs to the firm to implement Internet-based (customization) services, the less likely it is that consumer contributions will be integrated in the process.
	Strategic information quality of contributions	The greater the information asymmetries with regard to the value of consumer contributions made over the Internet, the less likely consumer contributions will be used.

hypothesized impact of the different variables for each set of characteristics is summarized in Table 2.

First, consumer characteristics may be an important driver of this choice. Consumers with a higher *income* and therefore a higher value of time are expected to find contributing to the Internet less attractive, because the costs of contributing to them are higher than to consumers with a lower value of time. Similarly, the costs of contributing to the Internet are expected to decrease as consumer *experience* with the Internet goes up and as *education* level increases. In contrast, when factors that drive consumer household production costs go up, consumers' willingness to contribute is expected to go down. Such other factors include whether or not the consumer's *primary language* is English and the level of the monetary *Internet access costs* to the consumer.

Secondly, product characteristics also may be relevant to consumers' choices whether or not to contribute. Products or services that can be *modularized* and/or *digitized* may have a higher potential for making use of consumer contributions on the Internet than products that cannot be digitized or modularized (cf., Peterson, Balasubramanian and Bronnenberg, 1997). The reason is that modular products are easier to customize based on consumer-producer interactions, while digital products can be presented and delivered more efficiently over the Internet.

Thirdly, characteristics of the Internet-based exchange process also may affect consumers' contribution choices. The implementation of consumer contribution exchanges on the Internet may create some additional costs for consumers and producers, because the *exchange process costs* may increase for the participants. For example, establishing a system by which value can be exchanged and measured on the Internet may require considerable investments by consumers and producers.

Most consumer contributions on the Internet can be classified as experience goods in the information economics sense (cf., Tirole 1988). Typically, consumer contributions involve information for which it is difficult for buyers to ascertain the quality before it is used or consumed. For example, a consumer cannot easily verify another consumer's claim that he or she is suggesting an attractive customization process before undergoing the process by him- or herself. Likewise, producers will find it difficult to evaluate a consumer's contribution to their design processes before the consumer's suggestions have been implemented.

Given that this *information asymmetry* may exist between buyers and sellers of consumer contributions on the Internet, there is some potential for strategic behavior. In particular, it may or may not be economically rational for parties participating in Internet exchanges to deliver the promised level of service quality. In fact, this potential for 'cheating' exists both for consumers and producers, as both can be sellers and buyers in the exchange of consumer contributions on the Internet. However, there typically also are mechanisms to overcome the information asymmetries between buyers and sellers such as independent quality certification. An important consequence of these information asymmetries and the mechanisms put in place to overcome the asymmetries is that some consumer contributions exchanges may still be relatively costly even though communication, interaction and exchange costs are low. Thus, the probability that consumers will choose to contribute to Web sites may be lower.

MODEL

Econometrically, consumers' choices to contribute to Web sites are modeled using a random utility model (e.g., Ben-Akiva and Lerman, 1985). This type of model assumes that consumers' choices can be represented as a process in which consumers evaluate the characteristics of the options that are relevant to a given choice situation in terms of the utility they provide. In the current study the options represent the choice whether or not to contribute to Internet Web sites under different conditions based on consumer, product and exchange process characteristics. The part-worth utilities associated with the characteristics of the choice conditions are assumed to be integrated cognitively into an overall utility, after which the option with the highest overall utility is selected (i.e., to contribute or not). The utility function in the model consists of two basic parts: i) a deterministic component that describes the structural utility that the consumer derives from contributing or not, and ii) a random error component that captures the errors in modeling this structural utility. Such errors can be due to various sources including measurement error, omitted explanatory variables, and unobserved variations in taste.

Depending on the assumptions one is willing to make with regard to the error component, the random utility model supports fairly straightforward estimation of coefficients that express the impact of each of the conditional characteristics on the total utility of a contribution. By applying the simple choice rule that the option with the highest utility is selected, the model also allows one to express the choice probability of making a contribution. This probability is modeled as a function of the characteristics of the conditions around the contribution and a generic *other* option capturing the expected utility of the consumer's best possible other way to spend his or her time. In formula, the random utility model is expressed as:

$$U_c = V_c + \varepsilon_c$$

$$= \hat{a}\mathbf{X}_c + \tilde{a}\mathbf{X}_i\mathbf{X}_c + \varsigma\mathbf{X}_p\mathbf{X}_c + \hat{o}\mathbf{X}_e\mathbf{X}_c + \varepsilon_c \qquad (1)$$

where: U_c is the utility of contributing, V_c is the structural utility of contributing, $\mathbf{X}_c$ is a dummy for contributing or not, β is the average parameter value of the utility of contributing, $\mathbf{X}_i$ is the vector of individual characteristics, γ is the vector of parameter values of the effect of individual i's characteristics on the evaluation of contributing, $\mathbf{X}_p$ is the vector of attributes of the specific product category, η is the vector of parameter values of the effect of the product category attributes on the evaluation of contributing, $\mathbf{X}_e$ is the vector of attributes of the exchange process, τ is the vector of parameter values of the effect of the exchange process on contributing, and ε_c is the random error component.

For the binomial case in which consumers choose whether or not to contribute (over the generic 'other' option), the choice probability is expressed as:

$$P(c) = P(U_c > U_{other})$$

$$= P(V_c + \varepsilon_c > V_{other} + \varepsilon_{other})$$

$$= P(\varepsilon_c - \varepsilon_{other} > V_{other} - V_c) \qquad (2)$$

where, $P(c)$ is the probability that the individual contributes to an Internet Web site, U_{other} is the utility of the generic 'other' option, of which V_{other} and ε_{other} are the structural and the random error component respectively.

If one is willing to assume that the random error components in the utilities of the alternatives follow independently and identically distributed distributions, for example, following a normal or Gumbel distribution, the well known probit and logit models arise respectively. Based on the different types of data available in this study, first, OLS regression is used to estimate a model directly on utility scores (eq. 1) and next, probit to estimate a model of consumer choices whether or not to contribute (eq. 2).

EMPIRICAL ANALYSIS

The hypothesized relationships were explored on the basis of data from the 10th GVU WWW survey (Georgia Tech Research Corporation, 1998). In particular, data were drawn from two parts of the GVU survey:

1. The 'General Demographics' (GD) questionnaire from which variables were used to conduct analyses on the relationships between *consumer* characteristics and consumer contributions to Internet processes, and
2. The 'Finding Product Information and Purchasing' (FPIP) questionnaire, from which data was used to analyze the relationship between *product* and *exchange process* characteristics and consumer contributions to Internet processes.

The GD questionnaire contained a number of questions that addressed consumers' skills and experience in using some of the more advanced options on the Internet. These questions were quite suitable to measure consumer contributions to Internet Web sites, because many of the options that were mentioned required activities that involve input of consumers' household production time. The options

Table 3: Consumer characteristics and consumer contributions [a]

Consumer characteristics	Standardized coefficient	t-value	Expected sign
Constant	1.134	8.675[b]	n.a.
Experience (yrs on Internet)	0.426	30.466[b]	+
Education (ordinal coding)	0.026	1.849	+
Primary language (English=1, other=0)	0.042	2.628[b]	+
Household income ($)	0.236	4.704[b]	-
Household income^2 ($)	-0.170	-3.437[b]	
Internet access costs (paid by work=1, self=0)	0.000	0.006	-

[a] Dependent variable *'Contributed to Web interfaces'*, composite measure based on multiple correspondence analysis of several types of consumer contributions to Web sites based (Appendix), n= 4113, OLS regression, adjusted R sqr. = 0.318, including corrections for heterogeneity due to age and gender
[b] $p<0.05$

that were selected for the analysis are listed in the Appendix (table A1). For each option, respondents indicated whether or not they had ever used it.

To map the options on some more general underlying dimensions of consumers' contributions to the Internet, a multiple correspondence analysis was conducted on the responses (for results see appendix). Of the two dimensions with the highest explanatory power resulting from the analysis the first was selected as the most appropriate indicator variable for consumer contributions because of its consistent substantive interpretation (e.g., it had a strong score on 'customizing a Web page'). The second indicator seemed more appropriate to describe purchase facilitation than consumer contributions (e.g., it had a strong score on 'filling out an ordering form on the Internet'). The multiple correspondence analysis score was taken as an indirect measurement for the individual's utility for contributing to Internet Web sites. Therefore, individuals' scores on the indicator were regressed on individuals' characteristics using OLS regression. The estimates of the regression model are reported in Table 3.

Consumer experience on the Internet was found to be an important explanatory variable for consumer contributions to Internet interfaces. Education and primary language were included along with the experience variable to provide some further indication of the likely impact of required effort and value of contributions on consumers' contributions. In particular, higher education and having English as a primary language were expected to increase consumer contributions. Both variables did indeed increase consumer contributions to Web site interfaces.

The effect of consumer income on contributions was somewhat complex. The results showed that increased consumer contributions to Web site interfaces went up, up to a point, after which income increases started to decrease consumer contributions. This may be explained by the fact that purchasing in general goes up as income increases, which is likely to be confounded with ordering on the Internet. Contrary to expectations, whether or not Internet access costs were paid for by respondents themselves had no effect on consumer contributions. Apparently once consumers have access to the Internet, access costs are not dominant in their decisions of whether or not to contribute.

The FPIP questionnaire of the GVU survey provided information on the relationships between product characteristics, exchange processes and consumer contributions. In this second questionnaire, information was available for 24 different product categories, allowing for comparisons between consumer contributions across product categories. Although the questionnaire did not provide equally detailed information about consumer contributions, it did include a variable indicating whether or not consumers interacted with vendors on the Internet after they had made their purchases. This variable was used as dependent variable.

The product categories that were analyzed are listed in the appendix (Table A2). To allow for tests of the hypothesized relationships between product characteristics and consumer contributions, these product categories were coded by the author in terms of the product and process characteristics ('modularization', 'digitization', 'cost of implementing Internet process', and 'information asymmetry

Table 4: Product and exchange process characteristics and consumer contributions[a]

Product and exchange process characteristics		Coefficient	t-value	Expected sign
	Constant	-1.739	-42.076[b]	n.a.
Product	Modularization (low, medium, high)	0.346	13.159[b]	+
	Digitization	0.013	0.059	n.a.
Exchange process	Costs of implementing Internet process (low, medium, high)	-0.082	-2.847[b]	-
	Information asymmetry in consumer contributions (low, medium, high)	-0.129	-5.281[b]	-

[a] dependent variable: '*Communicated with vendor*' (yes/no), for product classification see appendix, n= 645, probit model, Pearson Goodness of fit Chi Square significant at p = 0.000

[b] p<0.05

in consumer contributions'). The coding was done on a three point scale (-1,0,1) on which a lower score implied that the product was less suited from the perspective of implementing consumer contributions (also in appendix). The product and process characteristics were used as explanatory variables in a probit analysis on the dependent variable 'communicated with vendor' and the results of this analysis are presented in Table 4.

As expected, consumer contributions were more common for products that could be modularized relatively easily. Modularization may make it more likely that producers can respond effectively to consumer wishes for adaptations both before and after the product is delivered. However, whether or not a product could be digitized did not affect consumer contributions. This may perhaps be explained by the fact that although digitized products can be distributed more efficiently over the Internet, adapting them to consumer's wishes may still be difficult. Increased Internet system costs had a negative effect on consumer communications as was expected. Finally, for products for which it was relatively hard to judge the value of consumer contributions (information asymmetry), communications with vendors on the Internet decreased significantly, indicating that information asymmetries between producer and consumers in the area of consumer contributions may indeed reduce the likelihood of consumer contributions.

For comparison purposes, a probit model was estimated also on a second dependent variable, the consumer choice whether or not to purchase on the Internet. The results are presented in Table 5. Interestingly, the effects of the product and process characteristics on purchase probability differed from those on contribution choice. First, the possibility for digitization significantly affected the likelihood of

Table 5: Product and exchange process characteristics and probability of purchase[a]

Product and exchange process characteristics		Coefficient	t-value	Expected sign
	Constant	-1.002	-32.535[b]	n.a.
Product	Modularization (low, medium, high)	0.223	10.802[b]	+
	Digitization	0.096	5.430[b]	+
Exchange process	Costs of implementing Internet process (low, medium, high)	-0.191	-8.909[b]	-
	Information asymmetry in consumer contributions (low, medium, high)	0.009	0.450	n.a.

[a] dependent variable: *'Purchased online'* (yes/no), for product classification see appendix, n= 645, probit model, Pearson Goodness of fit Chi Square significant at p = 0.000

[b] p<0.05

purchasing over the Internet; whereas, it did not affect consumer contributions. This finding supports the notion that with respect to digitization, distribution benefits may be more important than communication benefits. Secondly, there was no significant effect of information asymmetry in consumer contributions on the probability of making a purchase. This result indicated that although consumer's contributions depended on the level of information asymmetry surrounding these contributions, online purchase decisions depended mainly on other factors.

CONCLUSION

The impact of the Internet on the consumer role in the value creation process may be far reaching. However, there still is considerable doubt as to how exactly the Internet will affect existing marketing and production channels. This article has attempted to shed some light on the effects that may influence the potential for consumer contributions to Internet Web sites.

Consumer experience on the Internet was found to be an important explanatory variable for consumer contributions to Internet interfaces. Increased consumer income increased consumer contributions up to a point after, which income increases decreased consumer contribution. Contrary to expectations, the question whether or not Internet access costs were paid for by respondents themselves turned out to have no effect on consumer contributions. As expected consumer contributions were more common for products that could be modularized relatively easily and for products for which it was relatively inexpensive to implement Internet-based processes. Whether or not a product could be digitized did not affect consumer contributions. Finally, for products for which it was relatively hard to judge consumer contributions on their value (information asymmetry), consumer communications with vendors on the Internet decreased significantly.

The primary objective of the current study was to analyze conceptually the value and likelihood of consumer contributions to value creation on Internet Web sites. Future research hopefully can take further steps in the direction of integrating consumer contributions into a full market model and into models of consumer and producer usage of such contributions. Internet-based consumer panels that focus on specific consumption areas combined with industry figures on production costs may be potential sources of data to conduct such analyses.

Therefore, a valuable further theoretical step in this line of research would be to integrate the current consumer model in a market mechanism model that also can capture strategic competitive effects that may occur as part of the dynamics in the supply side of the market. It would be interesting to explore under which competitive scenarios consumer contributions are likely to occur or not. For example, issues that could be addressed include manufacturer decisions to introduce Internet-based production, and market mechanism design for Internet exchanges between consumers and producers.

REFERENCES

Alba, Joseph, John Lynch, Barton Weitz, Chris Janiszewski, Richard Lutz, Alan Sawyer and Stacy Wood (1997). 'Interactive Home Shopping: Consumer, Retailer and Manufacturer Incentives to Participate in Electronic Commerce,' *Journal of Marketing* 61 (July), 38-53.

Ben-Akiva, Moshe and Steven R. Lerman (1985). *Discrete Choice Analysis: Theory and Application to Travel Demand*, Cambridge, MA: MIT Press.

Hoffman, Donna L. and Thomas P. Novak (1996). 'Marketing in Hypermedia Computer-Mediated Environments: Conceptual Foundations', *Journal of Marketing,* 60(July), 50-68.

Kooreman, Peter and Sophia Wunderink (1997). *The Economics of Household Behavior*, London: Macmillan Press.

Peterson, Robert A., Sridhar Balasubramanian and Bart J. Bronnenberg (1997). 'Exploring the Implications of the Internet for Consumer Marketing,' *Journal of the Academy of Marketing Science,* 25(4), 329-346.

Tirole, Jean (1988). *The Theory of Industrial Organization*, Cambridge, MA: MIT Press.

ACKNOWLEDGMENTS

The author's research is funded by the Dutch Science Foundation (NWO-ESR). The Georgia Tech Research Corporation (GTRC) and the Graphic, Visualization, & Usability Center (GVU) are gratefully acknowledged for making publicly available the results of the 10th WWW User Survey.

APPENDIX

Table A1: Variable base of consumer contribution indicators (n=5022)

Variable	Percentage contributing	Score dimension 1	Score dimension 2
Ordered a product or service by filling out a form on the Web	74%	0.296	0.340
Made a purchase online over $100	46%	0.286	0.326
Created a Web page	58%	0.451	0.095
Customized a Web page	48%	0.386	0.094
Changed a "start-up" page	80%	0.477	0.000
Changed your "cookie" preference	64%	0.505	0.000
Participated in an online chat	64%	0.215	0.226

Table A2: Product category variables analyzed in probit model (n=645)[a]

Product	Digitization costs	Modularization costs	Internet process costs	Information asymmetry
Hardware	-1	1	1	0
Software	1	1	1	0
Wine	-1	-1	0	-1
Generic groceries	-1	-1	-1	1
Branded groceries	-1	-1	-1	1
Recreational equipment	-1	0	0	0
Flowers	-1	1	0	-1
Magazines	0	0	1	0
Books	-1	-1	-1	-1
Video	-1	-1	-1	-1
Music CD's/tapes	1	0	0	-1
Concerts and plays	-1	0	-1	-1
Travel	0	0	0	-1
Electronics	-1	1	1	0
Autos	-1	0	0	0
Precious metals	-1	-1	1	-1
Jewelry	-1	-1	1	-1
Investment choices	1	1	0	-1
Stock market quotes	1	1	1	-1
Banking	1	1	0	0
Insurance	1	1	0	-1
Legal services	1	1	1	-1
Clothing/shoes	-1	0	0	1
Real estate	-1	-1	-1	-1

[a] Classification coding by the author

Chapter 11

The Theory Behind the Role of Leverage and the Strategic Alignment of Organisations While Creating New Markets (Internet Marketing and E-Commerce)

S.I. Lubbe
Vista University, South Africa

The quality of "alignment" is like the well-timed swoop of a falcon that enables it to strike and destroy its victim (With acknowledgment to Sun Tzu).

Over the past decade the Internet has taken off and organizations will soon reap benefits on it, as they have never seen. E-commerce will therefore hopefully emerge as an efficient yet effective mode of creating new markets although most managers still doubt the impact and profitability it has. Enabled by global telecommunication networks and the convergence of computing, telecom, entertainment, and publishing industries, e-commerce is supplanting (maybe replacing) traditional commerce. In the process it is creating new opportunities and challenges for today's businesses, creating new market structures, and changing the alignment of the organisation. Managers of tomorrow must therefore understand what e-commerce is; how the approach to this concept will be; and how it will affect the leverage of the organisation.

The questions could therefore be asked: What is the return on investment (ROI) on e-commerce? What is the effect of e-commerce on the strategic alignment of the organisation? and what is the leverage effect of the strategic alignment on the organisation? This research will be written explaining what leverage and e-commerce is and how this could be used to create new markets and to improve the strategic alignment of the organisation. Some factors that could be used to improve and affect e-commerce and the integration and development of business strategies are:

- *There is nothing absolute about Internet traffic measurement;*
- *The false claims to Internet traffic do not help to improve the marketing approach by organisations;*
- *There is no method that anyone can agree to that is the best way to measure Internet traffic;*
- *There are so many influencing factors and each one can influence the leverage on the e-commerce approach of any organisation;*
- *The off-line reading capacity of Internet browsers can affect e-commerce positively and should be kept in mind;*
- *Internal traffic can affect leverage badly.*

INTRODUCTION

Over the past decade the Internet has grown a lot and it is possible that organizations will soon reap benefits from using it, as they have never seen. E-commerce, as one of the 'products' of the Internet will therefore hopefully emerge as an efficient yet effective mode of conducting global commerce although most managers still doubt the impact and profitability it has. Enabled by global telecommunication networks and the convergence of computing, telecom, entertainment, and publishing industries, e-commerce is supplanting (maybe replacing) traditional commerce. In the process it is creating new opportunities and challenges for today's businesses, creating new market structures, and changing the alignment of the organisation. All organizations are challenged by an increasing focus on delivery speed and by an increasing degree of uncertainty. The question is: How do organizations keep up while still delivering business value?

The establishment of linkage between business and IT objectives has also consistently been reported as one of the key concerns of IS managers (Reich & Benbasat, 1996). They argued that there is firstly a need to clarify the nature of the linkage construct (socially and intellectually) and secondly to report on a project that was developed to test the social dimension of this linkage. It is important that all executives are involved during the establishment of the linkage because it could create a better understanding of each other's long-term visions and self-reported rating of the linkage and alignment. Reich & Benbasat argued that understanding of current objectives and shared vision for the utilization of IT are proposed as potential measures for all aspects of the reported social dimension of linkage and alignment.

This chapter will therefore address the importance of leverage on the strategic alignment of organizations. The chapter will firstly look at the strategic dimension of IT in the organization. Next, the chapter will address the issue of IT forecasting, IT alignment and e-commerce, the leverage effect and the measurement of alignment while keeping the effect of leverage in mind.

APPROACH TO THIS STUDY

This chapter will use the interpretive approach to research as an alternative to the more traditional positivist approach. By using the interpretive approach this chapter refers to such procedures as those associated with inferential statistics, hermeneutics, and phenomenology. The framework proposed is to formulate a specific goal (the Internet, e-commerce and Internet marketing), subject to certain constraints. This approach will call for the active role of people in strengthening a truly collaborative research effort to maintain a peaceful coexistence between all the boundaries. Behaviours such as pointlessness, absurdness or confusion can play a role during the alignment of the strategies in the organization. The phenomenological approach will therefore help with the validity of the interpretation that this chapter will conduct.

THE STRATEGIC DIMENSION OF THE ORGANIZATION

Being competitive in the next decade will depend on the effective application of information systems (IS) and e-commerce. Organizations also need to take a strategic perspective to ensure that investment in IS is contributing to the organization's business strategy. Increasingly, IS is therefore being used by innovative organizations to facilitate the alignment of technology strategies now that re-engineering has lost some of its lustre.

It can be argued that competitive advantage should be based on the capabilities of the organization. Competitive advantages are produced (Sohn, 1998) by organizational learning processes. The organizational learning processes obtain knowledge from IS, interpret, distribute to the organization, and memorize the knowledge. In order to have competitive advantage most organizations should have unique resources and capabilities. These resources and capabilities could help with the alignment of the strategies of the organization. Organizational learning therefore provides the opportunities to improve the existing IS and eventually help with better alignment of the strategies.

Whenever a positive culture exists employees are encouraged to learn and be ready to accept new information or strategies and this could eventually also help with better alignment of strategies. Ulrich & Lake (1990) as cited by Sohn noted that organizational capabilities have four components, that is shared mindset, management and human resources practices, capacity for change and leadership. These organizational capabilities have all the ability to affect alignment and should be kept in mind when alignment is discussed. Sohn argues that IS influences organizational learning and that each process of organizational learning is affected and adjusted by IS. These adjustments would affect the alignment of all strategies and should be kept in mind by the executives.

Organizations should utilize a set of measurements that could be used to measure key business goals and the results should be used to quantify its performance and emphasize its role in orchestrating alignment with all the strategies. In an age when cost-cutting and adding competitive value lie more squarely on the shoulders of the IS department it is no longer enough to successfully deploy systems – they should also be part of the alignment of all the strategies. Using metrics enables IS to spotlight its value to get additional funding for future technology projects and ensure that everything aligns. There had been lots of questions on whether IS contributes to the business and how efficient the organization is in aligning all strategies. Nobody had been able to effectively answer these questions. The tricky part of this question is how to align all strategies or measuring the contribution IT (including Internet marketing) makes to the organization.

The use of IT in organizations is subject to various kinds of risk and this is part of the alignment of all the strategies (Bandyopadhyay et al., 1999). As spending on IT rises organisations become increasingly technology-dependent and consequently become highly vulnerable to the risks of IT failure and eventual failure of the organisation. Risk management of IT is therefore one of the important issues facing IS executives today. A framework, as discussed by Bandyopadhyay et al., concentrates on the sequential linkage of the four components of risk management that make up the entire system of IT risk management.

According to them, this approach is an improvement because it enables managers to move smoothly from one component to another by identifying and understanding the possible courses of action in the different steps. What these managers should keep in mind is that the four steps could affect the alignment of IT although some of the external threats such as disasters are difficult to control and managers should acknowledge that these could affect alignment of the strategies. Risk-reducing measures should therefore keep in mind that the eventual alignment of IT should be enforced. The key to understanding strategic risks is dependent on the organization's ability to foresee the long-term benefits from a new system, assess the resources and capabilities of its potential competitors, assess its own financial strength, and align its IT strategy with its overall business strategy (Bandyopadhyay et al., 1999).

Organizational strategy provides the vision of where any organization needs to go. The problem is that many organizations focus too much on tactics and operations while the real value of IS is to open new opportunities to make money (such as e-commerce) to enter new markets such as e-commerce, and to use Internet marketing to induce potential customers to use the organizations products. Organizations could derive directly the IT and operational objectives from the overall objectives, ensuring that the IS and business strategies are aligned. One of the problems organisations face is that objectives and strategies can change according to market dynamics (e-commerce and Internet marketing).

Senior managers need a clear vision of the competitive impact of IS and how it will affect the alignment of IS. Business strategy provides the vision of where the organization wants to go like e-commerce and Internet marketing. It should be possible to ensure that technology objectives and operational objectives could be derived directly from the organization's corporate objectives, ensuring that the business and IS organizations are focused on the same goals and that alignment exists. Managers must keep in mind that a life cycle will provide an important perspective of the formulation of these strategies because each phase of the life cycle has distinct characteristics that affect the operation of the business. Each of these phases could 'experience' a gap and managers should ensure that leverage does not make these gaps bigger during any of these phases. These performance gaps should be managed and the organization should determine its overall market posture considering its relative position in the industry.

To forecast the incremental leverage effect likely to result from implementing alternative alignment planning, organizations should structure profile measures concentrating on industry market potential, relevant industry sales and real market share. E-commerce and Internet marketing should ensure that everyone who could reasonably be expected to use the product is using the product as often as possible and to its fullest extent. The problem however is that visitors' numbers as claimed by Internet Service Providers (ISP) cannot be verified, and until that can be done, will CEOs surely look at Internet marketing and the alignment factor as things that cannot be reconciled.

These gaps, as mentioned before, can contribute positively or negatively towards the alignment of the strategy of the organization and it can affect the actual performance of the organization during Internet marketing and the IT strategy of the organization. These gaps are:

- Product line gap: Introducing improved or new products that should ensure that the organization could compete on the Internet.
- Distribution gap: This is where e-commerce and Internet Marketing can help to expand the coverage, intensity, and exposure of distribution. This can help to better align the IT strategy and that of the organization.
- Usage gap: The Internet should help to induce current users to try the product and encourage users to increase their usage.
- Competitive gap: This is where e-commerce and the Internet marketing approach of the organization can make inroads into the market position of competitors as well as product substitutes.

The future marketing approach that can be used as a lever by the organization can be increased (and the alignment of the strategies of the organization can be improved) by increasing the organization's industry market potential, by increasing relevant industry sales while maintaining the present market share or by improving the organization's real market share at the expense of the competitor's sales.

Implications for IT Business Value During the Alignment of IS and Business Strategy

Tallon & Kraemer (1998) note that it had been argued that organizations' inability to realize sufficient value from their IT investment is because of an absence of strategic alignment. They cited Child (1992), who argued that the content of alignment should be a series on intersecting and mutually consistent choices across domains such as business strategy, IS strategy, organizational infrastructure and processes and IS infrastructure and processes. Other authors noted that these domains do not allow considerations of strategic alignment as a continuous process nor does it consider the management practices used in moving an organization towards alignment. There are tools available to oversee and manage the content and process of alignment.

According to Tallon & Kraemer (1998) there are a number of benefits associated with process-level measures of strategic alignment. Process-level measures are likely to yield greater insights into where the organization is misaligned, helping to isolate bottlenecks and other impediments to IT business value within the organization. If strategic alignment was measured at the organization level, IS and business managers might simply know that their organization was misaligned, but would not have sufficient information to isolate the source of the misalignment. It would be different if the organization adopted a process-level perspective and the strategy could be presented as a series of activities within each business process. Strategy can be described as a series of intersecting activities; it fits neatly with the definition of a process as a sequence or ordered set of activities. This would indicate that the organization should avoid having to force-fit strategy into one of the established generic strategy types and this could have a similar effect on the Internet marketing strategy organisations have to adopt. Measuring IS and business strategy at the process level allows organizations to take a closer look at key activities within each process configuration and to look at the IS that support those activities.

Opportunities for strategic alignment will arise if technological resources are directed towards the maintenance, improvement and creation of capabilities that underlie the business strategy. A link should therefore be established between resources and capabilities. It must be stressed that strategic alignment is not an event but a process of continuous adaptation and change, and it must be noted that the assignment of IS resources to capabilities must be continuously reevaluated to prevent the organization slipping into a state of misalignment. Organizations must also keep in mind that the ever-increasing pace of industrial, social, political and environmental change underscores the importance of strategic alignment. IT resources should thus be utilised to the fullest, ensuring effective use of IT.

Tallon et al. (1999) discovered a relationship between business value and strategic alignment in a sense that an absence of strategic alignment can lead to reduced payoffs from IT investment. Their analysis also found that the IS department plays a key role in enabling an organization to convert strategic alignment into higher levels of IT business value. It can be argued that as organizations focus their efforts on achieving intangible impacts in areas such as innovations (for example e-commerce) and customer relations (especially on the Internet), evaluating these impacts should therefore become a priority.

Information and the Internet's Influence on Alignment

Companies incessantly produce and use information, acquired by a variety of means, in part because it is perceived as a source of development. On the other hand, industries and organisations need accurate and up-to-date information about companies and their financial performance as well as reports on political, economic and market trends embracing environments such as manufacturing, wholesale and retail, government, etc., allowing many different people in different organizations to use this information. The information is important for things such as the operation of the organization and also alignment of strategies. In times of economic stringency information services seem to be regarded as the least essential arm of the organization. The magnitude and complexity of the business market are also largely unknown to the average customer, and very few businesses have the machinery to collect and coordinate information from a variety of sources and to apply it towards improving organizational decision making and alignment of strategies.

THE IMPORTANCE OF DECISIONS AND DECISION FRAMEWORKS ON STRATEGIC ALIGNMENT

A decision is a position, an opinion, or a judgement reached after consideration, according to the dictionary. It is of importance to note that the definition does not state anything about logical or illogical analysis or about good or bad results. Decisions are neither good or bad until put within the context of a decision framework on strategic alignment (Cutter Consortium, 1999).

The decision framework on strategic alignment should be an organized sequence of decisions that managers must make. Every decision should have a demarcation of the technical terms that could help outline the decision, and managers should also weigh organizational and technical issues (in other words issues that affect alignment) and make choices about products, IT investment, processes and resources. Without a context, decisions are meaningless – for example, to invest in newer models of hardware means nothing without understanding the framework within which the alignment decision was made. To understand the decision framework for strategic alignment is a prerequisite to delivering successful alignment. The decision-making process would affect successful alignment of strategies and would have to include answers to questions such as (Highsmith, 1999):

- What types of decisions need to be made?
- Who (person or group) makes each type of decision?
- How does the organization create sustainable decisions?

The decision framework for strategic alignment should consist of contents, context and process and should be followed closely. The content part is the information and knowledge while the context part is the circumstances such as e-commerce, Internet marketing and other events. Process defines how participants, during the strategic alignment process arrive at the decision of approaching the alignment. The decision to purchase a software product with known defects is an event that could affect strategic alignment. The circumstances (all IT investment plans such as quality goals, competition, etc.) provide the context that shapes how the decision was made to approach the alignment of all strategies.

IT FORECASTING PLANS
FOR OBSOLESCENCE

It is hard to make forecasts without offending both those who prepare them and those who receive them. The same could be said about the alignment of the strategies of the organization. As the organization approaches a wave of alignment, its time for honest estimates about the returns that organizations can get from different uses of scarce resources – financially and human – in the next decade. Short-term align-ments might work out because it is easy to suppress the knowledge that people affect the marketing of goods on the Internet. On the other hand, when organizations align these strategies on the longer term, organizations tend to under-predict the rate and extent of technology change because of the gap that exists. Surrounded by in-place IT assets that represent gruelling effort, sizeable investment and endless sleepless nights to align the strategies, few of the organizations are daring enough to say that the pioneering alignment of strategies today could be tomorrow's obsolete trash and the cycle will have to start all over again.

Bloodgood & Salisbury (1998) claim that organizations may find themselves in a position of needing to change the manner in which they operate. These changes could eventually affect alignment and should be kept in mind. According to them there are two characteristics, the degree of knowledge creation, transfer and protection and the degree of tacitness of the organization's knowledge, which are considered the most influential in determining the success of the use of IT in facilitating strategic change. It must be remembered that any change in strategy will also facilitate a change in the alignment of the organization's strategy and should be kept in mind.

Organisations that use a strategy of knowledge creation focus on creativity and experimentation to construct new knowledge that can be used to develop new products and services. The argument can be used that new services such as Internet marketing can and will affect the alignment of the strategies and should help with competitive advantage. Bloodgood & Salisbury argue that to understand tacit knowledge is important to understand how strategic change may be accomplished and how it can be supported by IT. They claim that reconfiguring with new resources combines both tacit and explicit knowledge in an effort to create something new and somewhat difficult to imitate. This new and difficult to imitate creation would have to be in alignment and this is what managers have to keep this in mind while planning the knowledge creation.

Long-range alignment and forecasts need unbiased evaluation of the use of technologies in actions such as e-commerce and Internet marketing, but users must remember that everything will change drastically during the next three years. If organizations do not align their strategies the alternative is to go out of business. The question that they must ask before they align the strategies is "What would they do if they were starting from scratch?" Competitors might just be doing that and they can compare at the same time what influence the e-commerce aspect of business could have on the organization.

When it comes to putting new business computing systems and applications such as e-commerce "progress" cannot be measured in terms of distance from where the organization started. This measurement would also measure how far the organization has gone along the road to align the strategies unless the organization cannot see where they are going. This 'blind' travelling could be because the organization did not align all their strategies. Well-planned journeys (alignment, etc.) make provision for measuring how much in line the alignment of the strategies are and how much further the organization could go before the alignment is out of shape and the resources would have to be monitored measuring the effect of e-commerce and Internet marketing.

The developments ahead include a lot of opportunities for organizations and as such create chances for development managers to deliver unprecedented value to the organizations. There are new practices worldwide that organizations could embrace in a number of ways. There are tools available such as Lean Development and Leadership-Collaboration Management that could be used. These tools should challenge the manager to question traditional ways and ensure that the manager creates an IT environment in which the organization can thrive.

BPR has lost some of the impetus and it is important to note that IS and organizational executives are again concentrating on aligning strategies (technology and corporate). Organization still struggle to align these – especially to match the two, and it seems most of the times as if the two are on opposite ends of the string. The IS budget is like a hole but in no way is it ever going to be filled, and also getting the right people for the IT department is a problem. Most of the times this could cause obsolescence because participating organizations do not always realize that achieving IT alignment involves not only personal dynamics but also some physical dynamics.

ORGANIZATION-IT ALIGNMENT AND E-COMMERCE

Aligning business and IT strategies continues to be an important management issue. The problem is that, according to the Cutter Consortium (1999), 65% of organizations have no e-commerce strategy while 25% of organizations have not yet developed an overall e-commerce strategy. Only 4.2% of the organizations contacted do have an e-commerce strategy. It is obvious from their figures that most organizations do not take e-commerce seriously and that this, once the affect has hit the organizations, would affect their alignment decisions. The Cutter Consortium claimed that many organizations have, however, noted the role that the Internet can play but they have not taken the steps necessary to fully realize its potential and again this would affect the alignment of their strategies should they try to realize these effects. E-commerce will affect the alignment of the organization and that people do not know what the initial and eventual effect will be. Technologies, however, affect all organizations – even the smallest one. While being able to pose an opportunity, e-commerce also poses a threat to the organizations and managers need to recognize all the factors that affect e-commerce, IT alignment and Internet marketing.

There is however, no framework that can be used by organizations to align strategies while doing e-commerce and Internet marketing. Some of the impediments on this alignment are: download delays, limitations in the interface, inadequate measurements of Internet traffic and successes, security weaknesses and lack of standards on the Internet. On the other hand, the results for the organization could be positive in the fact that the organization experiences improved usage of the effectiveness of the organization's resources and improved return on the investment in data, software applications, technology and IT staff—in other words, improved quality.

The Internet had been promoted as the essential way of doing business lately but it is still a retail medium (Whiteley, 1999). Organizations that establish successful Internet selling operations will need effective alignment and good logistics on the supply side of their operations. Organizations should remember that e-commerce is commerce enabled by the Internet-era technologies. These technologies are:

- Electronic markets
- Electronic data interchange
- Internet Commerce and analogous public ICT systems

In theory, the use of the Internet should give the consumer the opportunity to bypass the intermediary and, with appropriate interfaces, directly affect alignment. Any of the e-commerce operations should affect the alignment of all strategies and should not be resisted by the organization or the people working in the organization. Organizations trading on the Internet, if they are able to build up a substantial business operation and align their strategies, will need to be slick in all aspects of their business. Organizations with wide ambitions would also have to plan carefully in order to align all their strategies. Internet commerce, however, is seen as the great leveller as the size of the organization would not affect their e-commerce operations. Therefore, if the organization grows, they will have to keep in mind that they need to be backed up by a good decision framework to ensure fast and efficient alignment of the strategies that should be a long-term investment.

On the other hand, many development teams work hard on projects only to be told by their customers that it isn't enough, priorities are incorrect or the results were wrong, and these reactions could affect alignment. Technology changes and developments have been extraordinary in the last couple of years and all of these could also affect alignment. The problem with this is that there seems to be less emphasis on business trends and solutions and more on technology, and this could also affect alignment. Highsmith (1999) argues that in the next decade, application development strategies will be among the most important strategies any corporation will make. He also noted that sometime in the 1990s, software made the transition from an enabler of business processes to a driver of business strategies and thus would be helpful with alignment of IT strategies. According to Highsmith, software is the new economy while the author of this chapter reckons that all IT should be taken into account when aligning all strategies.

Alignment should be taken with the appropriate decision framework that suits the organization in the specific environment. As IT capability evolves, it should enable processes, products and opportunities never considered (like e-commerce). To be able to handle this and to ensure that all technology and business matters can handle this, organizations should ensure that they forge better partnerships with their employees and the decision frameworks they have designed.

In order to achieve the goal of being an organization that achieved alignment and ensures that the organization has aligned properly and WILL stay aligned they need to pay attention to the following key questions:

- What are the business trends that are driven by or are coevolving with e-commerce and Internet marketing?
- What are the key business and IT strategies that are evolving and how does the organization take advantage of this?
- What skills and capabilities are critical to make the transition to the new economy?
- What organization, infrastructure, and management changes are needed to implement e-commerce, Internet marketing and other strategies and how does the organization ensure that they are aligned and stay aligned?
- How does management assemble a decision framework for alignment of all IT strategies and how do they communicate it to all relevant people?

If the Internet (and this includes the e-commerce and Internet side of it) is a strategic business driver, how does the organization give direction to this and what does the organization do to keep the competitive advantage? Business strategy alignment is about innovative ideas and putting these ideas into action more effectively than the same competitors. IT should take a leadership role but it depends on the organization and its culture and the types of strategic plans. Business trends such as market fragmentation, information capacity to treat masses of customers on the Internet, shrinking product lifetimes and convergence of physical products and services are important ones, and the organization needs to concentrate more on these forces that are coevolving with the IT capability and opportunities that spring up.

There are some strategies that can be used to help with alignment because they are highly involved with business initiatives and IT is knowledge creation and sharing, collaboration, and agility. These are all overlapping and supportive of each other. Knowledge creation and sharing (as stated in this article) is the ability to create new knowledge from available information to help with alignment while collaboration is the process of shared creation to draw on the expertise of participants and to be able to create alignment from this collaboration. Agility is the ability of the organization to use new knowledge to adapt to external stimuli and use this to better or ensure total alignment of all strategies. All of these would work better if the staff's motivation were good enough and should be encouraged to ensure that there would be no atrophy.

Alignment is hard to see but managers would know it when they see it. The combination of all these mentioned above should ensure that alignment exists. Knowledge should be there to ensure that there is alignment. The organization should also ensure that all business trends are taken into account when aligning strategies. The question to ask is what skills will be necessary to align IT and organizational strategies. However, if managers really understand what the organization is trying to deliver, then they should be able to align all strategies.

On the other hand, reporting on user statistics on Internet sites is far below the required standards required for any IS department. These could affect the alignment of strategies because nobody can plan in anything that is not certain. That is why many CEOs have lost faith in the Internet as a communication and business medium of the future. Many ISPs cannot tell you why the people have ended up on their site and how long they have stayed. The latest tracking technologies should solve the problem but nobody can guarantee anything; it is like TV – it is a guessing game and although the developers of tracking technology are aware of these problems, they have not found a solution to combat the problems. The problem is to discover what people do when they arrive on the site and if they ever return. This information is invaluable to IS managers and carries a lot of credibility. User tracking on the Internet therefore needs to grow up and start to provide useful information those marketers and IS specialists and executives can use to align all the strategies of the corporation. Some of the problems are that there is nothing absolute about Internet traffic measurement and no one can agree on the best way to measure Internet traffic. The other problem is that publishers can include internal activities in their traffic or they can tamper with log files while the electronic counters are susceptible to server and network congestion and downtime. These facts would obviously affect Internet marketing and alignment of strategies.

Aligning the IS strategy with the organization's goals is also appropriate for those organizations in which there is a vision for items such as e-commerce. E-commerce is part of the actual choice any organization should have – to participate in e-commerce or not. This is where the IS-Department can play a major role – their primary responsibility should be to create opportunities of doing business (e-commerce) and not merely to ensure that the IT is there for the whole organisation.

White & Manning (1998) argued that the percentage of individuals on the Internet using the medium for shopping had increased by about 70% between 1995 and 1996. Users expect to get something of value for free and this type of marketing could affect the alignment of IT strategy with the corporate strategy. Personal opinion should affect the alignment of the strategies. Gender appears to be important in Internet marketing and would have to be kept in mind during alignment of strategies. They argue that it is important to find out how Internet marketing could be improved. Better use of the Internet could help with better alignment as well. Consumer demographics on the Internet could differ from normal demographics (if ever) and should be researched in full. The likelihood of purchasing from an online storefront would help with alignment on a new frontier and should be something that executives should keep in mind.

The explosion of the Internet as a resource for business information in all countries has taken off and has made business people aware of how easily data can be stored in different locations and in different formats that all these topics can use. All this can cause growth and can have an effect on strategic alignment. Some of the pitfalls are the following aspects:

- Cost – it can be very high and the organizations could not afford it.
- Capacity development – lacking strategic capacities.
- Visibility and security – use other providers?
- Inconsistency of telecommunications access – a problem in some areas as the Internet could not always be available.

Executives should communicate the mission of IS to both the people and other managers – this could mean half the battle is won during alignment. It is also important to show other people how the IS department operates because it is important for people to know how problems are being handled. Get feedback on the IS department's role and services they render. Check on end users from time to time —even if they have no problems—just to make sure that everybody knows that your department is around. It is important that communication channels exist that we can use. The inclusion of users during and when a big project is started is also important. Pay special attention to users with special needs and make sure that everybody receives the same amount of help. Make sure that the IS department understands what applications people are using and why they prefer to install their own software.

Gibson et al. (1998) note that with the onset of the 1990s came an unstable business environment, and businesses started to realise that the strategic vision of the business required a dramatic change in their business environment in order to at least maintain their competitive advantage. This meant that everybody had to realign their strategies to be able to stay in the market. According to them, the companies they investigated exhibited a change in strategic vision but these changes could not be reflected in their IS. It could be noted that this could create a problem because if IS cannot reflect the changes in the strategic vision, it would affect the alignment of these. It could be because certain business changes could prevent the advent of developments such as e-commerce and Internet marketing. As noted before, a gap is created and this gap could create a misalignment between the strategic vision of the organization and the route that is being followed. The gap, in this instance, is created by both business and IT dimensions and many of the organizations they investigated acknowledged that their IS was not a good fit for the organization. These companies that they investigated used a variety of approaches to realign the business model and IT with their strategic vision. Gibson et al. (1998) argued that these approaches have gone beyond technical solutions, which although they would eliminate the technical problems would probably not address the business issues, so realignment would not occur. New technology, such as ERP software, combined with business process requires the need to realign both the business model and IT with their strategic vision.

The aim of management should be to try and provide insights into identifying areas that help or hinder the alignment of the strategy for the organization with the IT. Alignment focuses on the activities that management performs to achieve cohesive goals across the organization. Certain activities can also assist in the achievement of the alignment while others are clearly barriers. To achieve this alignment is dynamic and can in a certain way be evolutionary. The alignment requires strong support from management at all levels, good relationships within the organization, strong leadership, points must be emphasized that should be paid attention to and communicated well enough so that all people can and should understand the organization's business environment, at the same time ensuring that the alignment is a success. All enablers and inhibitors should be focused on ensuring successful alignment and therefore all inhibitors should be minimized.

THE EFFECT OF LEVERAGE DURING THE ALIGNMENT OF STRATEGIES

Organizations have to assume that there are some basic definitions that need to be defined in order to ensure that all terminology is clearly understood. There are two types of leverage that managers can use, that is financial leverage and business leverage and there is a connection to both these leverages. Some of the basic definitions that can be used are: asset structure (assets the organization wants to finance or funds that they want to use to expand during e-commerce); financial structure (available funds or possible financing available to the organisation); financial leverage (the ratio of funds from outside the organisation to the total assets of the organisation. The act of borrowing is said to create financial leverage); operating leverage (refers to the extent to which total operating costs vary with changes in the operating revenues and these revenues could be affected with e-commerce); and business risk (financial leverage increases risk because it makes the return realised by the investor more sensitive to any event affecting the performance or the asset purchased).

It is of importance to look at the possible effect of leverage on alignment during IT investment and the expanding e-commerce. The argument could be used that IT assets and the finance of the IT assets as demonstrated could be financed by the use of equity and foreign financing. Leverage is a ratio that is calculated using certain financial figures and these ratios can show any possible investor or manager (especially the IT manager or IT director) how a possible opportunity to obtain funds can have an effect on the organisation and on alignment, as the decision would be a strategy that would affect another strategy.

Financial leverage affects both the analysis of interest and liquidity because of fixed commitments due to the use of funds from outside the organization. If the return on assets were higher than the cost of the debt, management would find that leverage can have a positive effect. Leverage can increase the return on owner's equity but there is a risk factor that managers have to keep in mind. Financial leverage involves the use of funds obtained at a fixed cost in the hope of increasing the return to the owners of the organization. If funds are thus being obtained to help with e-commerce then managers have to keep in mind that a successful project could increase the return on the funds while a negative project will reduce the return on the funds.

Business leverage has to do with the ratio of fixed costs to variable costs. This would have an effect on the profit of the organization. Fixed costs should always be recovered and assets with a fixed base cost should be used in the hope that more profit could be made during any operation. It would be wise for the organization to use financial leverage if profit is stable; otherwise, if the fixed cost represents the majority of the expenses, managers would find that profit is not stable. If customer numbers can not be guaranteed in e-commerce, project managers would find that profit would not be stable. Organizations are warned not to use financial leverage if business leverage plays a big role in organizational strategies. Managers should also remember that certain assets could affect fixed costs negatively. Also, remember that both these leverages could be combined, for example, a high Internet marketing risk could be combined with low financial risks and the other way around. The total risk of the organization could entail a swap between total risk and the expected return on any investment. There are some ratios that could help with leverage:

- Total debt to total assets. This displays the percentage total funds supplied by other people such as creditors. They prefer a low ratio while the owners prefer a big ratio to increase turnover and to keep control of the organization.
- Total interest earned. This ratio tells the organization how much turnover could be lowered without affecting the payment of these interest amounts. This ratio is calculated by dividing gross profit by interest.
- Fixed cost coverage. This ratio shows how the organization can pay fixed costs (interest added to long-term debt). The ratio is planned by calculating a total for profit before tax and tax and rent, and this total is then divided by the total for interest and rent.
- Break-even point is that mark where the total for fixed costs and variable costs is equal to that of the total turnover.
- The degree of financial leverage is calculated by dividing earnings before interest and taxes by earnings before tax minus interest.

There are other ratios that could affect financial or business leverage but are too many to mention and not dealt with during the course of this chapter. It is important to note that organizations should not ignore short-term credit. Some critics claim that short-term debt should be left alone because it might fluctuate a lot and the total cost of this is not known. They, however, should remember that there should be a constant ratio over long- and short-term debt. It would be difficult with e-commerce to calculate the break-even amount of sales that the organization needs because nobody can state for sure what the fixed and variable costs would be. This will affect leverage and one can safely note that e-commerce and Internet marketing would affect the alignment of the organization.

Break-even analysis could be used in three ways to modernise a program or if the organization wants to use a new market such as e-commerce (Internet), to study the effect of extensive build-up of the firm such as globalisation and with new product decisions. Again numbers are the crucial issue as nobody can guarantee the total number of people that would visit the WWW site.

Of importance for the organization is the effect of e-commerce and Internet marketing on leverage and the effect of leverage on the alignment of the organization. The cost to appear in the global market on the Internet could be affected as follows:

- The Internet market is perfect and all 'clickers' could get the correct information; these shoppers and browsers act rationally and no cost per transaction completed exists.
- Personal and manufactured leverages are perfect substitutes and they would affect alignment in equal amounts.
- Corporations and individuals can borrow money at the same rate.
- All organizations on the Internet can be placed in the same risk class so that all classes are homogenous.
- Since it will be difficult to control tax on the Internet it should be assumed that no tax would be levied.
- The average income of any organization can be represented by a variable that could be picked statistically.
  These arguments could be the following:
- The total value of any organization on the Internet should rise with the use of leverage.
- The turnover ratio on the book value of owner's equity should rise with the advent of leverage but should not affect debt of the organization on the Internet
- Leverage should not affect debt unless the organization uses debt to finance the e-commerce and Internet marketing operations.

Certain conditions could be analysed with the help of leverage – such as earnings before interest and taxes and also debt. Because the capital market is not complete it will also affect the capital structure. If organizations take the wrong decisions about leverage and alignment then the following could happen:

- Financing could be applied incorrectly.
- There could be a loss of qualified staff (especially Internet staff).
- Loss of suppliers.
- Loss of sales and the liquation of the organization.
- No financing.

- The loss of the market share – especially on the Internet.
- Formal liquation procedures.

Managers should keep leverage in mind while aligning of the strategies takes place because it could affect the organization adversely.

ORGANIZATIONAL INFORMATION VISUALIZATION – THE USE OF THE DIFFERENT INSTRUMENTS TO MEASURE ALIGNMENT

Customers of the IS department have recognized that the IS department and alignment of strategies are synonymous terms. These could affect measurement of alignment or value derived from the applications support process and eventual alignment. Historically there have been a number of challenges in aligning corporate strategies and creating an objective measurement of alignment improvement over time. It is important that measurement focuses on business objectives— end-user participation and satisfaction, reaching and sustaining alignment, tracking and measuring factors that affect alignment—and communicate alignment improvement. While remaining focused on these reported items, the alignment team must also be able to measure and report on its accomplishments.

They should be able to meet the challenges of being able to objectively measure alignment as performed by the management team and at the same time facilitate a process of continuous improvement of the alignment of the strategies; in other words there should be a process to measure the alignment as performed so far. Managers need to have a metric available that allows them to measure value in terms of business output, and the following are required:

- Good metrics of past and anticipated future Internet strategies
- Sound management
- Detailed and disciplined tracking
- An agreed approach for management
- Good internal communication to all role players.

Measurement should be adaptable to both traditional application support and to enterprise resource planning on alignments. For the alignment team, the measurement approach should provide a focus on the end product – alignment of all strategies (deliverables that provide value to the organization)—rather than simply tracking the alignment of strategies. It also ensures management visibility, in that communications show results in terms of accomplishments and milestones met. It should also provide a highly effective measurement capability that should be objective and reflects measurement capacity and alignment tracking.

Kiani (1998) argues that the current decade has witnessed evolution in the media environment and indicated that e-commerce could grow in importance. The opportunities offered by this new environment are still unknown and it is this fact that organizations should keep in mind while aligning all strategies. Kiani suggests

›

new concepts and models for marketers that should be kept in mind while aligning strategies. Organizations should keep in mind that they all compete in two worlds – a physical world that people can see and a virtual world made of information. It is thus clear that information should play a role while alignment of strategies takes place. The two-way communication channel between consumer and corporation, Kiani suggests, should be incorporated during the alignment process. This communication should be more in the way of dialogue.

The methodology could be to create a database of transaction histories and this database should be incorporated during the alignment process by management. This database would be moving all the time and it would mean that the alignment process would be more difficult and moving all the time to keep track of all factors that could affect alignment. The unit of measurement could be the value of each Internet and normal customer to the organization. Marketing strategy will be measured by changes in the asset value of the customer's base over time. Alignment of the strategies should be more flexible as niches too small to be served profitability could become viable as marketing strategies improve.

Opportunities on the WWW are equal for all players – regardless of size —and this would be affected by the information available to the consumers. Customers could thus help with the alignment of strategies and be a partner of the organization. Organizations have earned the right to the digital relationship and they have to shift their alignment all of the time if they continuously enhance the value they offer consumers. All of this should be kept in mind while measuring and aligning all strategies. Alignment of strategies should keep in mind that strategies on Internet marketing and e-commerce would be how to attract users, engage the users' interest and participation, learn about the preferences of consumers and ensure that there is interaction.

With the flood of data produced by today's IS, organizational decision makers must do something to allow all players to extract the correct knowledge from the available information. Recent advances on the Internet and visualization technologies provide many organizations the capability to start using human visual/spatial capabilities to solve abstract problems found in business and as such the e-commerce aspect of the Internet. This could allow the decision maker to separate the rubbish from the best that there is. To achieve this, organizations must use IT well and increase the value provided to normal and Internet customers. The Internet will force organizations to evaluate how and when they should start to use the Internet to create additional business value to their organization. Some organizations could rely on strategic use of enterprise-wide IT to enhance their competitive position as an established supplier of the goods they are marketing normally and on the Internet.

There are many measurement services that consultants provide. The statement that could be made is that if you cannot measure it you cannot align it. Once the organization establishes some objectives and goals, IS can facilitate them through a set of technology initiatives, and once organizations have that strategic sense, managers can identify criteria as to how this project creates value to the organization and how it can be used to help with alignment.

Many organizations employ the balanced scorecard technique to measure the IS department's overall success in an ongoing process. This scorecard gauges things such as internal stakeholders' satisfaction; it measures the system, rates the value and quality of that work and can be used in measuring and helping with the alignment of the strategies of the organization. The report card is broken into three categories: responsiveness, value and quality. The users rate things such as deliverables, establishment of timelines, accurately identified timelines and whether the solutions meet the expected ROI. This scorecard gives IS employees the opportunity for dialogue with business users if results fall short. The balanced scorecard report card can be used to link the alignment of the strategies regardless of the type of investment that was done. Things such as the business outcomes an organization desires, ensuring that key business holders are involved and the issues around change management would affect alignment. It is therefore about setting realistic, tangible and clearly communicated goals, ensuring that the entire team is speaking the same language and this could help with alignment.

To understand success better, organizations can use the balance scorecard to develop a model of organizational performance that could emphasize the contribution of IT and the Internet to different dimensions of the performance. Some organizations would be able to prove that IT, along with Internet marketing, when properly aligned with the strategies can contribute substantially to the organization's overall success and market leadership. Computer simulation and human thought could help a lot because strategic advantage could be obtained through effective utilization of the natural strengths each of these has to offer to improve the quality of the decision making on outcomes such as e-commerce and Internet marketing.

Instruments That Could be Used to Determine If the Organization's Strategies Are Aligned

The important thing to remember is always to determine if the organization has aligned their strategies, and one such tools that could be used is a questionnaire. The questionnaire could be scored as follows. Count each category and determine what the people think of the alignment of strategies. If there are more not sures or disagrees than agrees then you might have a problem. The steps to be taken would be to ensure that communication lines are open. Table 1, which represents a questionnaire, can help determine this.

The questionnaire available could be used in conjunction with the balanced scorecard approach. The balanced scorecard should keep enterprises such as e-commerce in mind and could be as follows: There should be different categories, combining it closely with the questionnaire, such as customer perspective, innovation and learning perspective, internal business processes perspective and the financial perspective. All of these categories should be discussed or be part of a decision framework where the different topics could include the goals for each perspective, the measurement of each perspective, the metrics being used, the targets and the actual that could be measured. For customer perspective, organiza-

Table 1: An example of a questionnaire that can help determine the level of strategic alignment

Questions	Agree	Disagree	Not sure
1. Executive management is involved in all strategic information decisions and references the formal business and information strategic plans.			
2. Customers, users and industry are regularly surveyed regarding the information needs and problems related to doing business with the organization.			
3. Technology is invested into only after establishing a business use for the decisions.			
4. The decision-making and operational roles of executives, managers and users are overlapping.			
5. Executives, managers and users understand and practice the concepts of managing data at all levels.			
6. Executives, managers and users understand and practice the concepts of changing information into knowledge at all levels.			
7. Information Services uses graphical, easy to understand methods of explaining how knowledge supports the organization's strategy.			
8. IT can help explain to you how the organization uses frameworks to align all strategies.			
9. More than half the IT projects are under budget and on time.			
10. You know exactly how many IT projects are currently being conducted.			
11. You know exactly why and how to use all information and knowledge available.			
12. You know how to apply the decision framework (if available) that will be used for strategic alignment.			

tions need to remember that this could help with better alignment but should not carry as much weight as the internal metrics.

The innovation and learning perspective should be important as this is where new categories, such as e-commerce and Internet marketing, would be added and this would affect the alignment of all strategies. All new innovations and possible innovations should be added here. The internal business perspective should be used, as we need to ensure that employees have kept track of all the perspectives and that they know how to work with data, information and knowledge. The financial perspective should concentrate on increased efficiency, effectiveness and transformation and investment. As different measurement issues exist for these, they should be placed into the BCD and used as and where needed.

SUMMARY

E-commerce will develop a lot over the next decade on the Internet, and it is possible that organizations will reap benefits from using it, as they have never seen. As one of the 'products' of the Internet, Internet marketing and e-commerce will therefore emerge as an efficient yet effective mode of conducting global commerce. The problem is, as mentioned in this chapter, that managers still doubt the impact and profitability it has. In the process it is creating new opportunities and challenges for today's businesses, creating new market structures, and changing the alignment of the organisation. All organizations are challenged by an increasing focus on delivery speed and by an increasing degree of uncertainty. The question: How do organizations keep up while still delivering business value? was hopefully answered.

This chapter has addressed the importance of leverage on the strategic alignment of organizations. The chapter looked at the strategic dimension of IT in the organization and addressed the issue of IT forecasting, IT alignment and e-commerce, the leverage effect and the measurement of alignment while keeping the effect of leverage in mind.

Organisations that survive and thrive in the new economy and use all to ensure that their strategies are aligned are those with better ideas than the rest. These organizations normally produce better products, novel interpretations of the market (e-commerce in this instance), innovative management strategies and the ability to create a unified strategic alignment where pools of talent, both inside and outside the organization, ensure that all stays on track and as the organization moves, the alignment moves to ensure that everything is in 'harmony'.

REFERENCES

Bandyopadhyay K., Mykytyn P. & Mykytyn M. (1999). A framework for integrated risk management in information technology, *Management Decision*, 37(5).

Bloodgood J.M & Salisbury W.D. (1998). If the IT strategy fits wear it: Matching strategic change efforts with IT efforts, *Proceedings of 1998 Americas Conference*, Baltimore, Maryland, August 14-16.

Child (1992). Cited in (1998) *A Process-oriented Assessment of the Alignment of Information Systems and Business Strategy: Implications for Business Value*, Proceedings of 1998 Americas Conference, Baltimore, Maryland, August 14-16.

Cutter Consortium (1999). Weekly e-mail service for IT professionals – *Using IT work units* (dated 14/09/99) and E-*business software practices* (dated 01/09/99).

Gibson N., Holland C. & Light B. (1998). *Identifying Misalignment between Strategic Vision and Legacy Information Systems in Organizations*, Proceedings of 1998 Americas Conference, Baltimore, Maryland, August 14-16.

Highsmith J. (1999). *Thriving in Turbulent Times*, White paper by Cutter Consortium.

Kiani G.R 1998: *Marketing opportunities in the digital world*, Internet Research: Electronic Networking Applications and Policy, Nov, 8(2).

Lubbe S. (1999). *Leverage effect*, Working paper – Department of Computer Science and Information Systems, Vista University, Bloemfontein.

Reich B.H. & Benbasat I. (1996). *Measuring the Linkage between Business and Information Technology Objectives*, MIS Quarterly, 20(1).

Sohn C. (1998). *How Information Systems provide competitive advantage: An Organizational learning perspective*, Proceedings of 1998 Americas Conference, Baltimore, Maryland, August 14-16.

Tallon P.T. & Kraemer K.L. (1998). *A Process-oriented Assessment of the Alignment of Information Systems and Business Strategy: Implications for Business Value*, Proceedings of 1998 Americas Conference, Baltimore, Maryland, August 14-16.

Tallon P.P, Kraemer K.L. & Gurbaxani V. (1999). *Fact or Fiction: The reality behind Executive Perceptions of IT Business Value*, Research paper July 29.

Ulrich & Lake (1990) *cited* by Sohn C. 1998 in *How Information Systems provide competitive advantage: An Organizational learning perspective*, Proceedings of 1998 Americas Conference, Baltimore, Maryland, August 14-16.

Whiteley D. (1999). *Merging Electronic Commerce Technologies for Competitive advantage*, Proceedings of 1998 Americas Conference, Baltimore, Maryland, August 14-16.

White G.K. & Manning B.J. (1998). *Commercial WWW site appeal: how does it affect online food and drink consumers' purchasing behaviour?*, Internet Research: Electronic Networking Applications and Policy, Nov, 8(1).

Chapter 12

Beyond CPMs and Clickthroughs: Understanding Consumer Interaction with Web Advertising

Patrali Chatterjee
Rutgers University, USA

Measuring effectiveness of online ads is of critical importance to the survival of the Web as an advertiser-supported medium. Present efforts in measuring performance of Web ads are concentrated on adapting measures used in traditional media to the online medium. However these measures do not take into account the unique interactive characteristics of the medium and the differences in how consumers process advertising stimuli on the Web. Further, ad processing and performance measurement capabilities differ across various advertising formats on the Web. This research proposes a framework to investigate how consumers interact with different advertising formats on the Web and identify metrics that reflect how effectively the ad is processed.

INTRODUCTION

Advertising revenues are critical to survival of many commercial Web sites on the Web. Since advertiser-supported Web sites bear important parallels to traditional media in the physical world, established advertising practices can be borrowed from traditional media environments to assist initial commercial efforts. However, the complexity of the medium and the wide variety of ad formats used online (IAB/CASIE ,1998) make direct adoption of performance metrics problematic. As advertisers and marketers debate the best ways to measure response to Web ads, rate cards currently use aggregate ad reach (CPM impressions or pageviews) and ad click (clickthroughs) measures to value advertising space for most ad formats. The fact that the impression and ad clickthrough measures have different implications in terms of effectiveness across various ad formats is largely ignored. A static banner ad impression and an interstitial impression lead to different processing outcomes – that rate cards ignore. For example, a banner ad that is clicked by a consumer out of interest offers a positive value to the advertiser compared to a click on a interstitial ad that may occur due to consumer interest or because the consumer must close the ad to continue browsing. In the former case, clickthrough measures are a measure of consumer interest in the advertiser's brand; in the latter the advertiser has no idea. This lack of understanding of how impression and clickthrough measures correspond to communication outcomes in various Web ad formats and reports of declining clickthrough rates is contributing to increasing skepticism regarding the value of Web advertising.

In this chapter we discuss the various ad formats used by practitioners in the Web advertising industry. We use the information processing framework to investigate how consumer interaction with ads relates to communication outcomes that are of interest to marketers. Further, we identify the minimum (and predictable) measurable outcomes that the various ad formats are able deliver. The role of tracking technology in measurement of interactive outcomes and the implications for use of ad formats will be discussed. Figure 1 presents an outline of our approach for deriving response measures for ad formats at advertiser-supported Web sites.

Figure 1. Framework for relating ad processing to performance measures

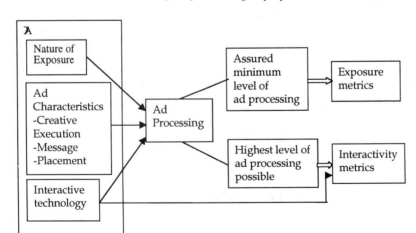

ADVERTISING FORMATS ON THE WEB

The Web with its audio, video, and interactive capabilities offers tremendous opportunity for effective and creative development of a variety of advertising formats. In this section we discuss ten ad formats commonly used by advertiser-supported sites on the Web. Together they account for 99% of ads posted at advertiser-supported Web sites at this time. Descriptions of ad formats can be found in Zeff and Aronson (1999). Since research on information processing implications of Web ad formats is lacking we classify them in terms of basic characteristics – nature of exposure, coverage of visual field and scope of interaction. Despite the rapid pace with which advertising formats on the Web are evolving, response measurement of most existing and future ad formats can be investigated in this framework. Table 1 shows how ad formats differ on the classification criteria and the metrics used to measure performance by the Web advertising industry.

Table 1: Advertising formats on the Web

Ad format	Nature of exposure	Coverage of visual field	Scope of interaction	Measurement unit used
Buttons & Static or animated banners	Incidental	Partial	Limited to click	CPM impressions, clickthroughs
HTML banners	Incidental	Partial	Radio buttons, Pull-down menu	CPM impressions, clickthroughs
Rich media banners	Incidental	Partial	Radio buttons, Pull-down menus, fill-out forms, search, complete transactions	CPM impressions, how long consumers interacted with it
Interstitials	Incidental	Complete	Limited to click	CPM impressions
Sponsorships & Advertorials	Incidental	Partial or complete	Limited to click	CPM impressions
Text links or listings	Incidental	Partial	Limited to click	CPM impressions
Ad navigation toolbars	Incidental	Partial	Limited to click	Number of down-loads, usage time
Browser bookmarks	On demand	Partial	Limited to click	CPM impressions
Ad cursors	Incidental	Partial	Limited to click	Number of downloads
Target ads	On demand	Complete	Click to advertiser site, search and full range of inter-active functions	Number of unique visitors, number of clicks to advertiser site, time spent, purchase and other behavioral outcomes.

Nature of Exposure: Exposures to ads on the Web may be incidental (similar to ads in traditional media) or on demand. Ad formats that are incidentally exposed or passive ads (Chatterjee, Hoffman and Novak, 2000), are typically encountered while the consumer is browsing through content at the Web site and hence controlled by the publisher. For these ad formats, exposure (while predictable by the publisher) does not necessarily imply that the consumer has noticed the ad or is aware of it unless it covers a significant portion of the computer screen (or the consumer's visual field). Hence, impressions merely indicate the number of opportunities for the ad to be noticed. If a consumer clicks on a passive ad, the consumer is either transferred to the advertiser's site or is exposed to the advertiser's page, what we term the *"target ad,"* dedicated to the advertiser's message (Chatterjee, 1996). A *clickthrough* is then recorded in the server access log.

Exposure to ads that are only displayed on consumers' demand or target ads (Chatterjee, Hoffman and Novak, 2000), in response to a click are under consumer control and hence performance numbers cannot be guaranteed by the publisher. Since exposure is solicited by the consumer, exposure necessarily implies that the consumer is aware of or has noticed the ad and hence has attended to it.

Coverage of Visual Field: Some ad formats occupy a relatively small portion of the screen (or consumer's visual field) and compete with other information on the Web page for the consumer's attention. Consumers can easily avoid seeing or noticing these ad formats (termed "ad blindness" in Web advertising industry) compared to more intrusive formats that occupy the entire screen. Hence, the probability that an ad will automatically get noticed and attended depends on its coverage of the consumer's visual field. Thus ads that occupy a relatively small portion of the visual field and lead to a click are more effective in delivering consumers interested in the advertiser's brand than those that occupy a greater portion of the computer screen.

Scope of Interaction: Interactivity emerges as a unique characteristic distinguishing advertising on the Web from that in other traditional media. Steuer (1992) defines interactivity as "the extent to which users can participate in modifying the form and content of a mediated environment in real time". Ad formats differ in the scope of interaction they allow. This may range from a limited click response in static banner ads to a full range of interactive features in rich media ads. Interactive technologies like InterVU (www.intervu.com), Narrative Communications' Enliven Technology (www.enliven.com), and Macromedia's Flash (www.macromedia.com/software/flash) allow users to interact by providing search facilities, audio and video capabilities, and the ability to play games, enter contests, send e-mail and complete purchase transactions through the banner itself without ever leaving the publisher's site.

A MODEL OF INTERACTION WITH WEB ADVERTISING FORMATS

Research in advertising indicates that in order to produce a response, all advertising stimuli must proceed through three stages: exposure, attention and processing (cf., Mitchell 1983), in order. The hierarchical model of ad processing (Greenwald and Levitt, 1984) suggests that if processing at one level fails to evoke the next highest level, processing of the ad is terminated and the capacity is allocated to some other task (i.e., navigating editorial information at the publisher Web site).

Chatterjee, Hoffman and Novak (2000) propose a model of a consumer's interaction with banner (passive) ad stimuli during network navigation at an ad-supported publisher Web site. A session at a Web site starts with the first access of any page at the site and ends with last page accessed before the consumer exits the site. Figure 2 depicts our proposed model of interaction with Web advertisement. Interaction with an ad stimulus starts when a consumer is exposed to a Web page that has an ad on it representing the opportunity to view the ad (or OTS).

If exposure to the ad is incidental and the ad occupies a relatively small portion

Figure 2. Model of consumer interaction with Web advertisement

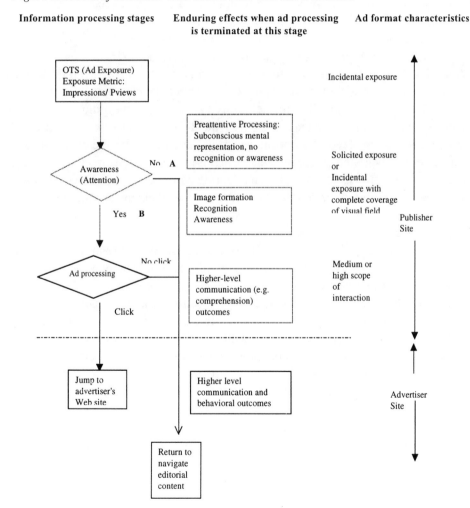

*Ad format characteristics that predict that a particular information processing outcome will necessarily occur.
Note: Objects with solid lines represent behavioral stages that may be tracked with clickstream data

of the screen (as in banner ads, text links, ad cursors or ad navigation toolbars, see Table 1) the consumer may either notice the ad or be unaware of its presence. Further processing of ad information is terminated if the consumer ignores the ad and continues navigating editorial content (A in Figure 2). In this case, research in preattentive processing would indicate that information that is present but is secondary is processed at a subconscious level without awareness or recognition (Janiszewski, 1993). Eye-tracking studies investigating awareness of banner ads have found that consumers do not see as many as half of the banner ads they have been exposed to (Dreze and Hussherr, 1999), termed "banner blindness" by the online advertising industry (Benway 1998). On the other hand, if the ad covers the entire screen (e.g., an interstitial) the consumer has no option but to notice the ad. If exposure to the ad is on demand, for example if the consumer clicks on a banner or text link to view a target ad awareness and attention is certain to occur. Hence while all ad formats provide opportunities to notice and see, awareness and recognition of an ad is assured if the ad is solicited or it covers the entire visual field of the consumer.

Further processing of the ad is done at the divided or focal attention level. Attentional capacity is required to determine what the ad is about and to decide if further processing or clicking on the ad will contribute to achieving the consumer's goals. In this stage, attending to the passive ad becomes the primary task, with editorial information relegated to the background. Once a consumer has noticed the ad, awareness and recognition occur regardless of whether he/she clicks on it. Ad information processing will be terminated at this level if the consumer does not click and moves attentional focus back to navigating editorial information (B in Figure 2). Hence attending to the ad is a necessary, but not sufficient condition for further processing or click to occur. Clicking is possible only if it offers an option to interact with the ad format.

Higher level processing of ad information leading to communication and behavioral outcomes is possible if sufficient information content is available (as in interstitials and target ads) and/or the consumer is able to interact with the ad (as in rich media banners and text links). Table 2 discusses the information processing stages that always occur and outcomes possible for the various ad formats on the Web. The consumer may evaluate brand information (brand processing strategy) or merely satisfy her/his curiosity or perhaps enter a sweepstakes (non-brand processing strategy). Higher level communication outcomes are not possible for static banners, ad cursors, ad navigation toolbars and browser bookmarks because of their limited informational content and scope of interaction. Behavioral outcomes are only possible for ad formats offering interactive options. Behavioral outcomes can be tracked with clickstream data and can be interpreted unambiguously; however, value of communication outcomes is subject to speculation. This lack of unobtrusive and objective measures of communication outcomes make effectiveness of ad formats that do not offer interactive features especially those hard to gauge and quantify.

Table 2: Ad information processing stages for Web ad formats

Ad Format	Ad Information Processing Stages			
	OTS (exposure)	Awareness *(attention)*	*Communication processing outcomes*	*Behavioral outcomes*
Static or animated banners	Always Occurs	Consumer controlled, not predictable	Minimal -Awareness and Recognition	None
HTML banners	Always Occurs	Consumer controlled, not predictable	Awareness, recognition, comprehension	Search and limited inform-ation exchange
Rich media banners	Always Occurs	Consumer controlled, not predictable	Awareness, recognition, comprehension, elaboration.	Purchase and search outcomes
Interstitials	Always Occurs	Always Occurs	Awareness, recognition, comprehension, elaboration.	None
Sponsorships & Advertorials	Always Occurs	Always Occurs	Awareness, recognition, comprehension, elaboration.	None
Text links or listings	Consumer controlled, not predictable	Predictable	Awareness, recognition, comprehension, elaboration.	Purchase and other behavioral outcomes
Ad navigation toolbars	Always Occurs	Predictable	Awareness, and recognition	None
Browser bookmarks	Consumer controlled, not predictable	Predictable	Awareness, recognition, comprehension, elaboration.	Purchase, search and other behav-ioral outcomes
Ad cursors	Always	Always	Awareness & Recognition	None
Target ads	Consumer controlled, not predictable	Always Occurs	Awareness, recognition, comprehension, elaboration	Purchase, search and other behav-ioral outcomes

WEB ADVERTISING MEASUREMENT MODELS

Consumer response to online advertisements can be tracked by analyzing the "log file" from which clickstream data is derived. In some ad formats (see Table 1) interactive technologies[1] allow marketers to track behavioral and transactional outcomes within the ad itself (e.g., Thinking Media's ActiveAds (www.thethinkingmedia.com/activeads/activeads.htm). Outcome-based metrics must be developed by specifying exactly what the marketer would like the ad to do. Examples of outcomes that can be tracked include purchase, software or document downloads, sending e-mail, filling out forms, or answering surveys. However communication outcomes present considerable challenge in terms of quantifying the value of an ad exposure.

Novak and Hoffman (1996) offer a detailed review of advertising metrics in the Web medium. They propose exposure metrics and interactivity metrics at ad, page and vehicle level. Exposure metrics of reach and frequency of Web ads namely banner impressions or page views, are based on the one-to-many communication model underlying traditional media and indicate that a visitor has had the opportunity to view an advertisement (page or site). Currently, CPM banner impressions are the dominant approach, with over 86% of Web publishers (IAB, 1999) using it as a basis for pricing advertising space. However, the value of an impression varies based on the ad format for which it is measured. For example, a static banner ad impression represents an OTS with very low probability that a consumer noticed it; however, an interstitial impression guarantees awareness of the ad by the consumer.

Interactivity metrics of duration time, interaction depth and width are based on the many-to-many communication model underlying the Web and indicate the extent to which the visitor actively engages with the Web content or ad. Unlike exposure metrics, interactivity metrics seek to quantify the quality of a consumer's navigation experience in terms of 'flow' (Novak, Hoffman and Yung, 2000) and represent a more accountable measure of communication and learning outcomes of the ad information. Collaboration between marketers, consumer psychologists and Web technology developers is required to identify ways in which interactivity metrics can be derived from clickstream data.

IMPLICATIONS FOR PRACTICE

This research provides a descriptive overview of consumer interaction with ads in the Web medium. We propose a typology to classify the wide variety of ad formats online in terms of their nature of exposure, coverage of visual field and scope of interaction. Ad formats differ in the way consumers interact with them. Hence developing metrics based on the ease with which they can be measured rather than how consumers respond to and process ads undervalues the performance of these ads. The same metric used for two ad formats offers differing values in terms of achieved communication outcomes for the advertiser. For a large number of advertisers who seek communication outcomes from their advertising efforts, this research offers a framework to evaluate their advertising strategies.

REFERENCES

Benway, J. P. (1998). "Banner Blindness: The Irony of Attention Grabbing on the World Wide Web," *Proceedings of the Human Factors and Ergonomics Society 42nd Annual Meeting*, 1, 463-467.

Chatterjee, P. , D. L. Hoffman and T. P. Novak (2000). "Modeling the Clickstream: Implications for Web-Based Advertising Efforts," working paper.

Dreze, Xavier and Francois Hussherr (1999). "Internet Advertising: Is Anybody Watching," working paper.

Greenwald, Anthony G. and Clark Leavitt (1984). "Audience Involvement in advertising: Four Levels," *Journal of Consumer Research*, 11 (June), 581-592.

IAB/CASIE (1998). Guidelines for Interactive Advertising Measurement. [www.iab.net/].

Internet Advertising Bureau (1999). "Net Ad Revenues Adding Up," August 23. [www.iab.net/news/content/new%20/q2.html].

Janiszewski, Chris (1993). "Preattentive Mere Exposure Effects," *Journal of Consumer Research*, 20 (December), 376-392.

Mitchell, Andrew A. (1983). "Cognitive Processes Initiated by Exposure to Advertising," *Information Processing Research in Advertising*, R. Harris (ed.), 13-42. Hillsdale, NJ: Lawrence Erlbaum Associates.

Novak and Hoffman (1996). "New Metrics for New Media: Towards the Development of Web Measurement Standards," Project 2000 white paper.

Novak, T.P., D.L. Hoffman, and Y.F. Yung (2000). "Measuring the Customer Experience in Online Environments: A Structural Modeling Approach," forthcoming, *Marketing Science*.

Steuer, J. (1992). "Virtual Reality: Dimensions of Telepresence," *Journal of Communication*, 42 (4), 73-93.

Zeff, R and B. Aronson (1999). *Advertising on the Internet*.

ENDNOTE

1 Examples: (www.macromedia.com/software/flash).

Chapter 13

Comparing Consumer Purchase Behavior on the Internet and in Brick-and-Mortar Stores: An Overview of Recent Research

Jie Zhang
University of Michigan, USA

A research area that has gained interest of marketing researchers in recent years is the comparison of consumer behavior on the Internet and traditional brick-and-mortar stores. We offer an overview of the recent developments in this research area and summarize the key findings along two dimensions: 1) factors that may cause behavioral differences in the two types of shopping environments; and 2) patterns of behavioral differences identified in the literature. We also outline our own recent work as an example to illustrate how this stream of research can help improve marketing strategies and tactics on the Internet. Directions for future research are discussed in the last section.

INTRODUCTION

In response to the dramatically expanding and evolving business activities on the Internet, academic research on electronic commerce is also growing rapidly. A broad spectrum of research topics has been explored by marketing researchers as well as scholars from many other disciplines. Topics contributed by marketing academics include, but are not limited to, conceptual works on consumer navigation behavior in the new hypermedia environment (e.g., Hoffman and Novak 1996) and the impact of the interactive shopping venue on consumers, retailers and manufacturers (e.g., Alba et al. 1997), strategic recommendations on how to build a new generation of electronic shopping infrastructures (e.g., Baty and Lee, 1995), analytical works examining the implications of the Internet as a new distribution channel (e.g., Zettelmeyer, 1998; Lal and Sarvary, 1999), and empirical studies that investigate various aspects of browsing and shopping behavior on the Internet (e.g., Dréze and Zufryden, 1998; Fader and Hardie, 1999; Bucklin and Sismeiro, 2000; Häubl and Popkowski Leszczyc, 2000).

One stream of research on electronic commerce is comparing consumers' purchase behavior on the Internet and in traditional brick-and-mortar shopping environments. Despite the explosive growth of Internet commerce and well recognized competitions between online and brick-and-mortar stores, there is a striking absence of empirical studies on behavioral differences across the two types of channels. The scarcity of empirical works is largely due to lack of usable data and is alleviated only very recently when high quality panel purchase data from online merchants become available to the academic community. Research topics in this newly developed area are mainly concerned with establishing systematic differences in consumers' decision-making processes and purchase behavior, identifying the moderating factors, and offering explanations to the observed behavioral differences (e.g., Alba et al. 1997; Degeratu et al. 2000; Zhang 1999; Zhang and Krishnamurthi, 2000; Nowlis and McCabe, 2000; Andrews and Currim, 2000; Danaher and Wilson, 2000).

In this chapter we would like to provide an overview of the recent developments in this important research area. We will summarize the key factors and findings identified in the literature first. We will then outline our own recent studies as an example to illustrate how this stream of research can help improve marketing strategies and tactics on the Internet. Directions for future research are discussed at the end of the chapter[1].

RESEARCH DEVELOPMENT
AND KEY FINDINGS

One of the earliest works related to this topic is Burke and colleagues' (1992) study on comparing dynamic consumer choice in real and computer-simulated environments. They designed a laboratory simulation to mimic a real supermarket shopping environment and compared actual store purchases and choice decisions collected in the laboratory setting over a seven-month period. Although the purpose of their study was to examine the external validity of using data generated in computer-simulated settings to study consumer purchase behavior, it provided some interesting findings which were very relevant to later studies on comparing the Internet and brick-and-mortar shopping environments. For example, they found that purchase behavior differences became magnified when specific information relevant to the decision was presented differently in the simulated store than in real supermarkets. They also found that consumers were likely to include fewer brands in their choice set and switch between brands less frequently in the laboratory than in the actual grocery store. As will be elaborated shortly, these patterns are similar to what is observed by later studies on comparing purchase behavior in brick-and-mortar stores and *real* online stores.

This stream of research formally took off with Alba and colleagues' (1997) conceptual work on examining the implications of electronic shopping for consumers, retailers, and manufacturers. In this influential article, they offer a framework of comparing alternative retail formats in terms of dimensions that could affect their relative attractiveness to consumers based on information acquisition and processing theories, and make conjectures on how the interactive electronic marketplace may cause consumers' shopping behavior to differ from traditional shopping environments.

Another stream of research takes the game theory approach to analyzing and predicting consumer behavior on the Internet. Lal and Sarvary's (1999) study is an example of this approach. They investigate when and how the Internet is likely to decrease price competition in the context of information uncertainty and competitions between online and traditional stores. They have identified some conditions under which consumers might be more brand loyal and less price sensitive in online stores than in brick-and-mortar stores and therefore provide opportunities for firms to increase profits on the Internet.

A third stream of research in this area is based on empirical analyses of actual consumer behavior and/or purchase data on the Internet. Developments in the theoretical and analytical domains call for empirical supports/challenges to their conjectures and predictions. Empirical studies are a nice complement to the first two approaches and often generate new findings that may need further theoretical testing and explanations. Despite the importance of empirical research, marketing scholars started working along this line only very recently, largely due to lack of usable data in the past. Nevertheless, the handful of recent studies has made nice progress and produced some interesting findings about how consumer purchase behavior differs between online and traditional brick-and-mortar stores. We will focus on these empirical studies in the rest of the chapter.

Despite the short history of this research stream, many conjectures and empirical findings have been offered in the literature. We organize these results along two dimensions: 1) factors that may cause behavioral differences in the two types of shopping environments; and 2) patterns of behavioral differences identified by empirical studies.

Factors Affecting Behavioral Differences

Two types of factors that may lead to behavioral differences in online and brick-and-mortar stores have been discussed. The first type is *shopping environment related* and the second is *consumer related*.

Shopping environment related factors can be summarized as follows.

Information search cost. Alba et al. (1997) point out that a key difference of online and traditional shopping channels is the online environment's ability to provide more readily accessible information about price and non-price attributes. They conjecture that given the lower information search cost on the Internet, more information about price could increase price sensitivity for undifferentiated products, while more information about non-price attributes could reduce price sensitivity for differentiated products. They also expect a stronger consideration set effect because consumers can more efficiently screen alternatives so that they can focus on the ones that match their preferences. Degeratu et al. (2000) also anticipate that lower search costs online for listed non-price attributes such as nutritional information and popularity of items in a category may shift consumer focus from price to non-price attributes and as a result lower price sensitivity.

Accessibility of information. Information can be more accessible in the online shopping environment due to lower search costs. In addition, there are some special tools offered in online stores to assist recording and retrieving information that would have been ignored by consumers otherwise, i.e., information that consumers may not intend to search for. For example, online grocery service companies such as Peapod and Netgrocer allow consumers to sort items in a given product category by brand, size, price, unit price, promotion status, and nutritional contents such as calories, fat, cholesterol, sodium, sugar, etc. In addition, they also provide tools like "personal lists" and "previous order lists" to simplify consumers' shopping processes[2]. Easier accessibility of past purchase information could increase the impact of previous purchases on current brand choice decision, i.e., a higher level of inertial behavior (Zhang and Krishnamurthi, 2000), and diminish the effects of price and promotion on choice decisions (Degeratu et al., 2000; Zhang and Krishnamurthi, 2000).

Richness of information. Lal and Sarvary (1999) make a distinction between two types of product attributes: *digital attributes* and *nondigital attributes*. Digital attributes can be communicated on the Web at very low cost, while nondigital attributes can only be obtained by physical inspection of the product in brick-and-mortar stores. Degeratu et al. (2000) emphasize a similar distinction. They partition product attributes into four categories: brand name, price, sensory attributes, and non-sensory attributes. Sensory attributes are those that are determined by touch, smell, sight or sound. Non-sensory attributes are those that cannot be directly determined by our senses (e.g., nutritional information). It is easier to obtain information on sensory attributes in brick-and-mortar stores than on the Internet, while the reverse is expected for non-sensory attributes. This difference in the richness of information on digital vs. non-digital or non-sensory vs. sensory attributes between the two types of shopping environments is expected to cause behavioral differences in the two channels. For example, Degeratu et al. (2000) suggest that consumers rely more on non-sensory attributes and less on sensory attributes in their decisions in online stores than in brick-and-mortar stores. Also, they conjecture that brand names will have greater impact in purchase decisions for product categories with more missing information in online stores. Nowlis and McCabe (2000) examine the effect of the ability to physically touch merchandise on consumer decision making based on an experimental study. They find that products with material texture and part properties are more likely to be purchased in brick-and-mortar stores, while products with geometric properties do not incur a disadvantage in online stores[3].

Purchase behavior differences in online and brick-and-mortar stores can be driven by differences in the shopping environments, as well as discrepancies in consumer attributes. We call the second type *consumer related factors*. The following consumer related factors have been identified as contributing to behavioral differences in the two types of shopping venues.

Demographics. Degeratu et al. (2000) and Zhang and Krishnamurthi (2000) report that online consumers have higher income and larger household size than brick-and-mortar consumers on average. Online consumers also have higher education and tend to hold professional or upper and middle management jobs (Kehoe et al., 1998). Higher income implies higher opportunity cost of time. More kids in the household means more domestic chores, which also leads to higher cost of time.

Lifestyle. Bellman and colleagues (1999) report that online consumers intend to be heavy users of the Internet for work, e-mail, reading news at home, etc. They label this "wired lifestyles". Online consumers are also found to have less discretionary time or be "time starved". All of the above factors make online consumers more likely to value convenience and be willing to pay a premium for it (Andrews and Currim, 2000).

Patterns of Behavioral Differences

The key empirical findings of behavioral differences between online consumers and brick-and-mortar consumers can be summarized along the following dimensions.

Price sensitivity. Zhang (1999) and Andrews and Currim (2000) find that consumers are less price sensitive in online stores than in brick-and-mortar stores. Degeratu et al. (2000) report that consumers are less price sensitive in some product categories (liquid detergent and light margarine spread), while they could be more price sensitive for other categories (e.g., paper towels). It is noteworthy that all three studies use purchase data from the same online grocery company Peapod[4]. Degeratu et al. (2000) and Zhang (1999) matched the samples of online consumers and brick-and-mortar consumers on some demographic variables (the former used education and the latter used income and household size) when comparing purchase behavior in the two shopping environments, while Andrews and Currim (2000) did not match the samples. In addition, Zhang (1999) and Andrews and Currim (2000) took into account the fact that variance of the random component in the brand utility function may differ across consumer samples and thus parameter estimates from a discrete choice model are not directly comparable (Swait and Louviere, 1993). One caveat of the above findings is that the result may not be generalizable to other product categories and other types of online stores which differ significantly from Peapod in terms of characteristics of products, store setup, pricing policy, enrollment method (membership-based vs. open-ended), etc.

State dependence. The term state dependence comes from the econometrics literature. It refers to the effect of past purchases on current buying decision. Two forms of state dependence are of particular interest to marketing researchers: *variety seeking* and *inertia*. Variety seeking is a consumer's intentional tendency to choose an item different from what was bought last time, which is not attributable to external influences such as the availability of promotion for another item. Inertia is a consumer's intentional tendency to choose the same item bought last time, net of external influences. Zhang (1999) finds that consumers show a higher level of inertia in the online store than in brick-and-mortar stores on average. She speculates that online tools such as personal lists and previous order lists are likely to make consumers rely more on past purchase information in making brand choice decisions and thus show a higher level of inertia. An early study by Burke et al. (1992) on consumer behavior in computer-simulated setting also reveals that consumers switch between brands less frequently in the computer shopping laboratory as compared to the actual grocery store.

Brand loyalty. Danaher and Wilson (2000) investigate data from an online grocery service developed by a leading food retailer in New Zealand and find that brand loyalty for larger brands is significantly higher in the online store than would be expected for the same brands in a traditional store. The reverse is found for smaller brands. They conjecture that consumers will rely more on well-recognized brands in online stores because it is more difficult to infer product quality on the Internet. The Degeratu's et al. (2000) study identifies the availability of key decision information as a moderating factor of the brand name effect. They find that, compared to offline stores, brand names are more important in consumers' purchase decisions for product categories whose information on fewer attributes is available online. Andrews and Currim (2000) separate the impact of brand name during the consideration formation stage and the brand evaluation stage and find that online consumers do more screening on the basis of brand names but show weaker brand loyalty when evaluating alternatives left in the consideration set. In general, it appears across these studies that brand names play a more important role in brand choice decisions in online stores than in brick-and-mortar stores.

Size loyalty. Andrews and Currim (2000) report that online consumers prefer larger sizes to smaller sizes. Due to their preference for larger sizes across brands, they do less screening on size to form the final consideration set.

Consideration set effect. It is a well-documented phenomenon in the marketing literature that consumers are not willing or able to evaluate all available alternatives in making choice decisions, especially for frequently purchased low involvement product categories. Rather, they often use heuristics to screen the alternatives and form a smaller consideration set before engaging in more elaborate evaluations of the remaining alternatives (e.g., Payne, 1976; Wright and Barbour, 1977; Lussier and Olshavsky, 1979). The *consideration set effect* refers to the importance of the initial consideration set formation stage on the entire decision process. Alba et al. (1997) predict that the consideration set effect will be greater in online stores because consumers can more efficiently screen alternatives and thus focus on alternatives that match their preferences. Andrews and Currim (2000) have offered empirical support to this view. They find that there is a larger percentage of consumers who screen alternatives in online stores than in brick-and-mortar stores.

Impact of sensory attributes. Degeratu et al. (2000) show that sensory attributes have lower impact on brand choice in online stores than in brick-and-mortar stores. Nowlis and McCabe (2000) examine the impact of the ability to assess one particular form of sensory attributes, i.e., to physically touch products, and its implications on behavioral differences between online and brick-and-mortar consumers. They report that products with material texture and part properties are more likely to be purchased in brick-and-mortar stores, while products with geometric properties do not incur a disadvantage in online stores.

A RESEARCH EXAMPLE

In this section we will outline our own recent research in the area of comparing behavioral differences in online and brick-and-mortar stores (Zhang, 1999; Zhang and Krishnamurthi, 2000). It is used as an example to illustrate how this stream of studies can help improve marketing strategies on the Internet.

We focus on differences in consumers' *dynamic* brand choice behavior between online stores and traditional brick-and-mortar stores. The term dynamic choice behavior is used in contrast to *zero-order* behavior. It addresses how past purchases may influence the current choice decision. The impact of past outcome on current outcome is termed *state dependence* in the econometrics literature. We study two forms of state dependence of choice behavior, i.e., variety seeking and inertia, both of which have been well documented and investigated in the marketing literature (e.g., Jeuland, 1979; Lattin, 1987; Lattin and McAlister, 1985; Erdem, 1996; Seetharaman and Chintagunta, 1998). Most previous models of variety seeking and/or inertia assume that they are constant within the same individual. We construct a time-varying state dependence model, which allows the degrees of variety seeking and inertia to vary over purchase occasions for the same consumer. Our proposed model offers a very flexible way of capturing within-consumer time varying pattern of state dependence and overcomes some limitations of previous methods of modeling time-varying patterns. The relationship between variety seeking/inertia and time is empirically estimated and thus a consumer's state dependence at a future time can be predicted using her purchase history. The model also captures market segmentation by estimating latent segments of consumers in the market, each segment with different brand preferences, price sensitivities, and degrees of variety seeking/inertia. Consumers can be assigned to one of the identified segments based on post-segmentation analysis.

We use data from Peapod Inc., a leading online grocery company, to study online consumers and data provided by A.C. Nielsen to study brick-and-mortar consumers. A subset of households from the Nielsen data is drawn to match two key demographic variables, income and household size, of the Peapod households in order to minimize differences in the two consumer samples. Data on stick butter and liquid laundry detergent are chosen to calibrate the model for each shopping channel.

For both types of shopping environments, we find that a consumer's degree of inertia or variety seeking changes over time depending on how long she has been in an inertia/variety-seeking state. For the majority of consumers inertia initially builds up over time and then declines gradually until the consumer becomes variety seeking. And variety seeking increases over time first and then decreases until the consumer becomes inertial again. *We also find that consumers are more inertial and less price-sensitive in Peapod-like online stores than in brick-and-mortar stores.*

Our model reveals distinctive latent consumer segments in terms of brand preferences, price and promotion sensitivities, and degree and time-varying pattern of inertia and variety seeking. Each household in the data is classified into one of the segments depending on which of its posterior segment probabilities is the highest. We compare the brand switching behavior in each segment and find that more variety seeking segments have higher percentages of brand switching instances.

We also compare the information usage and decision processes across the segments. Nineteen decision process patterns have been identified based on Peapod's online navigation data[5]. We further categorize the processes into two types: *on-the-spot decisions* and *habitual decisions*. An *on-the-spot decision* is defined as a brand choice decision that involves evaluation of certain product information, such as but not limited to price, promotion, nutrition, etc., before choosing an item. A *habitual decision* is defined as a brand choice decision that relies on the choice(s) made on previous purchase occasion(s) without any evidence of information elaboration at the current purchase instance. (An example of a habitual decision is to pick an item directly from a personal list or previous order list.) Two coders, who were unaware of the nature of the analysis, classified the 19 decision processes into one of the two categories. Disagreements between the coders were resolved upon our discussion with both of them. We find that the segment which exhibits higher level of inertia underwent a smaller percentage of on-the-spot decisions and had a greater percentage of habitual decisions than the segment which exhibits more variety seeking. This provides further support that the segments we identified indeed were different in their inertia and variety seeking tendencies. It also implies that marketing managers should work out different promotion strategies to target the different segments (Zhang, 1999).

The ultimate objective of understanding behavioral differences on the Internet and brick-and-mortar stores is to offer strategic recommendations and help managers make better marketing decisions. We focus on one important issue concerning the electronic commerce world, that is, how to utilize the interactive nature of the online shopping environment and offer customized promotions to selected consumers. We look at both *targeting* and *timing* when addressing the research problem. *Targeting* refers to *who* the best consumers are for a certain promotion. *Timing* refers to *what time* is optimal for a promotion. The emphasis of our research is the *timing* issue. We believe that timing could make targeting more efficient and help achieve the full potential of micro-marketing. The ultimate research objective is to provide a set of actionable decision algorithms about *when to promote which brand to whom.*

Our time-varying state dependence model is the foundation of this research. The time varying patterns of variety seeking and inertia have a direct implication on how promotions should be targeted and timed. For example, a promotion aimed at inducing a consumer to switch to the promoted brand may not be successful if she is in a high inertia state, because the required amount of discount might be too deep to achieve. On the other hand, the promotion may not be profitable if she is in a high variety-seeking state, because she is not likely to buy the same brand next time. It illustrates that targeting promotions *at the right time* is an important decision, if a consumer's variety seeking or inertia tendency changes over time as found by our empirical analyses (Zhang and Krishnamurthi, 2000).

Based on the proposed descriptive model, we derive a set of detailed decision algorithms for customizing promotions under two promotion objectives: 1) to induce a consumer to switch to the promoted brand; and 2) to prevent a consumer from switching to another brand[6]. These algorithms can be built into a decision support system to help managers make just-in-time promotion decisions. We compare our decision recommendations to what actually occurred in the data and find that our algorithms can greatly improve the effectiveness and efficiency of current promotion practices. Specifically, the algorithms can help identify the occasions when promotions could have been saved (the "wasted promotions") and the occasions when promotions either should have been offered or offered more deeply to achieve a given objective (the "lost opportunities").

This research also offers interesting insights into the competitions between Internet stores and brick-and-mortar stores. For example, we find that the average amount of price discounts required to induce brand switching is lower in brick-and-mortar stores than in online stores, while the average amount of price discounts required to prevent brand switching is lower in online stores than in brick-and-mortar stores. This is consistent with Lal and Sarvary's (1999) suggestion that brick-and-mortar stores are important for customer acquisition while the Internet can help leverage the acquired customer base.

We are not able to list all the results due to space limitation. Nevertheless, we hope that the above example shows how research in this area can offer better understanding of the rapidly growing Internet shopping channel and help improve marketing strategies and tactics in both online and brick-and-mortar shopping environments.

FUTURE RESEARCH

We have summarized some key findings of recent research in the area of comparing online and brick-and-mortar purchase behavior. We could not overemphasize the fact that this is a newly developed area and much more research needs to be done to generate new findings and insights and to provide external validity to the results covered in this overview. The following are a few directions that future research may take on.

The empirical studies in this area have focused mainly on brand choice behavior. Many other types of purchase behavior need to be investigated. These include, but are not limited to, purchase incidence decision (whether to buy the product category), purchase quantity decision (how much to buy for the chosen brand), inter-purchase timing (when to make a purchase of a category), purchase acceleration (whether to buy earlier), stockpiling (whether and how much to buy more than usual and stock up), consumption expansion (whether to consume more), etc.

Most studies to date have focused on investigating frequently purchased low involvement products, especially grocery products. We need to examine more types of online stores and product categories. This will help establish external validity to existing findings and identify moderating factors of the behavioral differences between the two types of shopping environments.

Despite the general consent that both shopping environment related factors and consumer related factors may contribute to the observed differences in purchase behavior between online consumers and brick-and-mortar consumers, little is known about the relative importance of each type of factor and possible moderating conditions. Experimental research is most suited to address this issue where the researcher has control over the composition of consumer samples and information presented in the shopping environment.

Finally, it is important to study cross-channel associations of consumers' decision-making and buying processes. Most existing studies analyze the online or brick-and-mortar shopping environment in isolation. In reality, however, consumers could rely on both channels for one purchase process. For example, when shopping for an automobile, some customers go to online auto stores to search information but make the purchase at a traditional brick-and-mortar dealer. Examples of research questions to be explored in this direction are: Does exposure in online stores increase purchases in brick-and-mortar stores and vice versa? Does the source of information (online vs. brick-and-mortar) moderate purchase behavior in a given channel? Do promotions in multiple channels have a positive or negative interaction effect? These questions are especially relevant to firms contemplating on selling products through both traditional and electronic marketplaces.

The marketing research literature offers a rich body of methodologies to address issues regarding various aspects of purchase behavior. Therefore, we do not expect any significant difficulties in terms of research techniques for future research in this area. The biggest challenges facing marketing scholars are likely to be obtaining proper online browsing and purchase data, and efficiently processing the data which usually appear in much more complicated (for example, clickstream data) structure than traditional scanner panel purchase data. With more communications and collaborations between the Internet industry and academic community and developments in fields like data mining and data reduction, we are very optimistic that this stream of research will grow steadily and keep generating interesting insights for the marketing field.

REFERENCES

Alba, Joseph, John Lynch, Barton Weitz, Chris Janiszewski, Richard Lutz, Alan Sawyer, and Stacy Wood (1997), "Interactive Home Shopping: Consumer, Retailer, and Manufacturer Incentives to Participate in Electronic Marketplace," *Journal of Marketing*, 61 (July), 38-53.

Andrews, Rick L. and Imran S. Currim (2000), "Behavioral Differences Between Consumers Attracted to Shopping Online vs. Traditional Supermarkets: Implications for Enterprise Design and Marketing Strategy," working paper, University of Delaware.

Baty, James B. and Ronald M. Lee (1995), "Intershop: Enhancing the Vendor/ Customer Dialectic in Electronic Shopping," *Journal of Management Information Systems*, 11 (4), 9-31.

Bellman, Steven, Gerald L. Lohse and Eric J. Johnson (1999), "Predictors of Online Buying Behavior," Communications of the ACM, 42 (12), 32-38.

Bucklin, Randolph E. and Catarina Sismeiro (2000), "How 'Sticky' is Your Web Site? Modeling Site Navigation Choices Using Clickstream Data," working paper, Anderson School, University of California at Los Angeles.

Burke, Raymond R., Bari A. Harlam, Barbara Kahn, and Leonard M. Lodish (1992), "Comparing Dynamic Consumer Choice in Real and Computer Simulated Environments," *Journal of Consumer Research*, 19 (1), 71-82.

Danaher, Peter J. and Isaac Wilson (2000), "Consumer Brand Loyalty in a Virtual Shopping Environment," presented at the Marketing Science Conference 2000, University of California at Los Angeles, June 22-25.

Degeratu, Alexandru, Arvind Rangaswamy, Jianan Wu (2000), "Consumer Choice Behavior in Online and Traditional Supermarkets: The Effects of Brand Name, Price, and Other Search Attributes," *International Journal of Research in Marketing*, 17 (1), in print.

Dréze, Xavier and Fred Zufryden (1998), "Is Internet Advertising Ready for Prim Time?" *Journal of Advertising Research*, 38 (3), 7-18.

Erdem, Túlin (1996), "A Dynamic Analysis of Market Structure Based on Panel Data," *Marketing Science*, 15 (4), 359-78.

Fader, Peter and Bruce Hardie (1999), "Forecasting Repeat Sales at CDNOW: A Case Study," working paper, Wharton School, University of Pennsylvania.

Hoffman, Donna L. and Thomas P. Novak (1996), "Marketing in Hypermedia Computer-Mediated Environments: Conceptual Foundations," *Journal of Marketing*, 60 (3), 50-68.

Häubl, Gerald and Peter T. L. Popkowski Leszczyc (2000), "Going, Going, Gone—Determinants of Bidding Behavior and Selling Prices in Internet Auctions," working paper, University of Alberta.

Jeuland, Abel P. (1979), "Brand Choice Inertia as One Aspect of the Notion of Brand Loyalty," *Management Science*, 25, 671-82.

Kehoe, C., J. Pitkow and J. Rogers (1998), GVU's Ninth WWW User Survey Report, Office of Technology Licensing, Georgia Tech Research Corporation, Atlanta.

Lal, Rajiv and Miklos Sarvary (1999), "When and How Is the Internet Likely to Decrease Price Competition?" *Marketing Science*, 18 (4), 485-503.

Lattin, James M. (1987), "A Model of Balanced Choice Behavior," *Marketing Science*, 6 (1), 48-65.

Lattin, James M. and Leigh McAlister (1985), "Using a Variety-Seeking Model to Identify Substitute and Complementary Relationships Among Competing Products," *Journal of Marketing Research*, 22(3), 330-39.

Lussier, Denis A. and Richard W. Olshavsky (1979), "Task Complexity and Contingent Processing in Brand Choice," *Journal of Consumer Research*, 6, 154-165.

Nowlis, Stephen M. and Deborah Brown McCabe (2000), "Online vs. Offline Consumer Decision Making: The Effect of the Ability to Physically Touch Merchandise," working paper, Arizona State University.

Payne, John L. (1976), "Task Complexity and Contingent Processing in Decision Making: An Information Search and Protocol Analysis," *Organizational Behavior and Human Performance*, 16 (August), 366-387.

Seetharaman, P. B. and Pradeep Chintagunta (1998), "A Model of Inertia and Variety-seeking with Marketing Variables," *International Journal of Research in Marketing*, 15 (1), 1-17.

Wright, Peter L. and Fredrick Barbour (1977), "Phased Decision Strategies: Sequels to Initial Screening," in North Holland TIMS studies in the Management Science: *Multiple Criteria Decision Making*, Vol. 6, M. K. Starr and Milan Zeleny, ed., Amsterdam: North Holland, 91-109.

Zettelmeyer, Florian (1998), "Expanding to the Internet: Pricing and Communications Strategies When Firms Compete on Multiple Channels," working paper, University of California at Berkeley.

Zhang, Jie (1999), *Investigating Dynamic Brand Choice Processes: A Comparison of Online Shopping Environments and Store Shopping Environments*, doctoral dissertation, Northwestern University.

Zhang, Jie and Lakshman Krishnamurthi (2000), "Customizing Promotions in Online Stores: Methodology and A Comparison to Brick-and-Mortar Stores," working paper, University of Michigan.

ENDNOTES

1 We are trying to include as many representative works in this area as possible to the best of our knowledge. Nevertheless, this review is by no means intended to be exhaustive, especially given the rapidly growing nature of Internet marketing research.

2 Sources: www.peapod.com, www.netgrocer.com.

3 According to Nowlis and McCabe (2000), a geometric object's most dominant attribute is size or shape. People rely most on vision when perceiving geometric objects.

4 Degeratu et al. (2000) and Andrews and Currim (2000) use IRI scanner panel data and Zhang (1999) use Nielsen scanner panel data to analyze purchase behavior in brick-and-mortar stores.

5 An example of a decision process is "Go to a category shelf screen, then sort the items by a certain criterion, and then look at the nutrition panel of an item, and then select an item and add it to the order list." See Zhang (1999) for a complete list of the 19 decision processes.

6 See Zhang and Krishnamurthi (2000) for details of the algorithms.

Chapter 14

Satisfaction, Frustration, and Delight: A Framework for Understanding How Consumers Interact with Web Sites

Jennifer Edson Escalas and Kapil Jain,
University of Arizona, USA

Judi E. Strebel
San Francisco State University, USA

This research project develops a framework for understanding how consumers interact with Web sites on the Internet. Our goal is to understand the interaction of individuals and Web sites from the perspective of the marketer, or third-party, who has created the site. Internet technology enables marketers to customize their interaction with consumers in order to better meet consumer needs. We are interested in whether and how this works. Our framework builds on four interdependent elements: first, the individual Internet user's mindset as he/she enters a particular Web site, which includes, importantly, the user's expectations; second, the Web site itself (consisting of four components: structure, content, connectivity, and malleability); third, the individual/Web site interaction; and fourth, the user's evaluation of the Web site, which affects behavior.

In this chapter, we begin with a fairly detailed examination of our framework. Next, we present the findings of an experiment that asked subjects to browse four actual live, electronic greeting card Web sites. Overall, the pattern of our results supports the components of the framework that we tested. Specifically, individual and Web site differences influence how users perceive the Web sites and these Web site perceptions influence both consumers' evaluations of the site and their behavior regarding the site.

INTRODUCTION

Recently, there has been great interest in increasing our understanding of consumer behavior in computer-mediated environments (CME) (e.g., Hoffman and Novak, 1996). Our framework expands on previous research by focusing on the interaction of Internet users with Web sites as they "surf" through the net environment, taking into consideration the unique attributes of the Internet as an entirely new communication medium. Our goal is to understand the interaction of individuals and Web sites from the perspective of the marketer, or third-party, who has created the site. How can marketers capitalize on Internet technology, which

Figure 1. The framework

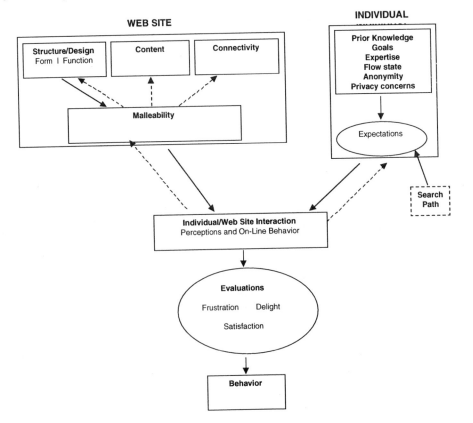

provides them with unique ways of communicating with and meeting the needs of consumers? In this way, we believe our framework is a significant step forward in understanding the very different medium of the Internet and provides a fresh approach designed specifically to understand consumer-Web site interactions, rather than narrowly applying consumer behavior theories developed before the advent of the Internet to a new context.

Our framework consists of four interdependent elements (see Figure 1). First, we propose that Web sites have four characteristics that have distinct effects on consumers: the site's design structure, content, connectivity (to other sites and other users), and malleability. We define malleability as the degree to which the marketer or user is able to change the site's structure, content, and connectivity. In this sense, technology enables Web site structure to facilitate "smarter" content. Second, the model incorporates variables representing the user's state of mind when entering a Web site, for example, consumer goals, expertise, and prior knowledge. These aspects of the individual affect expectations about the Web in general and about categories of Web sites in particular (e.g., sites for automobiles, auction sites, stock-trading sites, etc.). Third, we make predictions about how the individual, with his/her mindset and expectations, interacts with the Web site, including his/her perceptions of the site's structure, content, connectivity, and malleability and his/her behavior online. Finally, we propose that the consumer's evaluation of the site depends on the user's perceptions of the actual experience compared to a-priori expectations. The resulting evaluation can be varying degrees of satisfaction/dissatisfaction, delight, or frustration. These evaluations influence the consumer's behavior with the Web site (e.g., spending time vs. exiting, placing a bookmark, making a purchase, etc.).

To present a tangible example, consider for a moment that you find yourself at 1800flowers.com. As you enter the site, you may have some expectations. These expectations are influenced by a number of factors, including your level of expertise with the Internet and commercial Web sites. If you have high expertise, you will most likely have very precise expectations about the site. If you are a novice, your expectations about the site may be very diffuse. We differentiate four Web site elements that affect your interaction with the site: the structural design of the site (e.g., Does it have a pleasant appearance? Is it easy to navigate?), the content of the site (e.g., Are the flower arrangements appealing?), the connectivity of the site (e.g., can you link to flower information sites? can you link to other flower buyers on-line?), and the malleability of the site (e.g., Can you specify which types of flowers you're interested in and therefore limit your search?). Your evaluation of 1800flowers.com depends on your perceptions of the Web site interaction in relation to your expectations. You can be satisfied or dissatisfied with the site, based on how well the perceived interaction lives up to your expectations. The site may frustrate you because you are unable to accomplish a goal, perhaps one of sending flowers to your mother. On the other hand, a valued, but unexpected, feature of the site may pleasantly surprise you, creating "delight." For example, 1800flowers.com may be able to deliver your bouquet the same day you order it. These different evaluations will affect your behavior on the Web site. You may bookmark the site for future purchases if you were delighted or decide not to send your mother flowers if you were frustrated.

We will present the theory behind our framework sequentially, working from the Web site and the individual to interaction perceptions and evaluations and behavior. This is followed by a discussion of an experiment conducted using actual live Web sites, designed to provide some empirical evidence for a limited set of propositions, followed by directions for future research based on our framework.

THE WEB SITE

We conceptualize four Web site elements that are important for our framework (see Figure 1): structure, content, connectivity, and malleability. The first aspect is the site's structure or design, which is parallel to interacting with the store environment in a traditional shopping experience. Design structure further breaks down into two pieces: form and function. The first, form, refers to the Web site's appearance. Are the colors and graphics pleasing to the eye? Does the site have "cool" animation? But a site's structural design encompasses more than just what the site looks like. It also includes how well the site is organized, which we call structural design function. A site's design functions well if it is organized logically, allows users to navigate through the site easily, and allows them to accomplish the things they wanted to do. The second component of Web site interaction is the site's content, which maps onto the merchandise of a traditional shopping experience. Different types of Web sites provide different types of content: commercial Web sites provide traditional merchandise, news Web sites provide information content, auction sites allow users to bid for products, and so on.

From a marketer's perspective, many aspects of the Internet differentiate it from the brick-and-mortar world. Two Web site elements that are relatively unique to this new communication medium are site connectivity and malleability. These two technological advantages of the Internet medium allow marketers to customize their communication to meet consumer needs. First, connectivity refers to the extent to which a Web site allows the user to connect to other entities on the Internet. This includes links to other Web sites and communication with other Web users through chat rooms, bulletin boards, and even e-mail. It is particularly this last feature of Web sites that allows users to feel connected to a larger community.

Malleability is significantly different from structure, content, and connectivity in that it interacts with all three of these Web site components. We use the term malleability to refer to the characteristic of the Web site that enables the marketer (i.e., Web creator) or user to customize and change the site. For example, when a customer enters a site through a search engine, the home page may be different than if they enter through a particular banner ad. Malleability often responds to structural cues, such as the typed in name or recognition of a cookie, and then alters the structure, content, and connectivity of the site to better meet the user's needs. For example, consider the interaction of the Pets.com Web site with a customer whose only pet is a dog. Pets.com can be malleable in a variety of ways. First, once it has identified the user and linked to the user's dog-related purchase history, Pets.com could include pictures of dogs on all the pages (structural form). The site could also link internally to only dog-related pages (structural function) or present a limited set of dog food, dog toys, and dog books (content). Finally, Pets.com could provide a list of links to dog-related information sites and allow the user to enter a dog chat room (connectivity).

We believe that all four Web site components (structure, content, connectivity, and malleability) will have a significant impact on an individual's interaction with and perception of a Web site. We look now at some of the more interesting aspects of the mindset and expectations of individuals in the Web environment.

THE INDIVIDUAL

While there are many aspects of an individual's state of mind while "surfing" the Internet that are important in understanding how Web site expectations are influenced, we will highlight just a few of the most interesting ones. First, two important aspects of the individual are his/her prior knowledge and level of expertise. Prior knowledge can be divided into two types: procedural and declarative knowledge. Procedural knowledge is the knowledge or ability the consumer has developed for interacting with the Internet. For example, is he/she able to use hypertext or search engines effectively? People with high levels of procedural knowledge can be considered experts, since expertise has been defined as the ability to perform Web-related tasks successfully (Alba and Hutchinson 1987). Declarative knowledge is how much the consumer knows about the Web site topic and content. Is he/she able to understand the information presented in the site or able to make "smart" purchase decisions, using relevant information?

A related issue concerns the level of prior knowledge, or how consumers use category structures to organize aspects of the Internet. The level of knowledge can range from very general Internet knowledge (e.g., knowledge about how quickly sites should boot up, what a banner ad is, and how links work) to site category schema, which are specific to a particular category of sites (e.g., a consumer knows that commercial Web sites often have shopping carts while news Web sites will have a great deal of text and frequent updates). Site category schema may be considered the basic level category for the Web (see Rosch and Mervis, 1975). Below the basic level, there exists specific site knowledge (e.g., on Yahoo they use a categorization system to fulfill search requests). Another related variable is familiarity, or the number of experiences with the Web. Familiarity will affect the consumers' mindset when on the Internet by making it easier to categorize above and below the basic level (in this case, site categories). People who spend a lot of time on the Internet should have complex category structures that allow them to make inferences and process information efficiently (Alba and Hutchinson, 1987).

A third aspect of Internet users' state of mind is the extent to which they are immersed in the Web medium, with the highest degree of immersion considered to be that of achieving "flow." Flow, as a construct, has received increasing attention in the marketing in CME literature (e.g., Novak, Hoffman, and Yung 1999; Novak and Hoffman 1997; Hoffman and Novak 1996). In psychology research, flow is defined as the holistic sensation that people feel when they act with total involvement (Csikszentmihalyi 1990; 1977). Flow is a continuous variable ranging from none to intense. Trevino and Webster (1992) assert that flow characterizes the perceived interaction with technologies as more or less playful and exploratory. Hoffman and Novak (1996) propose four dimensions of flow. Flow is characterized as 1) a seamless sequence of responses facilitated by machine interactivity, 2) intrinsically enjoyable, 3) accompanied by a loss of self-consciousness, and 4) self-reinforcing.

Fourth, there is the degree to which the user has entered the Internet with a specific goal in mind. This variable represents a continuum from no goals whatsoever (e.g., "I'm just going to surf around for a while to kill some time") to very specific goals (e.g., "I need to buy an Olympus digital camera today"). In between these endpoints lie varying levels of goal specificity, such as broad goals (e.g., "I'd like to buy a digital camera if the price were right") and diffuse goals (e.g., "I wonder what they are selling on auction sites today"). The specificity of one's goals will affect which aspects of one's prior knowledge (schemas) are made salient in one's expectations. This goal continuum expands the browsing versus searching dichotomy identified by other CME researchers (e.g., Schlosser and Kanfer, 1999, Gupta, 1995). There are many additional antecedents of Web site expectations that can be incorporated into our framework in the future, including general attitudes towards the Web, privacy concerns, and the perceived desirability of maintaining anonymity.

Another interesting variable that may affect the Internet user's mindset and expectations is the search path through which they arrived at the site. If an Internet user comes to a site via a link from a related site, his/her expectations about that site may be very different from a user who arrives at the same site from a search engine. In the former case, the user may expect the site to provide specific information on the topic of interest. In the latter case, the user may not be sure if the site will be on topic or not, which would result in low expectations.

Expectations

In our framework, the consumer mindset variables discussed above combine to form expectations about Web sites. In our view, expectations may be made salient by the situation or they may be constructed in response to the situation at hand. Either way, consumers have/form expectations that influence their interaction with the Web and subsequent evaluation of the experience. Expectations exist at many levels of specificity, ranging from general Internet expectations to specific site expectations. There may also be expectations about the likelihood that a Web site will enable the consumer to achieve his/her goals.

Consumers will also form expectations about all four of the components of

Web site interactions (structure, content, connectivity, and malleability). First, consumers may have expectations about the structural design of a Web site, both in terms of form (appearance) and function (organization). For example, a consumer may expect "hip" product sites to have black backgrounds (form) or expect the home icon (that links to the first page of the site) to be the company's logo (function). Second, consumers may have expectations about the content of Web sites. If a consumer logs onto Volvocars.com, he/she expects to find automobiles. Third, consumers may have expectations about the connectivity of Web sites, including links to other sites and connecting to other users. For example, a consumer may expect a "fan" site for a television show to have many links to other fan sites as well as a message board or chat room. Finally, consumers will form expectations about the malleability of Web sites. For example, since sites like Amazon.com make book recommendations based on a consumer's purchase history, consumers may expect all book sites to do the same. Expectations, in turn, affect how the consumer evaluates the different levels of customer/Web site interaction that occur, because all three of our evaluation constructs (delight, satisfaction, and frustration) depend to some degree on consumer expectations (see Figure 1).

INDIVIDUAL/WEB SITE INTERACTION - PERCEPTIONS AND ON-LINE BEHAVIOR

This stage in our framework represents the point at which the individual and the Web site come together (see Figure 1). An individual's perceptions of site elements, which depend in part on their expectations and in part on actual Web site components, affect what they do on the site (their on-line behavior). This element of our framework is dynamic: expectations influence perceptions, which update expectations, and so on, within the context of a single site visit. For example, a consumer's goals may have been established before they enter a site, but it is possible that goals will be constructed, or at least modified, in response to one's interaction with a Web site. When consumers compare their perceptions to their expectations, they form an evaluation.

WEB SITE EVALUATIONS

We identify three evaluations Internet users are likely to make about Web sites: satisfaction, frustration, and delight (see Figure 1). Building on the research of Rust, Inman, Jia, and Zahorik (1999), Spreng, McKenzie, and Olshavski (1996) and others (e.g., Boulding, Kalra, Staelin, and Zeithaml, 1993), we assume satisfaction is achieved when the consumer's evaluation of the interaction meets or exceeds his/her expectations. For example, an individual is satisfied when a Web site is organized in a user-friendly fashion, particularly if he/she expected the Web site to be difficult to negotiate. Satisfaction increases as the site exceeds expectations to a greater extent. It ranges from negative to positive, with actual performance falling well below expectations (dissatisfaction) to well above expectations (satisfaction).

Frustration, on the other hand, occurs when the perceived performance of the site falls below user expectations, with the additional prerequisite that Web site performance also blocks a consumer's progress towards a valued goal (Lawson 1965; Rosenzweig 1934). For example, a consumer is frustrated when the site uploads more slowly than was expected because his/her goal of quickly scanning information is thwarted. As with dissatisfaction, users experience increasing levels of frustration as actual experience falls farther below expectations and as more goals are thwarted. But frustration is distinct from dissatisfaction in that an inability to achieve one's goals is necessary in addition to performance falling short of expectations. When a consumer becomes frustrated, the probability of him/her exiting the site increases significantly over merely being dissatisfied.

The third evaluation, delight, is achieved by not just increasing satisfaction. Rather, in addition to having one's expectations exceeded, delight occurs when a Web site also delivers on a valuable unexpected dimension or performs unexpectedly well on an expected, valued dimension. This novelty or surprise creates arousal and positive affect, which drive delight. For example, one may be satisfied with a Web site that is well-organized, but delighted by a Web site that in addition to being well-organized, has unexpected, exciting video clips to watch. This definition of delight is consistent with the original conception of delight as formulated by Kano, Seraku, Takahashi, and Tsuji (1984) and discussed in marketing by Oliver, Rust, and Varki (1997). Achieving delight has special rewards for marketers. In the context of the Internet, delight should result in such things as a purchase, e-mail communication, positive word-of-mouth, and/or placing a bookmark on the site.

INTERNET EXPERIMENT

The overarching objective of this chapter is to develop a framework for understanding how consumers interact with Web sites. A second goal is to report the findings of an experiment conducted to empirically demonstrate some of the relationships proposed by the framework. We begin this section by briefly reviewing the relationships tested in our experiment in the form of propositions. This is followed by a description of our method and the presentation of our results.

Propositions

In this experiment, we focus on demonstrating a manageable subset of the proposed framework relationships. Specifically, we empirically test two aspects of the consumer's mindset (attitudes and subjective expertise, Brucks, 1985); subjects' Web site interaction perceptions, which emerged from a large set of possible dimensions; three evaluations (satisfaction, delight, and frustration); and one choice behavior. Our study design held Web site content, connectivity, and malleability relatively constant. Therefore, the Web site interaction perceptions pertain primarily to Web site structural design form and function. There are five propositions that emerge from this subset of the framework.

First, the framework posits that the individual's mindset will influence his/her perceptions of the interaction with the Web site. Based on the discussion of expertise above, we predict that higher subjective Internet expertise will lead to poorer perceptions of site design. Experts should have higher levels of comparison than novices (P1A). Another individual difference is one's attitude towards the Web. We predict better Web attitudes will lead to high design perceptions, in essence a halo effect of having a positive overall attitude towards the Web (P1B). In addition to being influenced by aspects of the individual, the interaction perceptions component of our framework is also influenced by the Web site itself. Therefore, we predict a significant effect of the Web site itself on design perceptions (P2). In the case of this experiment, we focus specifically on Web site structural design form and function.

Next, interaction perceptions will influence consumer evaluations of the Web site, with more favorable perceptions leading to more favorable evaluations (P3). Specifically, we expect better perceptions of Web structural design form and function to lead to more satisfaction, more delight, and less frustration. Finally, these evaluations will affect Web related consumer behaviors (P4). In this study, the primary Web behavior is Web site choice. Essentially, with P3 and P4, we are

Figure 2. Components of the framework tested in experiment

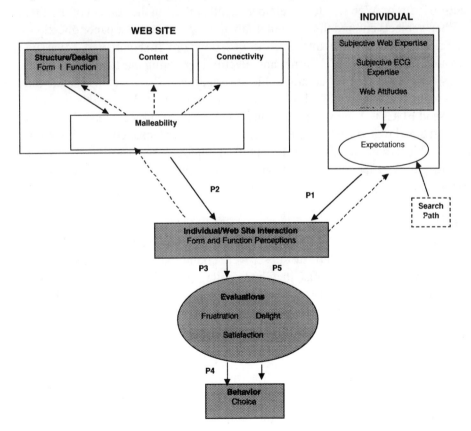

proposing a mediation process: the effect of consumer/Web site interaction perceptions on behavior will be mediated by consumer evaluations of the Web site (P5).
Figure 2 highlights those components of the framework that are tested in the
experiment.

Method

We tested these five propositions by instructing subjects to browse active
commercial Web sites and then measuring their perceptual, evaluative, and behavioral responses.

Subjects

Ninety-three undergraduate students subjects from a large, public, Southwest-
ern university completed our experiment. Participation was a course requirement
for their Introduction to Marketing course.

Procedure

We developed a cover story for this experiment based on the idea that we were
helping an electronic greeting card (EGC) company select a Web site design where
it could house its own collection of electronic greeting cards. Thus, we asked
subjects to focus on Web site design elements, rather than on the content of the site.

When subjects entered the computer lab, they were handed a paper questionnaire. Prior to entering the Internet, the questionnaire first gathered covariate
information on the subjects' Internet and electronic greeting card experience and
attitudes, along with some demographic information. Next, we instructed the
subjects to browse two EGC Web sites for five to ten minutes. We told them it was
okay to send EGCs to friends if they wanted to do so. The subjects recorded when
they entered and exited each site, using the computer's clock. After exiting from
each site, subjects completed the questionnaire, completing items designed to assess
their perceptions of the Web site design, their evaluation of the site, and choice
behavior.

Stimuli

Subjects were asked to browse two of four real-world Web sites for electronic
greeting cards (order and Web site subset were counterbalanced across subjects).
These sites were selected because they had similar quality EGCs (again, our goal
was to control Web site content as much as possible) and allowed users to send EGCs
for free. The four sites were ecards.com, cgreetings.com, great-greetings.com, and
thegreetings.com. The sites varied on design dimensions derived from Bucy et al.
(1999) and Ghose and Dou (1998), shown in Table 1.

Dependent Variables

The questionnaire measured perceived Web site interaction dimensions, three
evaluations (satisfaction, frustration, and delight), plus a behavioral choice item.

Table 1: Structural dimensions of the four EGC sites

Criteria	Codes	great-greetings	thegreetings	ecards	cgreetings
Site Aesthetics					
Design Consistency	1 – poor 5 – good	3	4	5	4
Design Appeal	1 – poor 5 – good	2	3	3	2
Design Uniqueness	1 – poor 5 – good	1	2	2	1
Card Selection Ease					
Catalog Structure	1 – poor 5 – good	3	4	3	3
Sorting Option?	0 – No 1 – Yes	0	0	0	0
Quality of Sorting option	1 – poor 5 – good	N/A	N/A	N/A	N/A
Search Option?	0 – No 1 – Yes	0	0	0	0
Quality of Search option	1 – poor 5 – good	N/A	N/A	N/A	N/A
"Hot" choices available?	0 - No 1 - Yes	1	0	0	0
Recommendations available?	0 - No 1 - Yes	0	0	0	0
Is history of cards sent available?	0 - No 1 - Yes	0	0	0	0
Ease of Card Purchase					
Ease of form entry	1 - poor 5 - good	3	4	4	4
Ability to automate sender info	0 - No 1 - Yes	0	0	0	0
Ability to spot errors	0 - No 1 - Yes	0	0	0	0
Message customizability	1 - poor 5 - good	3	5	3	3
Flexibility in card sending	1 - poor 5 - good	4	5	3	3
Sender informed when card is sent?	0 - No 1 - Yes	1	1	1	1
Sender informed when card is seen?	0 - No 1 - Yes	1	1	1	1

Table 1: Structural dimensions of the four EGC sites (continued)

Criteria	Codes	great-greetings	thegreetings	ecards	cgreetings
Site Aesthetics					
Navigation Ease					
Site depth	1 - Low 5 - High	2	4	2	3
Site breadth	1 - Low 5 - High	4	4	3	4
Presence of bookmarking option	0 - No 1 - Yes	1	0	0	0
Ease of knowing location within the site	1 - poor 5 - good	2	2	1	3
Ease of jumping non-linearly within the site	1 - poor 5 - good	2	1	2	4
Page Design / Structural elements					
Background pattern (home page)	1 - Solid 2-Patterned 3 - Non uniform	1	1	1	1
Background pattern (interior pages)	1 - Solid 2-Patterned 3 - Non uniform	2	1	1	1
Background Color (home page)	1 - White 2 - Other	1	1	2	1
Background Color (interior pages)	1 - White 2 - Other	2	1	2	1
Presence of Banners (home page)	0 - No 1 - Yes	1	1	0	1
Presence of Banners (interior pages)	0 - No 1 - Yes	1	1	1	1
Corporate Logo as home page link?	0 - No 1 - Yes	1	0	0	1
Use of frames	0 - No 1 - Yes	0	0	1	1
Page height (15" monitor)	1 - no scrolling needed 2 - scroll-ing needed	1	1	1	1
Page width (15" monitor)	1 - no scrolling needed 2 - scroll-ing needed	1	1	1	1

Table 1: Structural dimensions of the four EGC sites (continued)

Criteria	Codes				
Site Aesthetics		great-greetings	thegreetings	ecards	cgreetings
Home Page Elements					
Use of Flash	0 - No				
	1 - Yes	0	0	0	0
Page titles displayed?	0 - No				
	1 - Yes	1	0	0	1
Non-content pictures/line drawings?	0 - No				
	1 - Yes	1	0	0	0
Moving text/scrolling text/marquee?	0 - No				
	1 - Yes	0	0	0	0
Blinking text?	0 - No				
	1 - Yes	0	0	0	0
Color-changing text?	0 - No				
	1 - Yes	0	0	0	0
Image/icon movement?	0 - No				
	1 - Yes	1	0	1	0
Audio clips?	0 - No				
	1 - Yes	0	1	0	0
Video clips?	0 - No				
	1 - Yes	0	0	0	0
Provider / User Interaction					
Online diagnostics?	0 - No				
	1 - Yes	0	0	0	0
Phone number	0 - No				
	1 - Yes	0	0	0	0
Email support?	0 - No				
	1 - Yes	0	0	0	0
Postal address?	0 - No				
	1 - Yes	0	0	0	0
Comment forms?	0 - No				
	1 - Yes	0	0	1	1
Feedback option?	0 - No				
	1 - Yes	0	1	0	1
Provider Disclosures					
About Us	0 - No				
	1 - Yes	1	0	0	1
Sales policies?	0 - No				
	1 - Yes	1	0	0	1
FAQ?	0 - No				
	1 - Yes	0	1	0	1

First, 15 items were used to assess perceptions of design form and function, drawn from Nielsen (1998) and Schneiderman (1998). Site design form perceptions were measured by five 7-point items, including whether the appearance of the site was "cool" and whether the site's design was consistent (the five items were averaged to form one variable, $\alpha = .81$. For a list of all items, see Table 2). Site design function perceptions were measured by ten seven-point items, including whether the site was organized in a logical fashion, whether the site was easy to navigate, how reversible one's actions were, and whether the user was able to accomplish his/her goals (the ten items were averaged to form one variable, $\alpha = .89$, see Table 2).

In order to measure satisfaction, we used six seven-point scale items from Oliver, 1980, 1997 and Tse and Wilton, 1988. These items include "this site is one of the best commercial Web sites I've seen," "this Web site exceeded my expectations," "considering everything, I am very satisfied with this Web site," "my visit to this Web site didn't meet my expectations" (reversed), "this Web site is exactly what I want," and "browsing this Web site was enjoyable." These six items were averaged to form one overall satisfaction score ($\alpha = .94$). We considered this variable to measure the satisfaction to dissatisfaction continuum.

In order to measure delight, we followed the example of Oliver et al., 1997, and used one 7-point scale item: "compared to how satisfied I expected to be, I found I was much less/much more satisfied." Those respondents who circled a "7,"

Table 2: Measures of Web site design form and function

Web Site Design Form Items
1. This web site used a consistent design across all the pages
2. The pages that comprised this web site seemed to go together well
3. This web site had a unique design
4. I thought the design of this web site was cool
5. This web site's design captured my attention

Web Site Design Function Items
1. I was able to accomplish the things I wanted to do on this web site easily
2. This web site had short cuts that enabled me to move easily where I wanted to go
3. I was able to navigate through this web site easily
4. This web site provided me with informative feedback
5. This web site gave me useful directions on how to do what I wanted to do
6. It was easy to reverse actions on this web site
7. This web site was very well organized
8. If I did something or went somewhere I didn't want to go, I could easily fix it on this web site
9. This web site was easy to use
10. This web site was organized in a logical fashion

indicating they were much more satisfied than they expected, were considered to have been delighted, and were given a "1" for delighted. All other respondents were considered to have not been delighted and were given a zero. To compare this dichotomous variable with some additional delight measures, we ran a series of t-tests across five five-point emotion scale items (which were all highly correlated, $\rho = .47$, $p < .0001$): excited, surprised, happy, pleased, and delighted. All five t-tests were significant (detailed results can be found in Table 3) and provide some convergent validity for our dichotomous delight measure.

In order to measure frustration, we used one five-point scale item: "please circle the degree to which you felt frustrated while looking at this Web site" anchored by not at all/very much. Finally, we asked subjects to make a recommendation to the EGC company looking for a Web site design to house their own EGC collection (in our cover story), basing their choice on which Web site design of the two they visited they preferred. This choice task is our one behavioral measure.

Independent Variables

Four individual difference variables were measured to evaluate P1A and P1B: subjects' subjective Web expertise and subjects' subjective EGC expertise (each with the average of two seven-point items, measuring knowledge and interest in the Web/EGCs, $\rho = .60$ and $\rho = .58$, respectively) and subjects' general Web attitude and subjects' attitude towards EGC Web sites (each with the average of two seven-point items, anchored by very negative/very positive and very unfavorable/very favorable, $\rho = .91$ and $\rho = .92$, respectively). These four between-subjects variables (Internet and EGC subjective expertise, Internet and EGC general attitudes) were included in all GLM models and tested for significance with the subject mean square error term to test P1A and P1B.

Additional covariates include the order in which the sites were visited (each subject saw two of four sites, with the order and subset of sites counterbalanced across subjects), the self-report measure of the amount of time spent browsing each site (time exited subtracted from time entered), and whether or not the subject sent cards to friends from each site visited. Additionally, we included the subjects'

Table 3: T-tests for five delight related emotion variables across dichotomous delight scale

Emotion Variable	Non-Delighted Mean	Delighted Mean	t-value (significance)
Excited	2.65	3.95	-4.49 (p < .001)
Surprised	2.54	4.00	-4.49 (p < .001)
Happy	2.94	4.41	-5.85 (p < .001)
Pleased	3.19	4.68	-10.04 (p < .001)
Delighted	2.74	4.05	-4.41 (p < .001)

assessment of card quality to further control Web site content and a covariate for whether or not the subject had a server problem while browsing either site (23 out of 186 site visits (12%) had some server or site problem during the experiment).

Results

To examine the propositions where the dependent variable is continuous (the perceived design form and function dimensions, satisfaction, and frustration), we use a GLM model that includes the four between subjects covariates, a subject dummy variable, and the five within subjects covariates. To examine the propositions where the dependent variable is dichotomous (delight and choice), we use a multinomial logit model.

Propositions 1A and 1B

One individual difference affects subjects' perceptions of a site's design form, or appearance. Subjective expertise has a significant, negative relationship with design form ($\beta = -.29$, $F_{1, 87} = 5.46$, $p < .05$), supporting H1A. Two individual differences affect subjects' perceptions of a site's design function. General Web attitudes have a positive relationship ($\beta = .18$, $F_{1,87} = 3.90$, $p = .05$) as do general EGC attitudes ($\beta = .09$, $F_{1,87} = 5.42$, $p < .05$), supporting H1B.

Proposition 2

The site dummy variable was not significant in either the form or the function model ($F_{3, 180} < 1.5$ in both cases); thus, P2 was not supported.

Proposition 3

The findings for P3 support our framework: Web site design perceptions significantly affect Web site evaluations. Specifically, we find that design *form* perceptions positively affect both satisfaction and delight evaluations ($\beta = .81$, $p < .0001$ and $\beta = 2.06$, $p < .01$, respectively). Additionally, design form perceptions have a marginally negative effect on frustration ($\beta = -.20$, $p < .10$). Perceptions of site design *function* significantly enhance satisfaction ($\beta = .35$, $p < .01$) and marginally reduce frustration ($\beta = -.30$, $p = .06$), but do not affect delight.[1]

Proposition 4

In the logit model for the choice recommendation, all three evaluation variables are significant. Satisfaction and delight have a positive relationship with choice ($t = 3.64$, $p < .001$, $\beta = .67$ and $t = 2.00$, $p < .05$, $\beta = 2.37$, respectively). Frustration, as one would expect, has a negative relationship with choice ($t = -1.98$, $p < .05$, $\beta = -.39$).

Proposition 5

In order to prove mediation, four relationships must hold. First, there must be a direct effect of Web site design form and function perceptions on the behavior variable. This relationship is supported for form, but not function in the logit model for choice ($\beta = .83$, $t = 3.70$, $p < .0001$, and $/ t / < 1.0$, respectively). Therefore, we will only look at whether or not evaluations mediate the effect of form on choice. Second, there must be an effect of site design form on the evaluations. This was shown to be true for all three evaluation measures (positive for satisfaction and delight, negative for frustration) in P2. Third, there must be an effect of the Web site evaluations on behavior. This was shown to be true for all three evaluations (again, positive effects for satisfaction and delight, negative effect for frustration) in P3.

Finally, when both Web site design form and Web site evaluations are included in the logit model of choice, the effect of form must be eliminated. In this logit model, satisfaction, delight, and frustration all remain significant ($\beta = .76$, $t = 2.39$, $p < .05$; $\beta = 2.64$, $t = 2.10$, $p < .05$; and $\beta = -.42$, $t = -2.04$, $p < .05$; respectively) while form becomes insignificant ($/ t / < 1$). Thus, P5 demonstrates that the effect of the site design form on choice works through Web site evaluations.

Discussion

Overall, the pattern of results supports the tested components of our framework. First, there are aspects of an individual's mindset that affect his/her perceptions of a Web site. Specifically, we found individuals who are subjectively more expert about the Web rated the site designs to be less appealing (P1A), while subjects who have a positive attitude about the Web and those who have a positive attitude about EGCs both rated the organizational structure of the four Web sites to be better (P1B). People who like the Internet and EGCs find EGC Web sites to function better, while it appears to be harder to aesthetically please the experts.

We do not find support for P2, however: the individual sites did not differ in their assessment of form or function, when all other potential variables are included in the model (site order, card quality, time spent at the site, whether a card was sent, and whether a server problem was encountered). While it is intuitive that individual Web site differences should have an effect on subjects' perceptions of design form and function, our selection of four similar Web sites makes this test too conservative. In essence, by selecting active commercial Web sites that were similar in terms of the EGCs they provided and operations they allowed users to engage in, we reduced the variance across the sites to an insignificant level (refer to Table 1).

The findings for P3 support our framework by empirically demonstrating that Web site design perceptions affect Web site evaluations. Specifically, we find that the site design *form* variable positively affects satisfaction and delight and negatively affects frustration. Site design form measures the site's appearance. To be satisfied or delighted, the Web site's appearance must be acceptable (satisfaction) or unexpectedly pleasing (delight). To avoid frustration, the site's appearance must not be unattractive. The site design *function* variable positively affects satisfaction and negatively affects frustration. Site design function measures the site's organization and how well the site allows the user to meet his/her goals. Being well-organized enhances satisfaction, while being poorly organized creates frustration.

Frustration is conceptualized to be the emotion experienced when progress towards achieving a goal is blocked. Thus, it is logical that since poor Web site design function can prevent one from achieving goals, frustration results. Although our results do not find a relationship between Web site design function and evaluations of delight, it may be that we do not have enough variance in design function (s^2 function = 0.92, while s^2 form = 1.51) to account for the small number of subject/site interactions that achieved delight (only 22 out of 186 site visits resulted in the subject being delighted).

Our results also support P4: the three evaluation variables significantly affect which site design subjects recommend to our fictional EGC company. As expected, satisfaction and delight have a positive relationship with this choice, while frustration has a negative relationship with choice. While these results are intuitive, they nonetheless provide empirical support for our framework and begin to establish an overall pattern of results that is compelling.

Finally, we find that satisfaction, delight, and frustration mediate the effect of Web site design on Web site recommendation (P5). The effect of Web site design form works through satisfaction, delight, and frustration to affect choice behavior. However, there is not a significant effect of Web site design function on choice. Web site design form and function are correlated ($\rho = .59$, $p < .0001$). When run in two separate models, function has an effect on choice and is mediated by evaluation. When both are included in the model simultaneously, however, design form absorbs the variance and design function is no longer significant. We intend to examine these variables in greater detail in future studies by manipulating both form and function, rather than relying on actual live commercial Web sites (see directions for future research below). Thus, marketers can satisfy, delight, and avoid frustrating "e-customers" with a favorably perceived Web site appearance, and satisfy and avoid frustrating them with a favorably perceived Web site organization.

CONCLUSION

The goal of our framework is to provide an understanding of the complexities of consumer-Web site interactions. In order to do so, we consider the mindset and expectations of individuals when they enter a particular site and the different aspects of Web sites that are important. We differentiate Web sites from other marketing media (structure, content, connectivity, and malleability). The framework also examines how consumers interact with a Web site and the manner in which consumers evaluate their interaction with a site. We have empirical support for some of the relationships the framework predicts regarding how consumers perceive of, evaluate, and behave on a Web site. In order to strengthen our theoretical position, we plan to continue to investigate and empirically test the relationships advanced by our framework. We believe this research is a significant step forward in understanding the very different medium of the Internet, providing a fresh approach designed specifically to understand consumer-Web site interactions.

Directions for Future Research

The framework outlined in this chapter offers a plethora of interesting topics to explore. For example, there are many additional elements of our framework that were not examined in the study reported here, including such notions as consumer goals and site malleability. It may be that while site malleability enhances Web site perceptions when consumers have diffuse goals, malleability may actually interfere with goal achievement when consumers have specific goals, creating frustration. Other aspects of malleability would be interesting to study as well. For example, one could explore the differential effects of site-controlled malleability versus malleability controlled by the consumer. For example, rather than customizing the site for the consumer, a site can allow the consumer to customize the site for him-/herself.

Additional framework variables and relationships of interest include the effect of search path on an individual's mindset and expectations, and the notion of connectivity, which is an important point of differentiation for the Internet. The sense of community a user feels should have a significant effect on his/her Internet evaluations and behavior.

Another avenue of future research builds on some of our empirical findings relating to the form and function aspects of Web site design. The interplay between structure and content is of particular importance in the domain of Web based consumer behavior. Constructs such as malleability and personalization are premised on the notion that form can influence and/or enhance function. At the same time, form and function may not be completely separable elements of the Web site design, giving rise to both constitutive and operational challenges. A rich body of literature addressing this potential synergy already exists in areas such as advertising design and the study of narratives and can be used as a source of theoretically grounded propositions for empirical testing.

Finally, another interesting avenue for future research would be to extend the model itself, for example, by including a feedback mechanism in the model to examine the role of Web site evaluations and behavior on the consumer's mindset and prior knowledge when he/she reenters a particular site. A longitudinal study of consumer Web site behavior would be particularly interesting in this context because Web site interactions are not typically isolated occurrences. For example, initial visits to a site might be characterized as exploratory or browsing behavior, while later visits might become more purposeful. In conclusion, we plan to develop a programmatic approach to extending the theoretical implications and empirical support for our framework as we continue to investigate the nature of consumer behavior on the Internet. We hope that this chapter provides other Internet researchers and practitioners with some theoretical foundations upon which to build future research as well.

REFERENCES

Alba, Joseph W. and J. Wesley Hutchinson (1987), "Dimensions of Consumer Expertise," *Journal of Consumer Research*, 14 (March), 411-454.

Boulding, William, Ajay Kalra, Richard Staelin, and Valarie A. Zeithaml (1993), "A Dynamic Process Model of Service Quality: From Expectations to Behavioral Intentions," *Journal of Marketing Research*, 30 (February), 7-27.

Brucks, Merrie (1985), "The Effects of Product Class Knowledge on Information Search Behavior," *Journal of Consumer Research*, 12 (June), 1-16.

Busy, Erick P., Annie Lang, Robert F. Potter, and Maria Elizabeth Grabe (1999), "Formal Features of Cyberspace: Relationships between Web Page Complexity and Site Traffic," *Journal of the American Society for Information Science*, 50 (13), 1246-1256.

Csikszentmihalyi, Mihaly (1977), *Beyond Boredom and Anxiety*, second printing. San Francisco: Jossey-Bass.

Csikszentmihalyi, Mihaly (1990), *Flow: The Psychology of Optimal Experience*, New York: Harper and Row.

Ghose, Sanjoy and Wenyu Dou (1998), "Interactive Functions and Their Impacts on the Appeal of Internet Presence Sites," *Journal of Advertising Research*, March-April, 29-43.

Gupta, Sunil (1995), HERMES: A research project on the commercial uses of the World Wide Web. [On-line]. Available: http://www.umich.edu/~sgupta/hermes

Hoffman, Donna L. and Thomas P. Novak (1996), "Marketing in Hypermedia Computer-Mediated Environments: Conceptual Foundations," *Journal of Marketing*, 60 (July), 50-68.

Kano, Noriaki, Nobuhik Seraku, Fumi Takahashi, and Shinichi Tsuji. (1984), Attractive *Quality and Must-Be Quality. Translated* by Glenn Mazur. Hinshitsu 14, no. 2. (February): 39-48.

Klein, Lisa R. (1998), "Evaluating the Potential of Interactive Media through a New Lens: Search Versus Experience Goods," *Journal of Business Research*, 41, 195-203.

Lawson, Reed (1965), "Frustration: The Development of a Scientific Concept," *The Critical Issues in Psychology Series*, Melvin The Macmillan Company, New York.

Nielsen, J. (1998), *Designing Excellent Websites: Secrets of an Information Architect*, Indianapolis, IN: New Riders Publishing.

Novak, T.P. and Donna L. Hoffman (1997), "Measuring the Flow Experience Among Web Users," unpublished Working Paper, Vanderbilt University, TN.

Novak, T.P., D.L. Hoffman, and Y.F. Yung (1999), "Modeling the Flow Construct in Online Environments: A Structural Modeling Approach," in Donna Hoffman and John Little (Eds.), *Collected Working Papers, Marketing Science and the Internet*, INFORMS Mini-Conference, MIT Sloan School.

Oliver, Richard L. (1980), "A Cognitive Model of the Antecedents and Consequences of Satisfaction Decisions," *Journal of Marketing Research*, 42 (November), 460-469.

Oliver, Richard L. (1997), *Satisfaction*, New York, NY: McGraw-Hill.

Oliver, Richard L., Roland T. Rust and Sajeev Varki (1997), "Customer Delight: Foundations, Findings, and Managerial Insight," *Journal of Retailing*, 73 (March),

311-336.

Rosch, E. and Mervis, C.B. (1975), "Family Resemblance: Studies in the Internal Structure of Categories," *Cognitive Psychology*, 7, 533-605.

Rosenzweig, S. (1934), "Types of Reaction to Frustration: An Heuristic Classification," *Journal of Abnormal and Social Psychology*," 29, 298-300.

Rust, Roland, J. Jeffrey Inman, Jianmin Jia, and Anthony Zahorik (1999), "What You Don't Know About Customer-Perceived Quality: The Role of Customer Expectation Distributions," *Marketing Science*, 18, 77-92.

Schlosser, Ann E. and Alaina Kanfer (1999), "Interactivity in Commercial Web Sites: Implications for Web Site Effectiveness," unpublished Working Paper, Owen Graduate School of Management, Vanderbilt University, TN.

Schneiderman, B. (1998), *Designing the User Interface*, Berkeley, CA: Addison-Wesley.

Spreng, Richard, Scott MacKenzie, and Richard W. Olshavsky (1996), "A Reexamination of the Determinants of Consumer Satisfaction," *Journal of Marketing*, 60, (July) 15-32.

Trevino, Linda Kleve and Jane Webster (1992), "Flow in Computer-Mediated Communication," *Communication Research*, 19, (October), 539-573.

Tse, David K. and Peter C. Wilton (1988), "Models of Consumer Satisfaction Formation: An Extension," *Journal of Marketing Research*, 25 (May), 204-212.

ENDNOTE

1 In the model of frustration, the problem covariate is also significant and positive.

About the Authors

EDITOR

Ook Lee is currently senior lecturer at the University of Queensland, Australia. Dr. Lee also served as a professor of MIS in the Department of Management of University of Nevada at Las Vegas; the Department of Business Administration at North Carolina A&T State University in Greensboro, USA; as well as in the Department of Business Administration at Hansung University in Seoul, Korea. Previously, he worked as a Project Director at Information Resources, Inc., in Chicago, and as a Senior Information Research Scientist at Korea Research Information Center in Seoul, Korea. His main research interests include empirical software engineering, expert systems, neural networks, software engineering, digital libraries, electronic commerce, critical social theory, and global IT management. He holds a B.S. in Computer Science and Statistics from Seoul National University in Seoul, Korea, and an M.S. in Computer Science from Northwestern University in Evanston, Illinois, He also earned an M.S. and Ph.D. in Management Information Systems from Claremont Graduate University in Claremont, California. He has published in journals such as *Journal of Software Maintenance, International Journal of Electronic Markets,* and *IEEE Transactions on Professional Communications.*

CONTRIBUTORS

Christian Bauer, Ph.D., has been involved in the development of numerous commercial Web information systems since 1994. Christian holds a doctorate in information systems from the Vienna University of Economics and Business Administration, and has been published internationally on Web information systems and electronic commerce. He is currently General Manager of Research for Western Australian Internet and an e-health specialist for Working Systems. Previous employments include assistant professor at the Information Systems Department of the Vienna University of Economics and Business Administration, and a post-doctoral fellowship at Curtin Business School.

Pierre Berthon, Ph.D., is Chair of Marketing in the School of Management, University of Bath, UK. He also teaches at the Graduate School of Business, Columbia University and is visiting professor at the Copenhagen Business School, Denmark. His research interests are currently in the areas of e-commerce, branding, and management decision making. His work has been published in journals such as

California Management Review, Sloan Management Review, Journal of the Academy of Marketing Science, The Journal of Business Research and *The Journal of Advertising Research*.

Patrali Chatterjee is an assistant professor in the Faculty of Management, Rutgers University. She has master's degrees in Physics and Management, both from University of Bombay, India and a doctoral degree in Management (Marketing) from Vanderbilt University. Her research interests include modeling consumer response to advertising and decision-making in computer-mediated environments and service quality measurement. She has contributed papers and chapters to books on electronic commerce, and her research has appeared in several academic journals. Her Web page can be found at http://www.rci.rutgers.edu/~patrali/.

Benedict Dellaert is an Assistant Professor of Marketing at Tilburg University, The Netherlands. Benedict holds M.Sc. and Ph.D. degrees from Eindhoven University of Technology also in the Netherlands. His research interests are in interactive marketing, consumer choice modeling, developing optimal consumer experiences and tourism behavior. He has published in such journals as the *International Journal of Research in Marketing, the Journal of Marketing Research, Journal of Interactive Marketing* in the marketing field and in *Annals of Tourism Research, Leisure Sciences and Tourism Management* in the tourism field.

Jennifer Edson Escalas is Assistant Professor of Marketing at the University of Arizona, Tucson. She earned her Ph.D. in business administration from Duke University in 1996. Her research focuses on the use of narrative processing to create brand meaning, the effects of advertising narratives, and how consumers interact with the Internet. She has published articles in the *Journal of Public Policy and Marketing* and *Advances in Consumer Research*.

Michael Ewing, Ph.D., is senior lecturer in the School of Marketing, Curtin University of Technology, Perth, Australia. He teaches in the areas of advertising and marketing strategy as well as graduate courses in e-commerce. Prior to entering academia he held executive positions in Ford Motor Company. His research interests are eclectic and include TV advertising, the Internet and multi-cultural marketing communications. His work has been accepted for publication in journals such as *Business Horizons, Journal of the Academy of Marketing Science, Journal of Business Research* and *Journal of Advertising Research*, of which he is a member of the editorial board.

Eva Guterres holds an MBA from the Smith School of Business at the University of Maryland and an MS in Engineering from the Royal Institute of Technology of Stockholm, Sweden. She has worked with Dr. Kannan as a Graduate Assistant in 1999-2000. She has previously worked in several marketing and technical positions with companies such as AppNet, GE Information Services, The

Swedish Technical Attaches, and Atlas Copco. She can be reached at evaguterres@lycos.com.

Kapil Jain, Ph.D., is currently a Lecturer of Marketing at the University of Arizona's Eller College of Business and Public Administration where he teaches graduate and undergraduate courses in marketing research, product strategy, consumer behavior, and marketing decision models. In addition, Dr. Jain teaches courses in international marketing as a Visiting Professor for the Thunderbird Graduate School of International Management. Dr. Jain has a Ph.D. in Marketing from Columbia University. His research interests include consumer perceptions of product complexity and management of customer satisfaction and delight.

Nimal Jayaratna, Ph.D., is Professor of Information Systems and Head of School of Information Systems at Curtin University. Prior to joining Curtin University, he was head of Information Systems at two universities in the UK. He has worked in marketing, human resources, financial programming, medical databases and has consultancy experience in engineering, NHS, general practice, local authority and business environments. Professor Jayaratna is the Founding Chair of the British Computer Society Methodology Specialist Group and Co-chair with Professor Peter Checkland of the Advanced 'Soft' Systems Methodology Research Group. He has chaired several international methodology conferences and has edited eight conference/journal special issues. His research is on methodology in information systems and problem solving in general, frameworks for evaluation of business development and practices.

P. K. Kannan is associate director of the Center for Information Service and associate professor of marketing at the Robert H. Smith School of Business, University of Maryland. His current research interests focus on marketing information and information services on the Internet, pricing information products, and virtual communities. His articles in this area have appeared in *Management Science, Communications of the ACM* and *International Journal of Electronic Commerce.* He holds a Ph.D. in Management from Purdue University. He can be reached at pkannan@rhsmith.umd.edu.

Sam Lubbe has spent more than 14 years working in the field of information systems. He has served some time as a user and as an IT professional. He always ensured that the organisations obtain the maximum benefit for the amount of money they invested in IT. Recently he has specialised in the area of e-commerce metrics evaluation and benefit realisation. He has published some articles in the subject area of IT investment. He holds a B.Com., B.Com. (Hons.), M.Com and Ph.D. and is a Senior Lecturer at Vista University in South Africa.

Louis Minakakis is an Associate at Chase Manhattan Bank in New York City. He earned a Master's of Science Degree in Information Management from Polytechnic University in New York. Prior to joining Chase, he was a Webmaster at Carnegie Corporation of New York, where he managed the day-to-day operations of the Web site. Minakakis also worked on knowledge management initiatives and participated in the design and implementation of a firm-wide information system. His research has been published in the *International Journal of Electronic Markets.*

Amit Pazgal is an assistant professor of Marketing in the Olin School of Business at Washington University. He is recognized for his expertise in Electronic Commerce, Internet Marketing and Pricing. Dr. Pazgal teaches the graduate electronic commerce and pricing courses for Olin. He published numerous articles in leading Marketing and Operations journals and is a frequent speaker in academic as well as professional conferences both in the US and Europe. In addition to his teaching and research responsibility Mr. Pazgal has developed a number of computerized educational pricing simulations. He serves on the advisory board of several Electronic Commerce companies and is engaged in numerous consulting projects mainly in the Internet marketing arena. Prior to Olin, Mr. Pazgal served as a visiting assistant professor in the Kellogg Graduate School of Management, Northwestern University from June 1996-June 1997. Mr. Pazgal received his Ph.D. in Managerial Economics and Marketing from the Kellogg GSM Northwestern University, and Master of Science, *Magna Cum Laude*, in Mathematics, Statistics, and Operations Research and a Bachelor of Science, *Summa Cum Laude*, in Physics and Mathematics from Tel-Aviv University, Israel.

Rex Eugene Pereira is Assistant Professor of Management Information Systems in the College of Business Administration at Drake University - Des Moines, Iowa, USA. He received a Ph.D. in Management Information Systems from the University of Texas at Austin. His research focuses on human computer interaction, electronic commerce, and decision support systems. His articles have appeared in *Logistics Information Management, The DataBase for Advances in Information Systems,* and *Journal of Electronic Commerce Research.*

Leyland Pitt, Ph.D., holds joint positions as Professor of Marketing in the School of Marketing, Curtin University of Technology, Australia, and as Fellow in marketing and Strategy in the Cardiff Business School, University of Cardiff, UK. He has also taught marketing and electronic commerce on MBA and executive programs at school such as London Business School, the Graduate School of Business at Columbia University and the Graham School of Continuing Studies at the University of Chicago. His particular areas of interest in research and teaching involve marketing and the new electronic media, the staging of consumer experiences and marketing strategy. His research has appeared in *California Management Review*, *Sloan Management Review*, *Journal of the Academy of Marketing Science*, *Communications of the ACM* and *MIS Quarterly*, of which he also served as Associate Editor.

Barbara Kline Pope is director of the National Academy Press (NAP)—publisher for the National Academies (National Academy of Sciences, National Academy of Engineering, Institute of Medicine, National Research Council). Prior to her position as director, she was NAP's marketing director for 15 years. She holds an M.S.(1990) in textile science with a marketing concentration from the University of Maryland and a B.S. (1981) from Indiana University of Pennsylvania. She may be reached at bkline@nas.edu.

B. Ramaseshan, Ph.D., is currently Professor of Marketing and head of the School of Marketing at Curtin University of Technology, Perth, Western Australia. Professor Ramaseshan holds a Ph.D. in marketing and joined Curtin University (formerly the Western Australian Institute of Technology) in 1985. He teaches marketing, marketing research and business research methods. Prior to joining Curtin University, he worked in several business organizations holding senior positions in the areas of marketing, marketing research and business strategy. His research is currently in the areas of international strategic business alliances, international marketing channels, marketing strategy formulation and implementation and export barriers. He has presented and coauthored papers for numerous international conferences and has chaired competitive tracks at these conferences.

Ashok Ranchhod is Professor and Head of Marketing at Southampton Business School. Ashok has published extensively on e-marketing in Journals such as the *International Journal of Advertising* and the *Journal of Information Technology.* In addition to the published papers he has received prizes for his papers at the Academy of Marketing and The British Academy of Management. Currently his research is into e-commerce and the marketing of biotechnology companies. He leads a team of research students. His chair is sponsored by the Remedy Corporation Inc. Ashok is a Senior Examiner for the Chartered Institute of Marketing (CIM) and is a Visiting Professor at the University of Angers in France.

Bharat Rao is an Assistant Professor of Management at Polytechnic University in New York City. He leads several strategic research initiatives for the University's Institute for Technology and Enterprise in the areas of innovation in new media environments, supply chain management, strategic alliances, retailing and new product development. He earned a Ph.D. in Marketing and Strategic Management from The University of Georgia, and was a post-doctoral Research Associate at the Harvard Business School. His research has been published in *International Business Review, Journal of the Academy of Marketing Science, International Journal of Electronic Markets, Technology in Society, Journal of Computer Mediated Communications, Engineering Management Journal,* and in various conference proceedings and book chapters. He is the also the author of several business case studies, in both paper and digital formats, published by the Harvard Business School and the Institute for Technology and Enterprise, among others.

Malu Roldan is on the faculty of the Management Information Systems Department of the College of Business, San Jose State University. She has taught and done research on e-commerce in the Bay Area since 1996. Her research has appeared in MIS journals and books including *Communications of the ACM, EDI Forum* and the *Journal of Informatics Education and Research*. She is co-author of the book *In Search of Digital Excellence* published by McGraw-Hill. Her current research interests center around the application of Wireless Technologies in Education and IT management in entrepreneurial settings.

Arno Scharl is associate professor in the Information Systems Department at the Vienna University of Economics and Business Administration (Electronic Commerce Research Group), where he completed a Ph.D. and an M.B.A. Additionally, he received a Ph.D. and M.Sc. from the University of Vienna, Department of Sports Physiology. Between 1998 and 2000, he worked as visiting research fellow at the University of California at Berkeley and at the Curtin University of Technology in Perth, Western Australia. Besides the focus on automated analysis of Web-based information systems, his research and teaching interests include the various aspects of information modeling and visualization, commercial electronic transactions, adaptive hypertext, and the customization of electronic catalogs.

Sandeep Sikka is a software engineer working in the Research & Development organization at Akamai Technologies. Prior to Akamai, Mr. Sikka was a graduate student in the Computer Science Department at Washington University in St. Louis, Missouri from August 1997-July 1999 where he received his master of science degree in Computer Science in July 1999. He received a bachelor of Technology, Computer Science & Engineering degree in December 1996 from the Indian Institute of Technology, Bombay, India.

Marla Royne Stafford earned a Ph.D. in marketing from the University of Georgia in 1993, and has been listed by the Current Issues and Research in Advertising journal as a leading publisher in the advertising literature. Her research focuses on advertising and promotional strategy for services and electronic commerce. She is Associate Professor of Marketing at University of North Texas in Denton, Texas.

Thomas F. Stafford earned a Ph.D. in marketing from University of Georgia; he is currently completing a second doctorate in MIS at University of Texas - Arlington. His research involves motivations of consumers for Web site use and supply chain management. He is an Assistant Professor of MIS and Research Methods at Texas Woman's University in Denton, Texas.

Judi E. Strebel is an Assistant Professor of Marketing at the College of Business, San Francisco State University. Her main research interests are modeling consumer decision making and consumer purchase behavior in high tech industries.

Julie Tinson is a senior lecturer in Marketing at Southampton Business School. She has recently completed her Ph.D. on consumer perceptions of service in the NHS. She has presented several conference papers at doctoral, working and competitive levels. She has close links with the IPA Twinning Initiative. She is an examiner on the Planning and Control paper of the CIM Diploma and her current interests focus on segmentation.

Jie Zhang is an assistant professor of marketing at University of Michigan Business School. She earned her MA degree in demography and social statistics at The University of Chicago in 1995 and Ph.D. in marketing at Northwestern University in 1999. Her general research area is applying econometric and statistical models to study consumers' purchase behavior and decision-making processes. She is particularly interested in consumers' purchase decisions on the Internet. Her current research focuses on investigating consumers' inertia and variety seeking tendencies on the Internet, how to customize promotions in online stores, and how consumers' purchase behavior may change over time in online stores as they get more accustomed to the new shopping environment. She is also interested in pricing, promotion and consideration set formation issues in the off-line world.

Fan Zhou is a Ph.D. student at Southampton Business School. He holds a BA degree in English from Shanghai International Studies University (SISU) in the People's Republic of China and a Master's in Marketing from Leicester University in the United Kingdom. He has previously worked for several Hong Kong companies in China. His research interests include strategic marketing communications on the Internet.

Index

A

actual consumer behavior 220
advertiser-supported Web sites 211
advertising revenues 209
affective reactions 108
animation 63

B

branding 37
Browser-accessible applications 31
business strategy 192
business trends 197

C

change management 156
classical scaling 80
clickstreams 20
clickthroughs 210
cognitive factor 101
common gateway interface 18
comparison shopping 41
competitive advantage 189
competitive gap 191
components analysis 100
connectivity 233
consideration set effect 224
consumer behavior 218
consumer reporting services 44
convenience orientation 40
correspondence analysis 83
customer orientation 41
customer target groups 19
customer tracking 24
customization 158
cybermarketing 62, 73
cyberspace 153

D

data collection 36
digital attributes 221
digital customer data 26
Digital Marketing Service 99, 104
"direct model" business processes 156
direct-mail 2
distributed (database) networks 26
distribution channel 165
distribution gap 191
download delays 196

E

e-commerce strategy 196
economic orientation 40
effectiveness of online ads 209
electronic business models 29
electronic data interchange 16, 196
electronic transactions 21, 24
entertainment factor 101
exchange process costs 179
experiential orientation 40

F

filtering 9, 33
firm integration 161
flow construct 152

G

game theory approach 220
global telecommunication networks
     187
gratification 94
gratifications research 95

H

handheld device 34
high-bandwidth transmissions. 35
household production theory 177
hypermedia 22, 219
hypermedia information system 78
hypertext 110
Hypertext Transfer Protocol 17
hypertextuality 16

I

identification 150, 164
incentive-based marketing 3
information usage 225
integration 150, 188
intellectual property 1
intensity 150, 165
interaction 150, 162, 231
interactive 209
interactivity 16, 31, 35, 154
International Reach 78
Internet access costs 178
Internet domain 19
Internet marketing industry 68
Internet marketing perceptions 72
Internet traffic 188, 196
IP number 18
IP-addressable embedded computing
    34
IS strategy 192
IT alignment 195
IT forecasting 189, 194
IT risk management 190

J

Java 20
judgment formulation 115

K

key indicators 93
key variables 101
knowledge creation 194

L

linkage construct 188

M

malleability 234
many-to-many communication 153
market reaction research 64
marketing activities 151
marketing effectiveness 66
marketing management process 155
marketing perceptions 72
marketing strategies 61
mass customization 154
mass marketing 28
mass media advertising 16
measurement of alignment 189
measurement of Web site effective-
    ness 79
media sources 78
motivation 4, 94
multimedia usage 63
multimedia capabilities 42
multiple regression analysis 100

N

Netcentives 1
network reach 33

O

on-line database 63
on-line effectiveness 67
on-line interviews 64
online marketers 41
online marketing process. 159
Open Profiling Standard 17
organizational infrastructure 192
organizational learning processes 189
organizational strategy 190

P

part-worth utilities 179
PDA 42

Platform for Privacy Preferences
    Initiative 17
portability 31
price sensitivity 222
privacy 1, 26
privacy laws 35
product category 112
product class 108
product line gap 191
product-oriented market research 29
profile strategy 108
publishing industries 188
purchase acceleration 227
purchase behavior 227
purchase quantity decision 227
purchasing products 109

R

recreational orientation 40

S

search factor 103
security 18
sensory attributes 224
Social Factor 101
software agents 108
SPSS analysis 70
strategic alignment 188
structure 234
supply chain 176

T

technology capabilities 32
telecom industry 77
total customer cost 28
total customer value 28
traditional commerce 187

U

universal connected medium 152
usage gap 191

V

Viral marketing 43
virtual business partners 15
virtual communities 151
virtual reality 63
visualization 21

W

Web Information Systems 15, 21
Web marketing developers 63
web marketing practice 31
Web marketing proposers 66
Web presence 90
Web site statistics 62
Web surfing 96

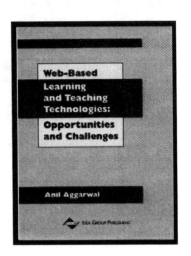